Punctuation

21 COMMA ,

a. Coordinate conjunctions
b. Introductory elements
c. Series
d. Movable adjectives
e. Nonrestrictive elements
f. Dialogue
g. Direct address
h. Dates, addresses
i. Letter salutation, closing
j. Short interrogatives
k. *Too*
l. Mild interjections; *yes, no*
m. For clarity

22 OVERUSE OF COMMAS *no ,*

a. Between subject, verb; verb, complement; direct object
b. With series
c. After *such as, like*
d. Between compound elements

23 SEMICOLON ;

a. Between closely related sentences
b. With conjunctive adverbs
c. With transitional phrases
d. In a series
e. Multiple references in footnotes

24 COLON :

a. With series
b. With final appositive
c. Between sentences
d. With quotations
e. Letter salutation
f. Biblical, time references

25 DASH —

26 PERIOD .

27 EXCLAMATION POINT !

28 QUESTION MARK ?

29 QUOTATION MARKS "/"

a. Direct quotations
b. Dialogue
c. Incorporated quotations
d. Quotations within quotations
e. Displayed quotations
f. Titles
g. Special, invented words
h. With words, letters, numerals
i. With other punctuation

30 SLASH /

31 ELLIPSIS . . .

32 BRACKETS [/]

33 PARENTHESES (/)

Mechanics

34 APOSTROPHE '

35 HYPHEN *hyph*

a. Compound words
b. Prefixes, suffixes
c. Common roots
d. Ambiguity, awkward letter combinations
e. Word division

36 UNDERLINING (ITALICS) *ital*

a. Titles
b. Names of vehicles
c. Emphasis
d. Foreign words
e. Words, letters, numerals
f. Scientific names
g. Key words, special terms

37 CAPITALIZATION *cap*

38 ABBREVIATIONS AND NUMBERS *ab/nos*

39 SPELLING *sp*

Diction

40 THE DICTIONARY

41 EFFECTIVE LANGUAGE *lang*

a. General, specific language
b. Abstract, concrete language
c. Archaic words, neologisms
d. Jargon
e. Inflated diction
f. Euphemism
g. Wordiness
h. Clichés

42 FIGURATIVE LANGUAGE

a. Metaphors
b. Similes
c. Personification
d. Overstatement
e. Unconscious echoes

Paragraphs

43 EFFECTIVE PARAGRAPHS ¶/no ¶

a. Structure
b. Coherence
c. Development
d. Introductions
e. Conclusions

Reasoning

Writing Assignments

Glossary

SECOND EDITION

Brief Handbook for Writers

JAMES F. HOWELL

DEAN MEMERING

Central Michigan University

Prentice Hall

Englewood Cliffs, New Jersey 07632

Library of Congress Cataloging-in-Publication Data

HOWELL, JAMES F.
Brief handbook for writers / James F. Howell and Dean Memering. — 2nd ed.
p. cm.
Includes index.
ISBN 0-13-082363-5
1. English languages—Grammar—1950– 2. English language—Rhetoric. I. Memering, Dean, 1936– . II. Title.
PE1112.H69 1989 88-28285
808'.042—dc19 CIP

Editorial/production supervision: Virginia Rubens
Interior and cover design: Kenny Beck
Manufacturing buyer: Laura Crossland

A Division of Simon & Schuster
Englewood Cliffs, New Jersey 07632

Printed in the United States of America
10 9 8 7 6 5 4 3 2 1

ISBN 0-13-082363-5 01

Prentice-Hall International (UK) Limited, *London*
Prentice-Hall of Australia Pty, Limited, *Sydney*
Prentice-Hall Canada, Inc., *Toronto*
Prentice-Hall Hispanoamericana, S.A., *Mexico*
Prentice-Hall of India Private Limited, *New Delhi*
Prentice-Hall of Japan, Inc., *Tokyo*
Simon & Schuster Asia Pte. Ltd., *Singapore*
Editora Prentice-Hall do Brasil, Ltda., *Rio de Janeiro*

Contents

Preface

TO THE TEACHER

The second edition of *Brief Handbook for Writers*, like the first, treats writing as a recursive process, from prewriting, to drafting, to revising and proofreading. In this view, writing becomes repeated rewriting, an organic process in which writers review, rethink, re-evaluate, and rework their ideas from simplest beginning notes to polished, finished drafts. Within this process, the individual skills contribute to the overall composition. Rules of grammar and punctuation, for example, are not simply criteria of correctness for students to apply mechanically, but are instead guidelines by which to reach an audience with the desired effect. There can be no such thing as a well-planned composition or a well-constructed paragraph or a well-written sentence or a well-chosen word without the context of situation, purpose, and point of view. Within such a context, the writing process calls for repeated efforts to find material, to focus ideas, to organize information, and to perfect expression.

The *Handbook* emphasizes revision. Students must be shown *how* to revise, how to make decisions about writing based on context, on the writing situation, on the effect they wish to have upon readers. Revision, we believe, is the true art of writing, and it applies not as a discrete activity at a particular point in the writing process (after a draft has been written, for example) but throughout the process, from the very beginning until the writer is satisfied with the composition.

Not every student needs or can benefit from a large, comprehensive grammar and composition text. Indeed, our experience has been that the larger such books are the more intimidating they become, especially where the composition text is intended as merely supplemental to another, equally intimidating tome. Our guiding premise in both the first and second editions has been that students are much more likely to use a *brief* handbook, and therefore teachers will find the second edition even more concise and easy to read. The second edition has been carefully edited to achieve the most economical presentation possible, yet it remains as comprehensive as the first edition. The section on summaries and reports has been absorbed into the research writing section. The glossary of grammatical terms has been absorbed into the appropriate grammar sections and can be found through the index. Everywhere possible we have tightened sentences, simplified explanations, cut redundant material, made the text more accessible to students.

New with the second edition:

- The second edition is easier to read. Careful editing has given us more space in which to use a larger, more readable print size. Overall the second edition has a less crowded format for pages.
- There is an appendix on the use of computers in composition including the advantages of using word processing programs, suggestions for incorporating computers into the writing process, and the relation of computers to the multiple-draft theory of *Brief Handbook for Writers.*
- The activities are new or revised. Based on reviewer feedback and extensive class testing, activities that were ineffective have been improved or replaced.
- The research writing section has more emphasis on preliminary reading and building a master bibliography.
- Research writing has been updated to illustrate the in-text documentation style of the 1988, third edition of the *MLA Handbook* as well as the third edition of the *Publication Manual of the APA.*
- There is a new student research paper: "Are Humpback Whale Sounds a Form of Meaningful Communication?"

- For the first time, an Instructor's Edition, containing the complete text of the *Handbook* with an Instructor's Manual bound in at the back, is available. The manual in the Instructor's Edition contains tips for teachers: a rationale for teaching composition, guidelines for organizing and running a composition class, research and principles for marking papers, material for using the handbook as a guide to revision, a model syllabus, and an answer key to the activities in *Brief Handbook*.
- For the second edition, the supplemental students' workbook has been completely rewritten. The workbook contains additional activities and exercises.
- New with this edition is a set of diagnostic tests covering most of the material in the *Handbook*. The diagnostic tests will help instructors identify writing problems and direct students to appropriate sections of the *Handbook*.

TO THE STUDENT

One of the chief characteristics of higher education is its emphasis on writing. At the upper levels you are expected to write informed papers about thermonuclear reactors, the international monetary fund, stress-related anxiety, Shakespearean drama, and so forth. The ability to write well is part of the definition of education.

Few jobs will be available to anyone who cannot read and write well. The technologically advanced societies have entered the "Information Age," in which information processing is the primary characteristic of "work" requiring a higher education. You must become a sophisticated user of language.

In addition to its practical uses in acquiring an education and getting a job, writing imposes advanced intellectual processes on the mind. To plan an utterance, to manipulate language, to shape discourse to a desired end—these are the skills of effective writing. Writers learn to anticipate the effects of language on distant readers and the effect on subject matter of expressing it in certain words and certain organizations rather than others. Writers learn subtle nuances of language and effective habits of composing.

You must learn a writer's view of writing. Few writers are inspired geniuses who "get" ideas and then copy them on paper. Few skillful writers compose without prewriting or rewriting. For thoughtful writing, analytical writing, writing that deals with abstractions, concepts, and values, and for writing about difficult and unfamiliar subject matter, the "inspired genius" theory of writing is not useful. Through the act of writing itself—through note-taking and scribbling and false starts and rewriting and rewriting—writers begin to find out what they have to say. Meaning isn't floating loose in the air; through struggles with language and ideas, writers make meaning.

Through writing, you have opportunities for extending yourself. Writing allows you to discover thoughts and ideas you didn't know you were capable of. While revising your words, you can see your ideas on the page. You can see that they often don't quite express your intended meaning. Your effort to reconcile these discrepancies, to bridge the gaps between what you think and what you write, will help you to grow intellectually. The ideas and words already on paper trigger other ideas; writing is thinking on paper.

Writing seems mysterious to many people because they don't see the hours upon hours of writing and rewriting. The end result looks so logically organized and well worded that it appears magical. But writing isn't magic. It's impossible to produce thoughtful writing as if it were a spontaneous oral performance, with no prior planning and no conscious control. The reader does not see the cross-outs and rewrites, the writer struggling; the reader cannot see the writer's greatest skill—revision. For even our best writers, writing is rewriting, rewriting, and more rewriting.

The true art—the craft—of writing is rewriting. In the process of working with language, ideas emerge. That is why many celebrities hire "ghost writers." It's not enough to have a story to tell; you must have the skill of telling. How to organize, how to develop, how to add missing information, cut extraneous language, clarify awkward sentences, supply the precise and effective words—these are the writer's skills. For this reason, we have emphasized revision throughout *Brief Handbook for Writers.*

HOW TO USE THIS BOOK

The handbook is organized in sections covering the writing process, a review of traditional grammar concepts, sentence errors, sentence structure, punctuation, mechanics, diction, paragraphs, reasoning, and writing assignments. Each major rule or heading is numbered. There are numerous activities throughout, approximately one-third new in this edition, to help students practice the concepts in each section. At the end of the book there is a glossary of specific usage items and a checksheet to help students revise. The table of contents and the comprehensive index will enable students to find anything in the book quickly. In addition, the endpapers set out in schematic form the numbering system and revision symbols used throughout the book.

When the handbook is used as a textbook, teachers may wish to proceed chronologically through each section, discussing the concepts and assigning the activities. Many teachers prefer to use the book as a reference guide when evaluating student drafts. When the book is used in this fashion, the numbering system or symbols can be used to help students find relevant sections. On their own, students can use the handbook at every stage of the writing process. The revision section will lead students through a careful analysis of each assignment, the title of their composition, its beginning, body, and conclusion, and each of the elements of good writing: purpose, tone, style, accurate and effective sentences and diction, and proofreading.

ACKNOWLEDGMENTS

The authors are pleased to take this opportunity to express our warmest thanks to all the Prentice Hall staff, past and present, who worked with the book.

Out thanks go also to the students of Central Michigan University who have allowed us to use their papers, paragraphs, and sentences in the book.

We are pleased to acknowledge the contributions of colleagues who offered feedback at various stages in the production of the book: Mark Branson, Davidson County Community College; Peggy F. Broder, Cleveland State University; Polly Glover, The University of Tennessee at Martin; JoAnna Stephens Mink, Atlantic Christian College; Robert Moore, State University of New York-Oswego; Carol Niederlander, St. Louis Community College at Forest Park; Carolyn O'Hearn, University of Texas at El Paso; Hephzibah Roskelly, University of Massachusetts-Boston; and Richard Thompson, Northern Virginia Community College.

To our wives, Joan and Kathy, we can only say thank you for patience, understanding, faith, endurance, and the fortitude that prevails.

James F. Howell
Dean Memering

Brief Handbook for Writers

The Writing Process

1 PLANNING

2 DRAFTING

3 REVISING AND EDITING

plan

1 PLANNING

A "writing situation" is an occasion that calls for writing. When you are in a writing situation, first decide what responses will be appropriate. Make sure you understand the assignment. Are you being asked for your opinion? Are you being asked to defend a thesis? In any writing situation, there is a writer (you), a subject, and an audience, each of which must be considered as you work toward a rough draft.

1a Analyze the assignment.

OPEN-ENDED ASSIGNMENTS

An open-ended assignment suggests a general subject but does not impose any restrictions on your writing. You may be asked to write about "something related to government" or "some aspect of Renaissance life" or "something that interests you." When an assignment is given in this open-ended fashion, you must *find* your subject. You are expected to transform the general assignment into a limited, specific topic.

STRUCTURED ASSIGNMENTS

A structured assignment specifies a limited subject to write about but may not suggest a focus. You may be given a specific assignment to write an essay about Shakespeare's animal imagery in *The Tempest* or a report about the Works Project Administration during the Great Depression. You are expected to find your own approach to the subject. The subject is *what* you are writing about, but you must answer the question, *What about it?* What *purpose* will your paper serve?

ESSAYS AND REPORTS

An essay requires a thesis—a statement of what the essay will attempt to show (see **2b,** Thesis)—such as "Hamlet was insane"; "America should return to the gold standard." An essay is an opinion, with evidence showing why the writer holds the opinion. If you believe Hamlet was insane, you should quote evidence of his insanity from the play. It isn't necessary to quote authorities who also hold that opinion. You might do some research for your paper, but an essay isn't a report and shouldn't be a compilation of other people's thoughts.

A report, on the other hand, is a compilation of information, not usually an opinion. Unlike essays, reports normally require quotations and paraphrasing and typically involve documentation. See Writing Assignments for use of documentation.

1b Determine your writing purpose.

Regardless of the assignment, you must analyze your own *purpose.* Purpose refers to the effect your writing will have on your audience. Do you want to entertain, persuade, inform? The clearer you are about your objectives, the more successfully you will fulfill them. A writer's purpose cannot be merely "to write about" something. Vague, inexact purposes lead to vague, inexact writing.

In his English class, Todd, a college freshman, was given an open-ended assignment: Write a brief essay on some subject that interests you. Todd has chosen his topic: fraternities. But this is only the general subject area; Todd doesn't plan to write everything about fraternities. He must search for his *point of view,* something specific *about* fraternities, some idea about which he can give his opinion. His purpose is to tell the reader something about fraternities, but what? and why? Will this subject interest Todd's readers?

Todd's purpose depends on who his reader is. If Todd were writing a letter to a friend, he might choose to tell stories about parties and fraternity events. But Todd is writing for a composition class; he may be asked to read his essay aloud. What can he tell this audience about fraternities that they would find worth hearing? Like Todd, you too must think *plan* about your reader. You will quickly discover that what you can tell your reader depends on what you *know* about your subject.

1c Explore various sources for finding subject matter.

EXPERIENCES

If you are writing an informal essay, you may be able to draw on your own experiences for material. For example, a thesis like "Our schools teach conformity and obedience" might be supported by examples from your own experience with school.

OBSERVATIONS

Sometimes you can develop a topic with material based on your own observations. For a botany report, you might be asked to find and describe various examples of flora. In sociology class, you might have to write a case study based on your observations of human behaviors.

COURSE WORK

In English class, you may read a novel, poem, or play. You can use your reading as a source for writing, analyze the theme of a poem, discuss the characters of a novel, and so on. (See Writing Assignments.) If you are studying American history, you may wish to write an essay about the colonial period, for example.

THE LIBRARY

You may be given assignments involving unfamiliar material. In such cases, studying library materials will enable you to come to know a subject well enough to write about it. (See Writing Assignments for more about library and research skills.)

1d Use various techniques for exploring and analyzing subject matter.

BRAINSTORMING

The easiest way to generate ideas is brainstorming: jotting down ideas in random order, "thinking on paper." Brainstorming means jotting down as rough notes everything you can think of related to the subject. The technique works best when it's done rapidly and without making judgments about the validity or relevance of the ideas.

When you have written down everything you can think of, sort your ideas and look for patterns. During this process, you will discover that you have more to say about some things than about others. This fact can be a clue to you either to drop some ideas or to develop them more fully (with research, for example). This second step in brainstorming helps you look for a controlling idea. Step two allows you to *focus* on your thesis question.

Since Todd's assignment calls for a *brief* essay, and he has some first-hand knowledge of fraternities, he tries to brainstorm. As ideas occur to him he jots them down:

BRAINSTORMING NOTES

fraternities (sororities?) frat houses 3 million in
societies history of
brothers pins, paddles, rings
frats getting popular again

Sigmas Greeks
snobs, rich kids? costs of fraternities?

pledging (why?) friends, companions, brotherhood,
contacts for business
(national organizations)
loyalty, commitment.

secret societies
beer, booze, girls – v.s. social relevance/socially useful:
blood drives
cleanup campaigns

hazing?
Should hazing be allowed?
injuries, abuses, etc.

ACTIVITY 1

Try a prewriting of your own. Assume you have an assignment like Todd's: write a brief essay on a familiar subject. Brainstorm to see how many ideas you can jot down.

INFORMAL OUTLINING

Create a rough outline of your major thoughts on a subject to determine whether they are worth pursuing and to see the relationships among them. For example, after brainstorming, Todd tries an informal outline for himself:

INFORMAL OUTLINE

```
  I. Thesis
     (Do frats do anything worthwhile?)
 II. Examples
     A (They help students get through college.)
     B (They donate services to the community.)
       1 Blood drives
       2 Cleanup campaigns
       3 Money for charity
     C (They train future leaders.)
III. Conclusion
     (Yes, frats are worthwhile.)
```

From his brainstorming, Todd has rejected possibilities like the history of fraternities, their cost, and their revival. He has attempted to select from his random thoughts a specific point of view, with concrete examples to support it. This outline represents Todd's first attempt to focus his subject, and it, like any other phase of writing, might be revised several times.

ACTIVITY 2

Write an informal outline for an essay you will write from your previous brainstorming, or start with a new subject.

FREEWRITING

Todd is still thinking about his subject. Something about his outline looks unsatisfying to him. Perhaps his idea is too easy, too obvious. Todd tries a "freewriting" or thinking-on-paper technique, shifting his point of view. His outline reflects a positive view of fraternities, but sometimes a better essay can come from an opposing stance, an unpopular point of view.

FREEWRITING

Does fraternity hazing have a place in our society. Do fraternities kid themselves when they think they aren't doing anything wrong. How can they justify something that has been proven to hurt so many people. Where do we draw the limit. I think that these ceremonies should be monitored by an elected staff of people from each fraternity. These people shouldn't be allowed to drink & should keep an open mind, but not be biased toward the fraternities side... their brothers side. With the limit self-imposed by people from the group this would insure as much.... Also there should be heavy fines for any individual that on his

plan

own or through his instigation causes any mental or physical punishment that might impair a persons health. Something has to be done This is apparent. Maybe it could be done in steps. Maybe the nationals could set up new forms of initiation. They would have to visit every fraternity & set this up. Too many people have been killed. 55 that I know of. Probably a lot more. These deaths are so senseless when you think that they never need to occur at all. What kind of things could prove the loyalty & commitment that hazing apparently provides.

ACTIVITY 3

Try a freewriting of your own. Write quickly, without trying to guide your ideas and without regard for spelling or grammar. Freewriting works best as a spontaneous flow of thoughts, even if the thoughts seem to wander.

FOCUSED ANALYSIS

From his first outline to his freewriting, Todd has uncovered two conflicting views of the subject. These techniques have helped him begin to understand his subject. Now he focuses on fraternity hazing.

FOCUSED NOTES

Fraternity Hazing

deaths	*proves a commitment*
physical abuse	*proves loyalty*
mental abuse	*proves reasons for joining*
humiliation	*assures secrecy*

bad outweighs the good

I. Fraternity Hazing
  A. What it is
  B. Thesis statement
II Examples
  A. The mental abuse
  B. Injuries
  C. Deaths
III Abolishing Hazing
  —restate thesis
  —go over three points made
  —personal opinion

At last Todd is beginning to find his idea. Though he is aware of positive aspects of fraternities, Todd intends to write about hazing. This rough outline may be enough to get him started in the right direction.

1e Limit the scope of the essay with a thesis statement.

After you have analyzed the writing situation, your material, and your purpose, you can write a thesis statement for your essay. A thesis statement is a clear expression of what you are going to write about; it is a single sentence that states precisely what the composition is about. For example, "The poor should not have to pay taxes."

A thesis statement for an essay has two components. It specifies some topic ("the poor") and makes a limited statement about it ("should not have to pay taxes"). The thesis limits your subject. You cannot write everything about poverty in a short paper; you must find a subtopic small enough to deal with. The more limited your thesis statement is, the easier it will be to bring your essay into focus.

Notice that in Todd's brainstorming (pp. 5–6) a number

plan of ideas occur to him: fraternities have a long history; fraternities are becoming popular again; fraternities are socially relevant. He knows he can't merely summarize all this; he cannot write everything about fraternities in a short essay. Therefore, he continues to think about the subject until he finds a limited thesis question: Should fraternity hazing be abolished? With this limitation on his subject, he no longer needs to concern himself with matters like history and cost.

Avoid overly broad, ambiguous, intangible concepts. Avoid thesis statements like the following that are too broad for a short essay: national defense policies should be revised; automation is changing our society; the English novel takes many forms. "Limiting" the thesis doesn't necessarily involve the physical size of the subject. A paper about Chicago isn't necessarily more limited than a paper about America, though Chicago is physically smaller than America. It isn't the subject that determines the size of a thesis but the *focus* on the subject. It isn't *what* the subject is but *what about it?* that determines size.

Nevertheless, some subjects are so big that almost no thesis can focus them sufficiently for a short paper. Abstract, philosophical subjects like communism, theology, human motivation, morality, and so forth are very large, general concepts suitable for books and doctoral dissertations. A good thesis for a college composition must be clear and specific. You should avoid ambiguous words and intangible concepts like *justice, ethics*, and *society*. Since these words mean different things to different people, they aren't good choices for a thesis unless and until they can be made specific and concrete. Note that Todd's first attempt at a thesis contains the idea that fraternities are "worthwhile," but this is a vague concept. What is worthwhile to one person may be worthless to another. Todd decides to continue revising his ideas; he is looking for a more specific, less ambiguous idea. (See his freewriting, pp. 7–8.)

Avoid self-evident, trivial, or overworked subjects. It is a mistake to try to avoid large, abstract subjects by selecting a very simple thesis. Avoid obvious, self-evident statements: murder is wrong; pollution should be controlled; smoking may lead to cancer. While such a thesis may be workable, it violates the basic purpose of composition. There is no point in telling readers what they already know. A thesis must be worthwhile for the writer, but it must also be worthwhile to the reader. Avoid trivial, immature subjects like "Getting ready for school each morning is hard work" or trite, overworked subjects like "Christmas has become too commercial." Every writing situation has three components—the writer, the subject, and the reader—and your thesis must account for each of them. You must revise your thesis until it satisfies you personally, does justice to the subject matter, and is appropriate for your audience.

1f Evaluate the thesis.

You can evaluate your own thesis on three criteria: (1) Is it specific enough? Does it name an unambiguous subject? (2) Is it limited enough? Is the focus narrow enough for a thorough treatment in a short paper? (3) Is it a worthwhile thesis? Does it satisfy the three components of the writing situation: worthwhile to you personally, appropriately focused for the nature of the subject itself, and appropriate for the intended audience?

GENERAL SUBJECTS	REVISED TO MORE SPECIFIC SUBTOPICS
love	love of country, romantic love, self-love
war	the arms race, the peace movement, the draft
the President	the President's economic policy, personal appeal, leadership qualities

BROAD TOPICS	REVISED TO MORE LIMITED TOPICS
romantic love	teenage marriages
the arms race	the Star Wars weapons
the President's appeal	the President's speech techniques

TRIAL THESES	REVISED TO THE WRITING SITUATION
Teenage marriages are a bad idea.	Teenagers are not mature enough for marriage.
Star Wars weapons will defend us.	Star Wars weapons are impractical.
The President delivers his speeches with style.	The President uses humor to show that he means well.

ACTIVITY 4

Evaluate each of the following statements. Write your analysis for each one. Which ones might make good thesis statements for short compositions? If you feel any of these are not good, explain why.

1. There are many advantages to a career in forestry.
2. The people of the world have many fascinating cultures.
3. Children of alcoholics are often abused and become drug dependent themselves.
4. There are many ways to improve the art of selling.
5. All college students should learn to operate a computer.
6. The MX missile is essential to our national defense.
7. Male college students should not wear earrings.
8. Friendships are valuable.
9. Dogs are easier to train than cats.
10. Mandatory public education violates citizens' freedom of choice.

Todd needs a *limited* subject. The overall subject, fraternities, was too big and too general. Through prewriting Todd has narrowed it to fraternity hazing. He must consider his own position and his readers' position: what will appeal to his composition class, educated general readers? At last Todd discovers his thesis: Hazing should be abolished. He is ready to try a rough draft. (See Drafting.)

ACTIVITY 5
Prewrite a topic for a possible composition. Describe your purpose. Jot down notes on the material you will use. Keep writing until you have two or three pages of notes; continue prewriting until you have exhausted your ideas. Evaluate and revise your thesis statement.

2 DRAFTING

When you have found sufficient information for your essay, you can begin a rough draft. In the drafting stage, you must begin to be specific about your subject, but this writing is tentative and rough, and you must expect to revise several drafts before arriving at the finished paper.

2a Clarify the aim of the composition.

For your first draft, you should be able to describe your overall intention as *informative, argumentative or persuasive*, or *expressive*. Your purpose must become clear to you if it is to become clear to your reader. Ask yourself, What do I want to achieve with this paper? Is the paper to focus on the information, on the reader, or on you, the writer?

INFORMATIVE

Informative writing reports and explains facts; it is the most widely used form of academic writing. The aim of such writing is to give information to the reader. For example, papers like "The New Tax Proposal," "The President's Human Rights Record," or "The Development of Modern Music" call for a straightforward presentation of facts—as opposed to arguments or opinions.

ARGUMENTATIVE AND PERSUASIVE

Argumentative or persuasive writing seeks to change the reader's mind. If the composition is strictly objective, presenting only facts and figures as evidence, it is called argumentation. The evidence by itself will move the mind of a reasonable reader. But if your composition uses emotional arguments and ethical appeals as well as logical ones, readers are likely to call your composition persuasive. These distinctions are usually too narrow to be of much consequence: readers believe they are *convinced* by appeals to the mind, but *persuaded* by appeals to emotions and morals. The truth is that many compositions of this type are both argumentative and persuasive.

EXPRESSIVE

Expressive writing attempts to show the writer's emotions, to share human experiences. It is most commonly used in nonfiction for autobiographical writing—the writer gives his or her personal experience, expresses feelings, explores ideas from a purely personal point of view.

2b Control the first draft with your thesis statement.

Once you have decided on the aim of your essay, you must find an appropriate thesis statement. For example, Todd has decided to write an argumentative/persuasive essay that will show why fraternity hazing should be abolished. This thesis statement will control his paper so that everything he writes will help to convince his reader. Thus Todd will write a unified essay that sticks to the idea he has selected.

The thesis statement will also suggest to Todd what material *ought* to be included. (See **1e.**) He knows he cannot simply make assertions and express moral disapproval. Todd's personal opinion of hazing won't move his readers, who may have different opinions. To *convince* his readers, Todd must illustrate his thesis with specific examples of what is wrong with hazing. His thesis is serious, and therefore he will write not about mere silly pranks but about serious dangers in hazing.

2c Select a developmental strategy for your whole composition.

Writers must determine the general strategy for their compositions. It's possible to use several in a composition, but you may find it easier to stick with a single strategy. Compositions aren't written by formula, and these strategies aren't patterns for writing. They are options to help you think about subject matter. (See **43c** for developmental patterns.)

NARRATION

Narrative writing uses chronological order. Stories use narration, but this pattern can also be used in many other kinds of writing. Events are listed in a time sequence such as beginning, middle, and end. The chronology needn't start at the beginning so long as the reader can follow the order of events.

> A Proposal for a Computer Lab
>
> Since 1975 faculty members have been using computers in their own research and writing. In 1976 two professors published a large textbook they had written entirely on computers. As more professors discovered the benefits of computers, they began to discuss ways in which students, too, might benefit from use of the machines. Then in 1980 a faculty committee wrote a proposal for "A Study of the Benefits to Students of Using Computers for Writing." The study described in that proposal was completed in 1984. The study showed positive results when students used computers. Based on that study and other research, the following proposal establishes the benefits of a lab in which students would be trained to use computers for writing.

DESCRIPTION

Descriptive writing presents items according to their relationships in space. For example, a description of a room can start with the items nearest the observer (the writer) and then move to items farther and farther away. Any pattern of arrangement is possible so long as the reader is given clear signals to follow.

> The lab is set up in a horseshoe pattern, with machines along three walls. As students enter the room, they are met by the

lab assistant, who sits at a table near the door. To the right of the door is the first wall of computers.

ILLUSTRATION

The most frequently used pattern of development is illustration: writers provide *examples* to illustrate their points. If you write an informal essay about your roommate's bad habits, for instance, you would need to illustrate those habits by giving examples.

> Students at first encounter many frustrating problems with computers. For example, after typing in several pages of a composition, some students forget that they must tell the computer to "save" their work. Without the "save" command, all the work is lost when the machine is turned off.

CLASSIFICATION

When writing about large numbers of things, it's useful to arrange them into groups, to classify them by type. For instance, you might write about students by classifying them with some criterion you select, such as reasons for coming to college: those who come to study, those who come to play, those who come because they were forced to, and so on.

> Students react in different ways to the computer. Some students are immediately intrigued by the technology. Seeing their work appear on the screen as they type is a novelty for such students. Others feel frustrated and anxious about the strangeness of the commands. Beeps from the machine, indicating errors, fluster these students. Still others, those who are excellent typists, prefer to use their typewriters. Their familiarity and expertise with the typewriter make the computer seem unnecessary.

DEFINITION

For some academic writing, you may need to define things. What is democracy? What is a social order? What is a sonnet? In the dictionary sense, a definition specifies a group or class (a sonnet is a poem) and a subgroup or distinguishing characteristic (of fourteen lines). Less formally, you may use other ways to define concepts, such as describing what the word means to you personally, what it means in actual practice, or what it means in comparison to other, similar terms.

Computer-assisted instruction uses the computer as if it were a teacher or a textbook. The computer can help students revise by asking questions and by showing principles of revision. Some CAI programs can identify errors and problems in writing and suggest possible ways to revise them.

COMPARISON

Compositions may use a compare-and-contrast strategy to show differences and similarities. You can compare the old with the new, the artificial with the natural, and so on. In academic writing, you may be called upon to compare two books, two theories, or two historical periods.

Writing with the computer is similar to using a typewriter, but there are a number of differences. The typewriter and the computer have similar keyboards. Both machines print on paper. However, revising on a traditional typewriter means retyping everything; revising on the computer means typing only the changes.

ANALYSIS (PROCESS)

A process analysis describes stages of development in actions or events. An objective description of the steps in designing a house tells the reader how to do it. If the composition is thought of as a recipe or set of directions for the reader, then the writer must be very specific, providing the reader with all the information required to repeat the process.

To start the Apple IIe with a program like Appleworks, a word-processing program, requires three steps. First you must insert a start-up disk into the disk drive and then turn on the machine. This prepares the computer to accept a program. Next you must remove the start-up disk and insert the program disk. When the program disk is fully loaded, the machine will ask you for the data disk. Finally, remove the program disk and insert your data disk.

ANALYSIS (CAUSAL)

A causal analysis describes a cause-and-effect sequence of events. You may analyze something physical, such as the causes of an accident, or something less tangible, such as the causes of the Civil War.

Sometimes the computer sends an error message: "Cannot read disk." This error may be caused by a variety of mistakes. Often the disk has not been properly formatted; you must start over and tell the computer to format the disk. Sometimes the disk has been put into the wrong drive; remove the disk and put it into the proper drive. Once in a while students accidentally put the disk in backwards or upside down.

ACTIVITY 6

Write a substantial paragraph on some subject you know well. Use one of the standard organizational strategies to guide your thinking.

2d Clarify point of view toward the reader, the subject matter, and the writer.

Point of view is the writer's attitude, a "slant" on the writing situation. Several writers might cover the same subject, for example, but each with a different point of view. Point of view is made up of the writer's attitudes (or views) toward the reader, toward subject matter, and toward self.

Adopt an appropriate attitude toward the reader. Many problems in writing arise from faulty assumptions about the reader. If you're writing for teachers, you can assume they prefer clear, concise, and accurate language. Readers don't expect to see ungrammatical writing or unproofread papers. You should also be careful about using big words and difficult sentences. Adult readers don't enjoy papers that sound immature, but that doesn't mean your teachers expect heavy writing from you. They do, however, expect sincerity. If you are indifferent, your readers will see that offensive attitude in your writing.

Maintain an appropriate tone toward the subject matter. It is a mistake to pretend to know more than you do; writers must study, collect information, and come to know their subjects well. A negative attitude, sarcasm, or cuteness are seldom appropriate: they indicate the writer feels superior to the subject. On the other hand, if your attitude is *too* serious, the result will sound heavy and pretentious.

Express an appropriate attitude toward yourself as writer. Your writing expresses your personality. Readers hear your "voice" in what you write. If you are bored, your "voice" will sound bored. If you are sarcastic, the sarcasm will come through the writing (not a good idea). Flippancy, misplaced humor, condescension, pretentiousness, pomposity, and other unnatural voices are mistakes. You must sound credible and trustworthy.

2e Construct an outline that shows the organization of your material and supports your thesis.

Outlines can be formal or informal, but either way an outline will help you to organize your material. The outline separates major and minor points and shows how they relate to each other. For example:

```
        The Legal Drinking Age Should Be Lowered

  I. Background to the question
 II. The conventional view: drinking at age 21
     A. Keeping alcohol out of high school
     B. Preventing addiction to alcohol
     C. Reducing alcohol-related accidents and crime
     D. Preserving conventional social values
III. The liberal view: lowering the drinking age to 18
     A. Preventing rebellion of minors
     B. Standardizing rights of all citizens
     C. Treating alcohol-related problems consistently
        1. Openly identifying nature and extent of
           problems
        2. Providing counseling, treatment for all
           citizens with abuse or addiction problems
     D. Contradicting accident and crime statistics
```

```
IV. Thesis question answered
    A. Summary of main points
    B. Closing statement
```

The outline provides a standard organizational pattern for otherwise random information. Use of the outline can help you to clarify your thoughts, identify the points you want to make, and set up a plan for your paper that the reader will understand. Note that standard parts of an outline like the introduction and conclusion are not labeled as such; use a descriptive heading instead.

The sequence of levels in a standard outline is as follows: roman numerals, capital letters, arabic numerals, lower-case letters, arabic numerals in parentheses, lower-case letters in parentheses.

```
I.
    A.
        1.
        2.
            a.
            b.
                (1)
                (2)
                    (a)
                    (b)
    B.
        1.
        2.
            a.
            b.
                (1)
                (2)
                    (a)
                    (b)
II.
```

There is no standard procedure for additional levels in this kind of an outline, and it is unlikely that you will need more divisions than this. However, if you did decide to add additional levels, you might try using brackets [A], [1]; lower-case roman numerals (i, ii, iii); or some other logical extension of the system.

Note that a formal outline uses parallel language: all the points are expressed in similar language. You can use full sentences or topical statements, as long as the outline is consistent. (Don't mix full sentences with topical statements.)

In a formal outline, there should be no such thing as a *1* without a *2* or an *a* without a *b*; there is no point in numbering if you have only one item. If you find any one-item categories in your outline, you should revise. The most common solution is to reword the main heading so that the subpoint is absorbed. For example:

ILLOGICAL (ONE-ITEM SUBPOINT)

```
 I. Cause of hypertension
    A. Excess sugar in the diet
II. Treatments of hypertension
```

REVISED (SUBPOINT ABSORBED IN MAIN POINT)

```
 I. Cause of hypertension: excess sugar in the diet
II. Treatments of hypertension
```

However, often these single-item divisions are clues that you need more research. In the example above, the writer should find additional causes of hypertension. Thus the outline can help you understand how well you have researched and can show you where your paper is weak.

ACTIVITY 7

Prepare a formal outline for an essay of several paragraphs. You may select the topic you used in activity 5 or some other topic that interests you.

---

draft

2f Give your composition an effective title.

Every paper should have a title. The title should give readers an idea of your subject and arouse their interest. Often a title can help you find your approach to a subject; however, sometimes the best time to select a title is after you have written the draft, when you are sure of your thesis. In either case, the title should be concise and fit the tone of your paper. A title of "Bombed Out" for a serious paper on the destruction of Dresden during World War II sets the wrong tone; it trivializes the topic. Avoid vague or inappropriate titles and ones that promise more than they can deliver. "An In-Depth View of the Problems of Disarmament" promises a serious discussion of a very big subject and probably can't be delivered in a short paper. A title like "Problems with the B1 Bomber" promises a more realistically limited paper.

2g Write your first draft.

After making decisions about the overall purpose of your essay, its organization, and your point of view, you may be ready to try a first draft. Concentrate on getting on paper the general idea and organization of your composition. Since there are going to be revisions anyway, you needn't labor too much over the first draft. Avoid crumpling up papers and starting over. Force yourself to go on to the end, even if you have to skip over hard parts.

Working from his informal outline, Todd has analyzed his point of view toward his audience (his composition class), his subject matter, and himself as author. He has produced the following rough draft. Describe his point of view: what is his attitude toward his reader, subject matter, himself? What aim or purpose has he selected? What strategy of development has he used?

Fraternities offer many good services to the community. When blood is needed at the hospital, the fraternity brothers quickly volunteer. And at least once a year several of the fraternities get out to help clean up the town. Through car washes, bottle collecting, and door-to-door collecting, fraternities help to raise money for charity. Yes, there are many good points to a fraternity, but one thing must be changed.

There are over 3 million college men in about 400 fraternities across the country. Through pledging these various fraternities there have been about 55 deaths. An amount that should be zero when you consider there shouldn't be any in the first place.

Injuries are also frequent and sometimes very serious. What promotes a person to pour a toxic chemicle on sombodies skin? This question & others are why fraternity hazing is looked at with such a criticizing eye. Other injuries & poinsoning are also frequent in today's fraternity rituals.

Mental abuse is also an important issue when discussing hazing. Can a person be the same after having relay races with sardines being passed with only the buttocks--what one does the rest follow. One would hardly think so. Many pledges have suffered mentally from pledging & even dropped out of school because of the embarrassment.

Fraternity hazing should be abolished because of the potential harm it creates. Deaths resulting from extravagant pledging rites, injuries due to sloppily done initiation ceremonies, & the possible mental

rev

```
implications from doing things one would never normally
do. These things convince me that our fraternity
systems must find another way to put pledges through &
fill the hazing abolition vacuum.
```

ACTIVITY 8

Using a brainstorming sheet you prepared earlier or a new one, write a rough draft. Assume you are writing for an audience of educated readers, like your composition class. Choose a subject you know well, as Todd did. Try to convince your readers to see the subject as you see it by providing examples, details, and reasons that illustrate your point.

3 REVISING AND EDITING

The writing process isn't linear; few writers can move forward from planning to drafting to final copy without circling back to rethink and revise. Even preliminary work—notes, freewritings, outlines, thesis statements—can be revised. At any time, anywhere in the writing process you may need to return to your notes and outlines for additions and clarifications.

Once you have a first draft, you may be tempted to proofread it, type it up, and hand it in. Writing is hard work, and you may be reluctant to do it over. But handing in a first draft would be like a furniture maker's selecting pieces of fine oak to build a table, then just tacking the pieces together without cutting, shaping, fitting, sanding, staining, or polishing them. The result may resemble a table, but it isn't finished.

Your ideas may be good, like the oak, but ideas need to be developed, language needs to be polished, and parts of the paper may need to be rearranged, added to, or deleted. You should look forward to revising as an opportunity to improve your work, especially if you have access to a computer.

3a Revise the first draft.

rev

The first draft should attempt to flesh out your outline—to capture the organization of the paper and the main points. If it can do more than that, so much the better, but no matter what is accomplished in the first draft, there is still significant work to do.

Always let a draft "cool off": wait at least a day before rereading it. The cooling-off period increases your objective distance and allows you to focus on problems, to see what needs to be changed, added, or deleted. Force yourself to read the draft slowly aloud, sentence by sentence, word by word. Assume that at least three types of revision are *always* necessary: (1) you need more information; (2) you need to delete extraneous words; and (3) you need to clarify your sentences.

ACTIVITY 9

Read Todd's first draft (pp. 23–24). What are its strengths and weaknesses? What kinds of revisions would you suggest?

Clarify the aim of your composition. Is your paper informative only, without opinions? Or are you trying to convince the reader with evidence or to persuade the reader with ethical and emotional appeals? You must clarify exactly what you are trying to achieve; revise to make sure your paper supports this aim (**2a**).

Make sure the draft and the thesis statement agree. All information in your paper must conform to the thesis; all matters of evidence, reasoning, and organization must reflect the thesis. Ask yourself about each element of your paper, Does this belong here? Does this illustrate the thesis? Many *no* answers may mean you need to develop a new thesis statement (**2b, 44, 45**).

Clarify the developmental strategy of the composition. Is the sequence of information or events clear enough for the reader? Hopping around from present to past to future, skipping over important events, and other problems of organiza-

rev tion will confuse most readers. Make sure that your readers can see the logic of your strategy (**2c**).

Clarify the point of view. Rethink your audience. Who will read your paper? What will be effective for this audience? Look at each sentence and each word in your draft. If your subject is a serious one, does everything in your paper contribute to that effect? What do your words and ideas say about yourself as the writer? (**2d**).

Make sure the draft and the outline agree. An effective way to check organization is to outline the draft, listing the points that appear in your paper. The progression of points must make sense to your reader. Look for ideas that don't seem to fit. Ask yourself, What point am I making in this paragraph? Why is this point here? Check this outline of your draft against the outline in your planning notes: do they agree? If they don't, revise the outline, the draft, or both, as necessary (**2e, 43**).

Revise for effective paragraphs. Each paragraph should make only one point and should have a purpose you can both name and relate to the thesis statement and to an outline. Moreover, the paragraphs themselves must hang together internally as well as connect to each other (**43a–c**).

The first paragraph of your composition is especially important and may be especially hard to write. We have provided some options for beginnings (**43d**); you decide which strategy best fits your purpose, tone, and topic. Check that your introductory paragraph is not one of the problem types (**43d**).

ACTIVITY 10

Practice revising for effective introductions. Assume you are writing a review of a recent film for your school newspaper. Write a rough draft introduction of several sentences, and then revise your introduction. Make a clean copy.

ACTIVITY 11

Revise the introduction you wrote for activity 10. Assume a different audience, such as a class in film criticism or a citizens' group that opposes the film. Revise the introduction to make it appropriate for this new audience.

Examine your paragraphs for repetitions; eliminate the excess. To avoid using the same word too often, find effective synonyms or consider combining sentences (p. 33). Also eliminate ideas that aren't directly connected to the purpose of the paragraph, even though they may be good ideas by themselves. ***rev***

ACTIVITY 12

Revise the following paragraph on UFOs for repetitions and irrelevant material. You may add needed transitions, but try to reduce the paragraph to its most economical form. Type up the revised version.

```
     There are many explanations of UFO sightings, and
beyond these explanations there are reasons to question
the legitimacy of so-called evidence of UFO sightings.
Hundreds of reports of UFO sightings are discovered to
be hoaxes. And most experts agree that ninety to
ninety-five percent of the pictures of UFOs and their
occupants are double exposures or some other contrived
hoax or deception. A double exposure occurs when one
picture is taken on top of another without advancing
the film. Of the evidence collected from purported UFO
landing sites, none has been identified by experts as
being other than "earthly."
```

Ending the paper can be troublesome: writers may try to do too much or may leave the reader hanging, expecting something more. Make sure your readers get a sense of closure when they finish the essay, so that they know there is nothing else coming. And make sure the paper has fulfilled the thesis obligation, has done what it said it was going to do (**43e**).

ACTIVITY 13

Study the following paragraph. Notice the changes in wording that have been made. Write a brief analysis of the effect of each revision.

When the lights came up, Mick Jagger, Keith Richard, and Ronnie Wood ~~came out together~~ lurch onto the stage in a cluster, and Bill Wyman, looking ~~uncourageous~~ timidly rather than ~~in an evil way like he didn't care~~ satanically withdrawn, goes into his spot in front of his stack. Wood, cigarette ~~held~~ mounted at a ~~happy~~ jaunty angle, ~~goes~~ scuttles over to his amp. Keith Richard ~~rubs his hand in~~ ruffles his hair and ~~picks~~ hitches up his ~~instrument~~ guitar. Jagger--wearing a ~~shiny coat~~ silver leather jacket that looks to be part of David Bowie's ~~old clothes~~ 1972 offstage wardrobe -- ~~goes~~ parades around the ~~place with his usually silly movements~~ stage with a gait like his pout expanded into an entire body style.

When Todd rethinks his first draft (pp. 23–24), he finds a number of places to improve. This draft isn't bad, but it is very general; there is little *information* in it. When Todd considers his audience, he realizes they probably don't need to be told that hazing abuses are bad; they need facts, examples, illustrations. The paper seems underdeveloped. Now read Todd's revision:

Fraternity hazing is any action taken that may produce mental or physical discomfort. It can be humiliating and degrading. University officials for a long time have been trying to abolish hazing. Nationals have also tried to help in ~~determing~~ their chapters hazing rituals. The problem still exists however, and is in ~~dire~~ immediate need of drastic action. I think fraternity hazing should be abolished because of ~~the harm it does~~ its particularly degrading and dangerous nature. This is Illustrated ~~in the~~ following points. ~~examples~~.

TAKE OUT: ~~Fraternities offer many good services to the community. When blood is needed at the hospital, the fraternity brothers quickly volunteer. And at least once a year several of the fraternities get out to help clean up the town. Through car washes, bottle collecting, and door to door collecting fraternities help to raise money for charity. Yes, there are many good points to a fraternity, but one thing must be changed.~~

Highway incident: There are over 3 million college men in about 400 fraternities across the country. Through pledging these various fraternities ~~there have been~~ are the cause of about 55 deaths. One such death involved a pledge that was walking across a highway blindfolded when a car struck and killed him. This death and others could have been prevented with stricter hazing laws. An amount that should be zero when you consider there shouldn't be any in the first place.

Injuries are also frequent and sometimes very serious. What promotes a person to ~~pour a toxic chemicle on~~ ~~badly burn~~ (STET) ~~sombodies~~ a pledges skin? This question & others are why fraternity hazing is looked at with such a criticizing eye. ~~Another incident was~~ One boy from the University of West Virginia was badly burned when lighter fluid ignighted his body during an init. rite. Other injuries ~~& poinsoning~~ are also frequent in todays fraternity rituals, such as: Alcohol poisoning, suffocation, and so on.

Mental abuse is also an important issue when discussing hazing. Can a person be the same after having relay races with sardines being passed with only the buttocks--what one does the rest follow. One would hardly think so. Many pledges have suffered mentally from pledging & even dropped out of school bexause of the embarrassment.

Fraternity hazing should be abolished because of the potential harm it ~~creates~~ can cause. Deaths resulting from extravagant pledging rites, injuries due to sloppily ~~done~~ run initiation ceromonies, & the possible mental implications from doing things one would never normally do show the urgency of the situation. ~~These things convince me that our fraternity systems must find another way to put pledges through & fill the hazing abolition vacuum.~~ The vaccuum hazing abolition would leave must be filled by a more constructive set of guidelines and ensure the safety of new inductees and the continuance of our frat. system.

Note that Todd has replaced or revised both his introduction and conclusion, two hard spots in any composition. He has added examples to illustrate his point, giving his essay a much more developed sound. These revisions improve the essay, and Todd types a second draft incorporating them.

Some students might feel the paper is now ready to hand in. Todd has already put a good deal of work into it, and it's now better than it was. But there is still work to do on this essay. Now that the general structure and substance of the paper have been decided, Todd can turn his attention to matters of clarity and accuracy and the style of his sentences.

ACTIVITY 14

Practice revision. Following is a paragraph excerpted from a story about an accident in which a young girl was killed. If you were trying to improve this first draft, what would you do to it? Use your imagination to supply missing details. After you have revised it, type a clean copy.

We were coming back from the game. My friend and I were heading back to school. I needed to change my rev

```
clothes for the dance. The game had been close, but we
lost. As we were driving back to school the dark road
was dark, naturally. Country roads, of course, do not
have lights. The radio was on loud. Suddenly I see
coming right up behind me, lights. They were coming
right along at a high rate of speed. All of the sudden
this car passes me quickly and goes into a curve. In
the dark I saw a flash of blue paint as it went by. The
only thing was that it never came out of the curve.
Here we had been going along, and suddenly—an accident!
The car was old and went sideways, and the next thing I
knew I saw headlights spinning through the air. It went
off the pavement and into a ditch. The car rolled
several times through the ditch and came to a stop
about forty yards out in a hay field. It turned right
side up. I could imagine what the farmer would say
about tire ruts in his field!
```

3b Revise the second draft.

Most professional writers write several drafts, striving for perfection. All this rewriting makes weary work for the author, but it also holds great promise: each draft comes closer to realizing the author's objectives.

Monitor style as well as content. Style is the result of the choices you make in selecting words and constructing sentences and paragraphs. Style projects personality, attitude, and point of view along with your information. First, decide whether you've maintained the proper distance with your audience (**2d**). Then look at the words you've used (**40–42**). Suit word choice to the topic and to your audience. Using every big word from the thesaurus when writing about relatively common subjects is seldom appropriate. For example: *rev*

```
After perusing the proffered documentation and its
concomitant germaneness to both the potable and
nonpotable aqueous matter available for utilization by
the indigenous population of the urban center, the
committee vacillated as to a recommendation.
```

Few readers will be impressed by such big words and difficult sentences. This is called the pretentious style—it pretends to be more important than it is. Any writer can make simple subjects seem complex by using a pretentious style; however, the goal is to present complex subjects simply: "The report on water pollution made no recommendation."

The preferred style for most writing is a "plain style": clear, concise, accurate sentences in a simple, "natural" English. Good style for academic writing is plain English modified for educated readers, meaning that you are required to use standard grammar, avoid slang, write readable sentences. use conventional spelling and punctuation. However, plain style does not mean dull or colorless writing.

ACTIVITY 15

What is wrong with the style of the following composition? Mark revisions to improve the style. Imagine a person entering a prison as part of a visiting ball team. Is this the way you would describe such an experience? After marking your revisions, prepare a clean copy.

```
    We arrived at the entrance to the prison at about
eleven o'clock in the morning. We were required to go
through a guarded gate in order to enter. After passing
```

rev

```
through several security tests we were allowed to
proceed into the parking lot. From there we were led
into a building which had a small locker room, and we
were told to keep our valuables in a strongbox, which
was under constant guard. Before we could proceed to
the field, we were searched by two security guards. We
were then led to a set of two sliding iron bar doors,
which led into a large visitor's lobby, where the
prisoners are allowed to see their families. This lobby
was unattractive. We then proceeded through two more
iron doors and were marked with a liquid on our hands
for identification. This liquid only shows up under a
black light. Finally after a long walk through a
corridor we approached the last iron gate, which led
into the courtyard.
```

Revise for accurate and effective sentences. Make your sentences clear. Look for sentences that might be awkward, badly worded, overly complicated, or ambiguous. If in doubt about any sentence, read it aloud slowly, either to yourself or to someone else. Every sentence *can* be changed; your job is to decide which changes will have the best effect on your reader (**20**).

Make your sentences economical. Say exactly what you want to say in the fewest words. This is not to suggest that you should write only simple little sentences but rather that you must eliminate unnecessary repetitions, irrelevant information, and any words that do not contribute to the effect you are trying to achieve. If it's possible to delete words without losing the meaning you are after, they should be eliminated (**20**).

ACTIVITY 16

Carefully evaluate each sentence in the following paragraph. Revise to make the sentences effective not only in themselves but also in the context of the other sentences.

In 1972 the policy of the Israeli people toward terrorism were put to a severe test. During the Olympic games in Munich Germany Arab terrorists seized nine Israeli athletes. And killed two others in the process. Their demand; two hundred Arab prisoners who are to be flown and to be released to the Arab capital. The Israeli government refused to negotiate, instead they decided by means of planning an ambush in which they hoped to either kill or capture the Arab commandos, the group of hostages and their captors were transported to a nearby airport. In the early morning hours five West German sharpshooters open fire on the hostages contained in the helicopter and kidnappers. There weren't any survivors.

Use sentence combining to revise for variety in structure and length. Pay particular attention to the number of short, simple sentences. If there are too many short ones, try combining sentences. **Sentence combining** means adding, deleting, replacing, or rearranging words in two or more sentences to produce a single, effective sentence.

SHORT SENTENCES	COMBINED
The officer ordered the man to halt. The man was running down the street. He was carrying a new TV set.	The officer ordered the man running down the street with a new TV set to halt.

rev As a general rule, short sentences should be reserved for emphasis, to make a point stand out (**20**).

ACTIVITY 17

Using your own sense of language rhythm, revise the following paragraph. Invent details to add information. Revise the sentences for greater variety and emphasis. Make the paragraph sound more realistic and mature.

I told my parents I was going away to college. I was praying they'd understand. It was hard to tell them. It was the hardest thing I did in my life. It's not fair to bring up anything like this so suddenly. They didn't even know I had applied to out-of-state schools. My mother thought I was kidding at first. All hell broke loose later when she realized I was telling the truth. She was crying and saying things, they didn't make sense. I tried explaining, I tried to defend myself against her accusations. She said I didn't love her and my father. She said I didn't want to help my father in the shop anymore. I wanted her to understand. I wanted him to understand too. All our hopes and dreams would have a greater chance of becoming a reality. But only if I went to college and learned how to really design machine tools. They settled down and thought it over. They decided I might be right.

Revise for accurate and effective word choice. Ask yourself whether your word choice is appropriate: Is it suited exactly to you as a writer and to what you are trying to accomplish with your reader? A single misused word can put the reader off and cause you to lose credibility. Even with the most precise language possible, there may be some readers who will not understand you; and your readers will surely misunderstand if your language is general, vague, inexact. For example, can you achieve your effect with a word like *collie, mongrel, cur, puppy, hound, mutt, stray?* Or is it sufficient to use the general word, *dog?* Are your verbs exact? Suppose you are describing a politician besieged by reporters after his trial for drug possession. Does he *talk, yell, speak, rant, bellow, whisper, shout, orate, posture, whine?* What picture are you trying to create for your reader? (**40–42**). ***rev***

ACTIVITY 18

Here are Todd's revisions of the second draft. Read the paper carefully. Be prepared to discuss the revisions. What has Todd changed? Are the changes helpful?

Fraternity Hazing

Fraternity hazing is any action ~~taken~~ that may produce mental or physical discomfort. It can be humi li ating or degrading. Universit y officials have, for a long time, been trying to abolish hazing. Nationals have also tried to ~~help in~~ deter ~~ing~~ in thier chapters ri hazing rituals. The problem still exists however, and is in immediate need of drastic action. ~~I think~~ Fraternity hazing should be abolished because of its particulary degrading and dangerous nature. ~~This is illustrated in the following points.~~

There are over a million college men in about 400 fraternities across the nation ~~country~~. Through the rites of pledging ~~these various fraternities are the cause of about~~ there have been an estimated 55 deaths. ~~An amount that should be zero when you consider there shouldn't be any in the first place.~~ One such death involved a pledge who ~~that~~ was walking across a highway blindfolded when a car struck and killed hin. This death and others could have been prevented with stricter hazing laws.

Injuries are also frequent and sometimes very serious. What promotes a person to pour a toxic chemical ~~cle~~ on a pledges' skin? ~~This~~ Questions like these ~~and others~~ are why fraternity hazing is looked at so critically ~~with such a criticizing eye~~. One young man ~~boy~~, from ~~the~~ University ~~of~~ West Virginia was badly burned when lighter fluid ignighted his

rev

body during an intiation rite. Other injuries are also frequent in todays freaternity rituals, such as: ~~A~~ alcohol poisoning, soffocation, and ~~so on~~ stabbing wounds.

~~Mental~~ Hazing abuse is ~~also an important issue when discussing fraternity hazing.~~ not only physical but mental as well. Can a person be the same after ~~having~~ participating in relay races ~~with~~ in which sardines ~~being~~ are passed with only the buttocks. One would hardly think so. Many pledges have suffered mentally from pledging initiation rites. Some have ~~and~~ even dropped out of school because of the embarrassment, harrassment, and ridicule. This must surely end if ~~uor~~ our fraternity systems are to survive.

Fraternity hazing sould be abolished because of the ~~potential~~ harm it can cause. Deaths resulting from extravagant bizzare, and cruel pledging rites; injuries due to sloppily run initiation ceromonies; and the possible mental ~~implications~~ consequences from doing things one would never normally do ~~show thw~~ make urgency + reasons for abolition. ~~of the situation~~. Instead of ~~The~~ hazing ~~abolition would leave must be filled by~~ we need a more constructive set of guidelines. ~~and~~ This would insure the safety of new inductees and the continuance of our fraternity system.

3c End the revision process.

It's always possible to make more changes, but at some point additional changes may become excessive fiddling with the manuscript. By the time you have revised a second draft and incorporated all your changes into the third draft, you may be ready to stop revising. You will not be through working, but if you have revised carefully, you should have a well-structured and worthwhile composition nearing completion.

3d Edit the third draft.

In the third draft, writers narrow their focus to small details. If you should find anything else to change at this point, any final changes in ideas, organization, language, by all means make the changes. But the chief function of the third draft is to *polish* your composition, give it the finished, professional look of a skilled writer. *rev*

Edit your sentences for formal grammar. Educated readers don't expect to find grammatical errors in serious writing. Editing for standard English shows that you respect your audience. Keep an eye on subject/verb and pronoun/antecedent agreement (**9–10**). The reader must be certain who is doing what in each of your sentences. Correctness of pronoun case (such as the difference between *who* and *whom*) and verb usage (like the difference between *lie* and *lay*) mark the differences between formal and informal writing. Check carefully to catch and correct any fragments, comma splices, or run-on sentences (**7, 8**).

Edit for punctuation and mechanics. Make sure your punctuation is standard and makes your sentences clear. Check for small things like the use of apostrophes, hyphens, underlining, capitalization, abbreviations and numbers, and spelling. Good writing must also *look* good; spelling errors may cost you credibility with your readers. Strive for professional-looking work. (See Mechanics.)

Eventually Todd produces an *edited draft,* the one that is as nearly perfect as he can get it. Not only has he made his draft correct according to the rules and conventions of standard English; Todd has switched his paragraphs around so that the most important point comes last. Compare this version with his second draft on pp. 28–29. What changes did he make? Did he miss any problems? Compare this version with his rough draft (pp. 23–24). Would you agree that Todd has improved his writing?

Fraternity Hazing

Fraternity hazing is any action that may produce mental or physical discomfort. It can be humiliating and degrading. For a long time, university officials have been trying to abolish hazing. Nationals have also tried to deter hazing rituals in their chapters. The problem still exists however, and is in drastic need of

rev

immediate action. Fraternity hazing should be abolished because of its particularly degrading and dangerous nature.

Hazing abuse can be not only physical but mental as well. Can a person be the same after participating in relay races in which sardines are passed using only the buttocks? One would hardly think so. Many initiation rites require pledges to remove part or all of their clothing; some of these rites are vaguely—others clearly—sexual in nature. Numbers of pledges have suffered mentally from such initiation rites. Some have even dropped out of school because of the humiliation, harrassment, and ridicule. This must surely end if our fraternity systems are to survive.

Injuries too are frequent and sometimes very serious. What causes a person to pour a toxic chemical on a pledge's skin? Questions like these are why fraternity hazing is looked at so critically. One young man from West Virginia University was badly burned when lighter fluid ignited his body during an initiation rite. Other injuries, such as alcohol poisoning, suffocation, and stabbing wounds, are also frequent in today's fraternity rituals.

There are over a million college men in about four hundred fraternities across the nation. Through the rites of pledging there have been an estimated fifty-five deaths among these young men. One such death involved a pledge who was walking across a highway blindfolded when a car struck and killed him. This death and others could have been prevented with stricter hazing laws.

Fraternity hazing should be abolished because of the potential harm it can cause. Mental disturbances from doing things against your own moral code; injuries due to sloppily run initiation ceremonies; and deaths resulting from extravagant, bizarre, and cruel pledging rites are urgent reasons for abolition. Instead of hazing we need a more constructive set of guidelines. There is no need for any student to become injured or to die in college. Abolish hazing.

3e Type the clean copy according to format standards.

Before typing your final draft, be sure you understand your instructor's requirements. If a title page is required, what information should appear on it? How is that information to be arranged on the page? If your paper involved research, how does the instructor want the references and bibliography handled? What quality of paper is acceptable? Is your typewriter or printer ribbon still dark? All these little things show that you are a careful writer, aware of your audience.

STANDARD TYPING GUIDELINES

1. Type all papers unless told otherwise. When handwriting is allowed, use neat, legible writing in dark blue or black ink. Give your work a professional appearance.
2. Use standard typing paper only. Do not use expensive, heavy-weight paper, nor should you use onionskin paper, nor easy-to-erase paper. Use inexpensive typing paper of medium weight. Type on one side of the paper only.
3. Do not attempt to erase or blot out errors. Learn to use correction liquid or tape to cover errors.
4. Type double-spaced. Double space everything, even indented quotations and bibliographies. (See Punctuation.)
5. Use a one-inch margin on all four edges. If your machine

rev

has no indicator for the bottom margin, mark your paper with a light pencil dot one inch from the bottom.

6. Title pages are usually not required. Unless told otherwise, put your name, the date, the assignment, and other information in the upper left-hand corner of the first page.
7. Center the title of your paper one inch from the top of the first page. Capitalize the first and last word and all important words in the title except conjunctions and prepositions. Do not put quotation marks around or underline your own title.
8. To fasten pages together, use a staple or paper clip. (Ask your instructor.) Do not pin, fold, or tear corners to fasten pages together.
9. Number every page, starting with page one, in the upper right-hand corner. Use only your last name as a header for page numbers: Smith 1.
10. Indent five spaces for each new paragraph. Indent handwritten paragraphs at least half an inch.
11. Avoid dividing words at the ends of lines. If you run into the margin, take the entire word to the next line.
12. Make last-minute corrections with a pen. You may make penned-in corrections on clean copy, if there aren't too many of them.

3f Proofread the clean copy.

The last stage in the writing process is proofreading. Check spelling, capitalization, and so on. Typographical mistakes may not seem serious, but they can make your sentences unclear and may convince your readers that you do not respect your audience.

Look carefully for material that might have been left out, for transposed letters, for all those mistakes that frequently occur during typing. Read the paper slowly, sentence by sentence, forcing yourself to look at each word. There is no such thing as a perfect, unalterable composition; follow the revisers' rule: if it *can* be changed for the better, it *should* be.

Prepare and hand in your clean copy. Perfection is the goal, but even skilled writers miss an error sometimes. If you should find a mistake at the last minute, draw one line through the error and write your correction neatly above it in ink. *rev*

ACTIVITY 19

Write a composition on some subject you know well. Make prewriting notes, outlines, brainstorming sheets, freewritings; show how you arrived at your rough draft.

Write the rough draft, leaving space for revisions. Let some time pass before marking the rough draft for revisions.

Type up the *revised* rough draft. Again, let some time pass before marking the draft for revisions.

Type up your new revisions. Let some time pass before editing this draft.

When you are satisfied with your composition, carefully type and proofread the clean copy.

Grammar

4 PARTS OF SPEECH
5 SENTENCE ELEMENTS
6 SENTENCE TYPES

gr Grammar may help you judge what is acceptable or not, understandable or not, in your writing. During editing, check your sentences for grammar.

4 PARTS OF SPEECH

A part of speech labels the way a word is used in a sentence. Many words can be used in more than one way, depending on context. For example, *paint* can be a noun: "The *paint* on this wall is faded." But it can also be a verb: "We will *paint* this wall soon." The eight parts of speech are nouns, pronouns, verbs, adjectives, adverbs, conjunctions, prepositions, and interjections.

4a Noun

A noun indicates a person, place, object, or idea: *person, Lee, Chicago, tree, justice, heroism.*

A noun test: any word that can be modified by an article (*a, an, the*) is a noun—*a* person, *the* explosion, *an* apple. (This test also works for proper nouns: "*The America* of today is very different from George Washington's America.")

Abstract nouns name ideas, intangible qualities (things not observable with the senses): *freedom, justice, intelligence.*

Collective nouns name groups of things: *family, company, group, organization.*

Common nouns name general categories and types of things: *dog, girl, house, man.*

Concrete nouns name physical objects and individuals: *ground, house, mountain, tree.*

Proper nouns name specific persons, places, and things: *Carole, Chicago, Fido, Easter.*

Some nouns (**compound nouns**) are formed with more than one word: *jack-in-the-box, high school, Fourth of July.*

4b Pronoun

A pronoun is a word that can "stand for," or take the place of, a noun: "John is a jazz musician; *he* plays a synthesizer." A pronoun refers to its **antecedent;** the pronoun *he* refers to its antecedent, *John,* in the example.

Demonstrative pronouns specify a particular noun: *this, that, these, those.*

A good example of modern art is *this.*

That is what is making all the noise, our dot-matrix printer.

Indefinite pronouns refer to nonspecific individuals, persons, or things in general: *all, another, any, anybody, anyone, anything, each, either, everybody, everyone, few, many, most, neither, nobody, none, no one, one, several, some, somebody, someone, something.*

All will be clear as soon as we talk to the President.

Lowering the tax rates will benefit *everyone.*

Interrogative pronouns indicate questions: *who, whom, whose, what, which.*

Who ordered the Kabuki costumes?

Whom can we invite to the baptism?

Personal pronouns refer to specific persons or things.

SINGULAR	PLURAL
I, me	we, us
you	you
he, him, she, her, it	they, them

Possessive pronouns show possession.

SINGULAR	PLURAL
my, mine	our, ours
your, yours	your, yours
his, her, hers, its	their, theirs

The computer belongs to Irene; the machine is *hers.*

gr **Reflexive and intensive pronouns** are the "self" forms: *herself, himself, itself, myself, ourselves, themselves, yourself, yourselves.* Reflexive pronouns show the subject of a clause acting upon itself; intensive pronouns are used for emphasis.

Reflexive: I accidentally shot *myself* in the foot.

Intensive: The Queen *herself* inspected the troops.

Relative pronouns begin dependent clauses: *that, what, which, whichever, who, whom, whoever, whomever, whose.* The relative pronoun serves either as the subject or the object of its own clause.

RELATIVE PRONOUN AS SUBJECT OF ITS OWN CLAUSE:

We all applauded the performer *who sang in Swahili.*

RELATIVE PRONOUN AS OBJECT OF ITS OWN CLAUSE:

The senator was a person *whom we could trust.*

ACTIVITY 1

Underline and label each noun and pronoun in the following sentences. Be prepared to identify the class of each noun and pronoun.

1. Does everyone believe that men and women should have equal pay for equal work?
2. The army no longer drafts eighteen-year-olds, but they still must register.
3. He does well who does what he should.
4. The quest for personal freedom often conflicts with society's conventions.
5. That racism could still be a potent force in our society was not possible, we thought.
6. The third secretary neglected his duties, so the ambassador decided to have him relieved.
7. This does not fulfill the assignment, but I admire your effort.
8. Each of you must decide for herself.
9. They wanted to give themselves a treat, so the brothers skipped class and went to see *Star Wars III.*

gr

10. When you go to the credit office, what will you say about the unpaid loan?

ACTIVITY 2

Using pronouns, revise each of the following sets of short sentences into a single, effective sentence. You may combine sentences, add words, change the form of words, delete words, and make other changes that will produce a single, effective sentence. Avoid using *and, but,* or *or* to string ideas together.

1. I lost something. It was a dollar. I lost it yesterday. I lost it in the cafeteria. Someone finds the dollar. Whoever it is can keep it.
2. We cause much misery. We do it to ourselves. It is misery we could avoid. We should have more foresight.
3. There are serious hunters. They are the ones who do something. They load their own shells. They don't drink in the woods. They don't brag about their kills.

4c Verb

Every complete sentence must contain a verb. Most verbs indicate action: *shoot, cut, run, strike.* A few (parts of the verb *to be*) indicate that something exists: *is, are.* And a few others indicate appearances or a state of being: *appear, look, seem, feel.* Verbs can be classified by their function as *helping* (sometimes called *auxiliary*) or as *linking.* And they can also be classified according to their relationship to each other as *main* or *secondary.*

Action verbs can be classified according to whether or not their action is aimed at an object. (See **5d.**)

Transitive verbs aim an action at an object.

The pilot *flew* the plane. [The object answers the question, "Flew what?" *The plane* is the object of the transitive verb *flew.*]

Congress *passed* a new law. [Congress passed what? *A new law* is the object of the transitive verb *passed.*]

gr **Intransitive verbs do not aim at an object.**

In the jury box, someone suddenly *laughed.*

Some verbs can be either transitive or intransitive, depending on context.

The Nazi war criminal *confessed* his crime. [Transitive]
The Nazi war criminal confessed. [Intransitive]

Helping verbs are used to form **verb phrases** that help a verb express tense or mood. Helping verbs include: *to be* (*am, is, are, was, were, be, being, been*), *to do* (*do, did, does*); *to have* (*have, has, had*); and *may, might, must; can, could; shall, should; will, would.*

The paper *had been* written. [The verb in this example is *written; had* and *been* are helping verbs.]

Linking verbs do not express action; instead they "link" a subject to a condition or state of being. Linking verbs include forms of the verb *to be* (*am, is, are, was, were, be, being, been*), and the forms of *appear, become, feel, grow, keep, look, remain, seem, smell, sound, stay, taste.*

They *were* tired.
The man *seemed* troubled.
We all eventually *grow* old.
At last she *became* president.
The album *sounds* scratchy.
Our coffee *tastes* sour.

None of the words following the verbs in these examples is an object; the word *president,* for instance, is not an object; only action verbs can take objects. (See Predicate Nouns, **5f,** and Predicate Adjectives, **5g.**) Some verbs can be linking in one context and transitive in another.

Grandfather *feels* tired today. [Intransitive]
The doctor *feels* your throat for lumps. [Transitive]

Main verbs are the verbs in main or independent clauses (groups of words that could stand alone, like a sentence).

Secondary verbs are verbs in dependent clauses (groups of words that cannot stand alone). (See **5i.**) *gr*

MAIN SECONDARY

The Cambodians *fled* when Vietnamese soldiers *invaded* their country.

SECONDARY MAIN

Until the bell *rings,* the students *must work* on their essays.

Note the difference between a verb and a noun. Nouns, like *explosion,* name an action; but verbs, like *explode,* express the action itself. Nouns can always be modified by one of the articles (*an* explosion, *the* explosion), but verbs cannot (*an* explode?). Note a difference between helping verbs and linking verbs. Helping verbs form phrases with other verbs; linking verbs form phrases with adjectives or nouns.

HELPING VERB WITH ACTION VERB:

Everyone *will see* the solar eclipse at noon.

LINKING VERB WITH NOUN:

Clayton *was captain* of the team. (See **5f.**)

LINKING VERB WITH ADJECTIVE:

Viola *seemed interested* in our work. (See **5g.**)

ACTIVITY 3

Underline the verbs in the following sentences. Be prepared to explain whether the verb is main or secondary; an action verb or helping, being, or linking; and transitive or intransitive.

1. Red, white, and blue, Old Glory fluttered above the crowd on the Fourth of July.
2. Young people in college today work very hard as they prepare for their careers.
3. Although tax reform appeared necessary, no one was doing anything about it.
4. The Boss led his group triumphantly onto the stage that had just been erected.

gr

5. The snake slithered across the hot sand to where the old man had collapsed.
6. The barrel careened noisily down the ramp and seemed to be heading for the open door.
7. The left-fielder hit the ball sharply into the hole that had opened up between first and second.
8. Jerry fished all day for bluegills, but he came up empty again.
9. Consider the work of the mortician: death can be profitable.
10. The square of the hypotenuse is equal to the sum of the squares of the other two sides.

ACTIVITY 4

Revise the following sentences into a single sentence. You may combine sentences, add words, change words, delete words, and make other changes that will produce a single, effective sentence. Avoid using *and, but,* or *or* to string ideas together.

1. Father raced toward the car. He was roaring. It was like a bear. I backed the car. I did it slowly. It backed toward the oak. It was standing at the end of the driveway.
2. It slipped out of my fingers. It was my bowling ball. It crashed across the lanes, six of them. It exploded. It went into a dozen fragments. It was like a bomb.
3. Lola was a sex goddess. She was aging. She could still slink across a room. She could be offering an invitation. She did it with her eyes. Her invitations were slow. They were sultry. They were offered to any man she liked.

4d Adjective

Adjectives describe, limit, change, or in some other way modify nouns and pronouns: *young* person, *gold* coin, *healthy* one. Adjectives identify *who, which, what kind,* or *how many.*

Articles (*a, an, the*) identify either a definite or an indefinite person, place, or thing:

The bird escaped from its cage. [A definite bird is indicated.]

A bird escaped from its cage. [An indefinite bird, some bird, is indicated.]

Demonstrative adjectives are demonstrative pronouns used like adjectives:

This lesson is very difficult.

That dog is a pointer.

Indefinite adjectives are indefinite pronouns used like adjectives:

Some books are meant to be read slowly.

Any questions about Milton will be answered tomorrow.

Each event will be introduced by the announcer.

Possessive adjectives are possessive pronouns used like adjectives:

His trial will be held in Colorado.

Her job pays $50,000 a year.

4e Adverb

Adverbs describe adjectives, other adverbs, and verbs: *very* pretty, *too* quickly, walk *slowly*. Most (but not all) words ending in *-ly* are adverbs. Adverbs indicate time (*now, then, soon*), place (*here, there*), manner (*softly, quickly*), degree (*frequently, often*), and reason in phrases and clauses (*for his own good, because he wanted to succeed*).

The orchestra *seldom* played rock music.

Our new car *very easily* fit our garage.

The prisoners ate the food *because they had no choice.*

Note the difference between an adjective ending in *-ly* and an adverb:

> The clowns were *silly*. [*Silly* is a predicate adjective, **5g**]
> The clowns behaved *foolishly*. [*Foolishly* is an adverb.]

ACTIVITY 5

Underline the adjectives and adverbs in each of the following sentences.

1. Young, strong, and handsome, Oren felt there was no reason women shouldn't adore him.
2. Slowly, carefully, Heidi began to put the shattered pieces of the antique vase back together.
3. Since the inexperienced doctor had never encountered those symptoms, he gratefully accepted the assistance of the older physician.
4. The garish brochure talked glowingly about golden sunshine, white sands, and blue surf.
5. Krissy's wire sculpture lay twisted in a heap, hopelessly bent and distorted beyond recognition.
6. Eyes wide and gleaming, Lindsay reached out carefully to touch the pet raccoon.
7. The moon appeared eerily, red and ominous, the night before Halloween.
8. Marshall gradually became aware of the young woman's presence.
9. The many grateful refugees eagerly embraced the woman as she walked through the door of the reception hall.
10. Laboriously he panted up the final hill, not at all convinced he could finish the marathon.

ACTIVITY 6

Using adjectives and adverbs, revise the following sets of short sentences into a single, effective sentence. You may combine sentences, add words, change the form of words, delete words, and make other changes that will produce a single, effective sentence. Avoid using *and, but,* or *or* to string ideas together.

1. The beer bottles erupted. They erupted in geysers. The geysers were foaming. They were homemade brew. It happened suddenly. It happened unexpectedly. It happened with a pop. The pop was loud.
2. The horror of death came to us. It was from AIDS. The horror filtered into our lives. It happened slowly. It was creating fear everywhere. It was the new reality. The reality was cold. It was grim.
3. An eagle flew. It was great. It was golden. It went into the area. It was where we had planted something. It was seedlings. They were pine. They were young.

4f Conjunction

Coordinate conjunctions connect equal structures, such as two or more nouns, two or more phrases, two or more clauses: *and, but, or, nor, so, for, yet.*

Mike *and* Jim went to the game.

Mike went to the game, *but* Jim stayed home.

Correlative conjunctions form pairs: *both/and, either/or, neither/nor, not only/but also.*

Both the President *and* the Vice-President spoke to the crowd.

Neither a borrower *nor* a lender be.

Subordinate conjunctions connect unequal structures, such as independent and dependent clauses.

after	because	though	whenever
although	before	unless	where
as	if	until	wherever
as if	since	when	while

Since you have had experience with computers, you may explain the lesson.

The camera failed to work, *although* it had just been repaired.

gr

4g Preposition

Most prepositions indicate positions: *in at, on.* A few do not indicate position (*during, except*), and some can also be used as adverbs. Unlike adverbs, prepositions take objects: in the *well,* at the *house,* during the *war,* except the *girls.* The preposition and its object form a **prepositional phrase.**

aboard	before	in regard to	regardless of
above	behind	inside	since
about	below	in spite of	through
according to	beneath	instead of	throughout
across	beside	into	to
after	between	like	toward
against	beyond	near	under
along	but	next to	underneath
amid	by	of	until
among	concerning	off	unto
around	despite	on	up
as	during	on account of	upon
aside from	except	on behalf of	with
as to	for	over	within
as well as	from	out of	without
at	in	outside	
because of	in front of	past	

4h Interjection

Interjections are exclamatory words and expressions: *Oh! Help!* An interjection needn't end with an exclamation point.

Ah, now I see what you mean.

ACTIVITY 7

Identify the part of speech of each word in the following sentences.

1. The *Titanic* tilted up and slowly slipped below the surface.
2. Long ago in a galaxy beyond the stars an ancient astronomer asked himself, "Do others exist, somewhere?"
3. Alas, she walked slowly toward the sea and stepped blindly into its too tender embrace.
4. Neither those who are ever cool nor those whose hot tempers burn with passion shall be our models.
5. "Wow!" the captain said afterward, "I had a very bad dream, and it frightened me terribly."

ACTIVITY 8

Revise the following sentences into a single sentence. You may combine sentences; add, change, or delete words; and make other changes that will produce a single effective sentence. Avoid using *and, but,* or *or* too often.

1. I said ouch. I stumbled back. I went blindly. I went from the doorway. I had managed to give myself a gash. It was bloody. It was across my forehead.
2. We will have to do something. It will be either one or the other. We will have to shovel out some of this junk. It will be in the morning. We will have to move. It will be to an apartment. It will be bigger.
3. The glasses sat in a row. They were on the porch railing. They were tall. They were crystal. They were filled with iced tea. They were where we could see. They were glistening in the sun. The sun was hot.

5 SENTENCE ELEMENTS

A sentence is a group of words containing a *subject* and a *predicate* expressing a complete thought.

sent el

5a Subject

The subject is the *actor* in sentences expressing action; the subject is usually a noun or pronoun (or some other *nominal*). In most sentences, the subject comes before the predicate. The *simple subject* is a single word: "The wooden *raft* was floating on the river." The *complete* subject is the simple subject plus all modifiers attached to it: "*The wooden raft* was floating on the river."

SIMPLE SUBJECT

The young *officers* read their orders.

A bright green little *snake* darted among the leaves.

COMPLETE SUBJECT

The young officers read their orders.

A bright green little snake darted among the leaves.

The subject of a sentence can be a *nominal*, a word or group of words used like a noun.

NOMINAL SUBJECT

Swimming is good for you.

Whoever broke the window must pay for it.

Some sentences have an *understood subject:* "Shut the door quietly, please." The sentence means: "[*You*] shut the door quietly, please."

UNDERSTOOD SUBJECT

Answer the phone. [*You* answer the phone.]

Take the kettle off the stove. [*You* take the kettle off the stove.]

5b Predicate

The predicate makes a statement about the subject. The *simple predicate* is the main verb (with its helping verbs): "The wooden raft *was floating* on the river." The *complete predicate* is the main verb and any modifiers or complements attached to it. "The wooden raft *was floating on the river.*" *sent el*

SIMPLE PREDICATE

We *opened* the door cautiously.

Congress *sent* a message to the President.

COMPLETE PREDICATE

We *opened the door cautiously.*

Congress *sent a message to the President.*

A sentence can have more than one verb: "The wooden raft *was floating* on the river that *ran* by our house." In such sentences, the simple predicate is the *main* verb: *was floating* is the main verb because it states what the raft was doing; *ran* is a *secondary* verb in a modifying clause describing the river. The main verb occurs in the part of the sentence that could stand by itself (see Independent Clause, **5i**):

SIMPLE PREDICATE — SECONDARY VERB

We *saw* the men who *built* the bridge. [*We saw the men* could stand alone.]

The play *closed* after the actor *died.* [*The play closed* could stand alone.]

Both predicates and subjects can be *compound.* Compound elements are joined by conjunctions.

COMPOUND SUBJECT

Boys, girls, and *adults* were all playing baseball together.

Neither the people on the hill nor *those waiting below* could see the plane circling the woods.

COMPOUND PREDICATE

The little dog *danced* and *did tricks.*

The President *addressed the nation* but *explained very little about his new economic policy.*

ACTIVITY 9

Identify the subject and the predicate in each of these sentences. Draw one line under the subject and two lines under the predicate. Be prepared to distinguish between simple and complete subject and between simple and complete predicate.

1. Steam locomotives have become nearly extinct.
2. Our janitor is a very wise man, someone the students can turn to when no one else will help.
3. The glowing ball of fire appeared suddenly in the eastern sky.
4. Running five miles every morning will certainly keep you in shape.
5. To everyone's amazement, the party had been going on since Friday and showed no signs of slowing down.
6. Dunking for apples, toasting marshmallows, and playing guessing games were our diversions.
7. Calmly and carefully, the manager of the large department store explained to her staff what to expect.
8. A most important decision was made about the timing of the grape harvest.
9. The old oak near the farmhouse had been struck repeatedly by lightning.
10. Because she was not a union member, the carpenter was not allowed to work on the new building project.

ACTIVITY 10

Revise the following sentences into a single sentence. You may combine sentences; add, change, and delete words; and make other changes that will produce a single, effective sentence. Avoid using *and, but,* or *or* to string ideas together.

1. The children were on our block. They had friends from the next street. They conspired to meet somewhere. It was in our backyard. They put on a carnival. It was of unimaginable noise and confusion.
2. Something shot out of the shadows. It was a powerboat. It was sleek. The shadows were under the willows. The boat sliced across the lake. It went in an arc. The arc was clean. It was curving.

3. He was slightly built. Hervey was an unlikely athlete except for something. His speed was phenomenal. So was his agility. His reflexes were catlike. His intuition was almost supernatural. This told him the right moves.

5c Complement

A complement "completes" the sense of the verb. A complement may be a direct object, an indirect object, a predicate noun, or a predicate adjective.

5d Direct object

Some verbs (called *transitive*) take objects: the object "receives" the action of the verb. For example: "The arrow hit *the target.*" The direct object is usually a noun or a noun substitute such as a pronoun, gerund, or noun clause. The direct object answers the question, who? or what? after the verb.

> We saw the *President* on television. [The direct object here is the noun *President.*]
>
> We saw *him* on television. [The pronoun *him* is the direct object.]
>
> We all enjoy *swimming* at the beach. [The gerund (see **5h**) *swimming* is the direct object.]
>
> I understand *what you mean.* [*What you mean,* a noun clause, is the direct object.]

A sentence may appear to have a second object, called an *objective complement: They elected her* ***president.*** In the example, *her* is the direct object, and *president* is the objective complement.

Not all verbs take objects. Some verbs are *intransitive,* meaning they do not express an action toward an object. (See **4c.**)

5e Indirect object

Sometimes a verb may have an indirect object *to whom* or *for whom* the action is done. For example: "We sent him a letter." In this sentence, the *letter* is the thing actually sent, the direct object. But note that the letter was sent "to him": *him* is the indirect object. Note the same sentence with a prepositional phrase instead of an indirect object: "We sent a letter *to him*."

INDIRECT OBJECT — DIRECT OBJECT

John's mother bought *him* a new *calculator*.

INDIRECT OBJECT — DIRECT OBJECT

We finally found *Ted* a *date* for the dance.

5f Predicate noun

Nouns in the object position that follow linking verbs are called *predicate nouns:* "The senator was *a powerful speaker.*"

Note the difference between predicate noun and direct object:

PREDICATE NOUN	DIRECT OBJECT
John is a senator.	John saw a senator.
Vivian became an ambassador.	Vivian married an ambassador.

5g Predicate adjective

Adjectives that follow linking verbs and refer to the subject are called *predicate adjectives.*

All the students were *terrified*.

The ground feels *moist*.

ACTIVITY 11

Identify the complements in the following sentences. Underline and label the direct object, indirect object, predicate noun, or predicate adjective.

1. War in the Persian Gulf seemed more likely every day.
2. The stock market is sending the country a message.
3. Deep down in the abandoned well, the little girl was trapped but alive.
4. Finches and chickadees scattered seeds around the base of the feeder.
5. The president began his press conference with a joke.
6. Everyone's favorite summer sport is probably swimming.
7. Swallows and gulls were the only birds he could name.
8. Arcade games gave him pleasure despite their cost.
9. The breeze swept the aroma of freshly mown grass through the open windows of the school.
10. Overripe onions smell sour and taste worse.

ACTIVITY 12

Revise the following sentences into a single sentence. You may combine sentences; add, change, and delete words; and make other changes that will produce a single, effective sentence. Avoid using *and, but,* or *or* to string ideas together.

1. There was a box. It was mysterious. It was cardboard. It contained something. It was a dollar's worth of something. It was assorted nails and tacks. It was a feather boa. It was long. It was from the twenties.
2. Matlock once sent us something. He was my great uncle. It was a tiki. It was old. It was wooden. He had found it somewhere. It was on his travels somewhere. It was to the islands.
3. She was an honor student. She was captain of the debate team. She was a promising athlete. She was ravenhaired and beautiful. Viki had reason to believe something. The world was her oyster.

sent el

5h Phrase

A phrase is any group of words acting as a unit that lacks either a subject or a predicate.

Absolute phrases modify entire clauses instead of individual words. Absolutes are created by deleting the main verb or the helping verb of a simple sentence or by substituting the present participle for the main verb (see **20f**).

His job completed, Stacy left.
They remained seated, *the bomb ticking loudly.*

Prepositional phrases are used like adverbs and adjectives; occasionally they may be used like nouns. The prepositional phrase is composed of a preposition and its object.

After the interview, the mayor relaxed.
My father was a colonel *during the last war.*

Verb phrases are formed by verbs and their helping verbs.

The shot *had been fired.*
We *did see* him just a moment ago.

Verbal phrases are verb forms and their complements used like nouns or modifiers. Verbal phrases include gerunds, participles, and infinitives.

Gerunds are verbal phrases used like nouns. A gerund is the present participle of a verb. (See **11.**) The gerund may have modifiers or, because it is a verb, objects.

Swimming in the ocean takes courage.
The best part of the show was *Jason's singing.*

Infinitives are formed with the word *to* and a verb: *to go, to talk.* An infinitive may have its own complement. The infinitive phrase functions like a noun or a modifier.

To be champion was her goal.
I need a place *to park my car.*

Participles, which are used like adjectives, are formed with the past or the present participle of a verb. (See **11.**) Participial phrases may have modifiers and objects.

Cracked in many places, the vase was completely worthless.
The whistling wind rattled the eaves of the house.

5i Clause

A clause is a group of words containing a subject and a verb. A simple sentence is an *independent clause;* it can stand alone. Dependent clauses have subjects and verbs, but are not complete sentences. Each of the following groups of words is an independent clause.

SUBJECT VERB
The great *ship sailed* out to sea.

SUBJECT VERB
Dogs bark.

Each of the following groups of words is a dependent clause because it contains a subject and verb but does not make a completed statement:

SUBJECT VERB
Where *we were going. . .*

SUBJECT VERB
That *she can swim. . .*

Adjective clauses are dependent clauses used like adjectives, to modify nouns and pronouns and other nominals. Adjective clauses begin with relative pronouns (and are therefore sometimes called relative clauses) or the subordinators *when, where,* or *why.* (See **4b.**)

We found a man *who would cut the grass for us.*
One poem *that you should read* is "Ozymandias."
Now is the time *when we must all work together.*

Writers frequently omit the relative pronoun of an adjective clause: The card *we gave to John* was inexpensive.

Adverb clauses are dependent clauses used like adverbs. In addition to time, place, manner, and degree (see Adverb), adverb clauses can be used to show cause, comparison, concession, condition, and purpose. Adverb clauses begin with subordinate conjunctions. (See **4f.**)

When the rain stops, we can go.
We are going to the show *after we finish dinner.*
This is tougher *than it looks.*

Noun clauses are dependent clauses used like nouns, as subjects, objects, and predicate nouns. Noun clauses begin with relative pronouns or the subordinators *when, where,* and *why.* (See **4b.**)

NOUN CLAUSE AS SUBJECT
Why we had to go to war was never explained.

NOUN CLAUSE AS OBJECT
We gave them *what they wanted.*

NOUN CLAUSE AS PREDICATE NOUN
She was not *whom we expected.*

ACTIVITY 13
Identify the type of phrases and clauses underlined in the following sentences.

1. Anyone <u>who gives drugs to a child</u> should be punished.
2. Our job was to clean the house <u>after the party was over</u>.
3. <u>What we want to know</u> is <u>who is the guilty party</u>?
4. Near the clearing by the stream <u>Jack built the blind</u>.
5. <u>When the bell rings</u>, contestants may begin dancing.

6. The students in his class were chosen first because they had studied that period of history most closely.
7. Hitting a golf ball 250 yards requires skill in timing and coordination.
8. To want to do well is not enough.
9. Since recent studies have determined that cigarette smoking is even more harmful than previously believed, the Surgeon General wants to word his warnings more strongly.
10. Although home computers are enthusiastically endorsed by many, some people question their effects on family life.

ACTIVITY 14

Identify the sentence elements in the following sentences:

1. A mature rattler is a very dangerous snake.
2. Why Congress passed the bill, we will never know.
3. Anyone who smokes should be aware of the dangers.
4. After the ceremony the mothers and fathers were too tired for the party.
5. The old couple bought Ellen flowers for her birthday.

ACTIVITY 15

Identify the underlined sentence element in each of the following sentences.

1. The citizens of a democracy must participate in government.
2. Cafeteria food tastes bland to me.
3. Our ambassador received an insult aimed at our President.
4. Each night the students spent hours in the library.
5. Nancy's computer was extremely fast.
6. Whoever answers first will be our winner.
7. They were required to buy a diskette for the English class.
8. As soon as the car stopped, Wally and Janelle jumped onto the roof.
9. She wanted to know what was required.
10. To be a biophysicist was Lorna's only ambition.

6 SENTENCE TYPES

6a Sentence purpose

Declarative sentences make statements. Use declaratives to express facts, opinions, and propositions.

It is twelve o'clock.
London is the capital of England.

Interrogative sentences ask questions. Use interrogatives to request information or permission or to express interest or affirmation. Any sentence ending with a question mark is interrogatory. (See **28.**)

Where was Beethoven born?
You bought that scarf at the rummage sale, right?
The apple trees are in full bloom?

Imperative sentences state commands or requests. Use imperatives to give orders or directions.

Go left to highway 27.
Please send me a dozen brochures.

Exclamatory sentences indicate strong feelings. Use exclamations to express surprise, anger, fear, joy, and other emotions. Any sentence ending with an exclamation mark is exclamatory. (See **27.**)

The bear is out of its cage!
Don't you ever speak to me that way again!

6b Sentence structure

A **simple sentence** is one independent clause. (See **5i.**) *Simple* need not refer to shortness or elementary ideas.

> Birds sing.
>
> The Italian government cracked down on underworld gangsters.
>
> The members of the House of Representatives had undertaken a serious proposal, a matter of great urgency, and something of a unique challenge.

The sentences are "simple" because each contains only one subject and one main verb. Contrast these simple sentences with the compound and complex sentences below.

A **compound sentence** contains at least two independent clauses but no dependent clauses. (See **5i.**) For punctuation of compound sentences, see **21a** and **23e.**

> The bread was stale, and the tea was weak.
>
> We must never fear to speak against tyranny, for tyrants use fear as a weapon.

The independent clauses of a compound sentence can be written as separate sentences.

AS COMPOUND SENTENCE	AS SEPARATE SENTENCES
We called Kitty for hours, but she refused to answer.	We called Kitty for hours. She refused to answer.

A **complex sentence** contains one independent clause and at least one dependent clause. (See **5i.**) Dependent clauses start with subordinate conjunctions (**4f**) or relative pronouns

sent type (**4b**). All clauses must have a subject and a verb, but only the independent clause can be written as a separate sentence:

INDEPENDENT CLAUSE

The men began coming up out of the mine after the whistle blew.

Until Castro changes his tactics, *Cuba must be watched carefully.*

Although Miss Emily was poor, *she remained proud.*

A **compound-complex sentence** contains two (or more) independent clauses and one (or more) dependent clauses.

INDEPENDENT CLAUSES

After the whistle blew, *the men began coming up,* and *their wives hurred to meet them.*

The Prime Minister met with her cabinet, and *together they worked out a plan* while the nation waited.

ACTIVITY 16

Identify the sentence types that follow.

1. In the dim light of dawn, the deer remained motionless at the edge of the meadow.
2. They had sent spies into Tunisia before, but none of them ever came back.
3. When the danger was noticed, they opened all the safety valves, and the temperature gauges slowly returned to normal.
4. That anyone could have deliberately set the old barn on fire was too much for Uncle Cyrus to believe.
5. Long into the night the enemy guns pounded away at the forward lines, the supply depot, and our western gun emplacements.

ACTIVITY 17

Using sentence variation, revise the following sentences into a single sentence. You may combine sentences; add, change, and delete words; and make other changes to produce a single, effective sentence. Avoid using *and, but,* or *or* too much.

1. The tank was faster than any other armored vehicle. Its firing system was more effective than any other mobile weapon. The system was computer controlled. The government refused to buy the tank. It was too heavy. It could not cross bridges.
2. Slowly something dawned on Aaron. He wanted to graduate. If so, he would have to choose between two images of himself. Was he the dashing young man about campus? Or was he the dreary bookworm? It was lurking in the library.
3. We bought a goat for Sarah. It was young. We bought it after she broke her arm. It was really a pet. But it grew older. As it did so it became obnoxious. It was so obnoxious that we considered something. We were serious. We would butcher it.

Sentence Errors

frag

7 SENTENCE FRAGMENTS

Formal writing requires complete sentences. A sentence fragment is incomplete. Part of the sentence is missing; the writer has written only a "fragment" of a sentence. Make sure that each of your sentences has a subject and a verb and can stand alone as an expression of an idea. Revise fragments to form complete sentences.

Though fragments are most often punctuation errors (see **26a**), they can sometimes be the result of sentence length. In a long sentence the writer may accidentally omit a word:

INCOMPLETE

The long line of gray ships passing across the horizon on the way to a rendezvous somewhere at sea with a carrier task force and the reserve squadron of the Pacific fleet.

REVISED FOR CLARITY

The long line of gray ships *was* passing across the horizon on the way to a rendezvous somewhere at sea with a carrier task force and the reserve squadron of the Pacific fleet.

When sentences are grammatically complete, they will make sense, even out of context. Read each sentence aloud by itself. If you have any doubts about the completeness of a sentence, read it aloud to a friend. For example, read each of these sentences aloud, one at a time:

Sesu was overcome with curiosity about the great snake his brother had brought home in the basket. Although he knew such snakes could be very dangerous. The scratches and swishes coming from the basket as the snake moved were too exciting to ignore.

In the context of other sentences, the fragment may temporarily seem to make sense. However, when read aloud by itself, the fragment sounds incomplete: "Although he knew such snakes could be very dangerous." Clearly these words are only part of a sentence; they must be connected either to a preceding or following sentence.

7a Avoid punctuating parts of sentences as complete thoughts.

Prepositional phrases should not be split off from the words they modify. (See **4g.**)

PREPOSITIONAL PHRASE FRAGMENT

We all stood quietly. *In the shadow of the old oak.*

REVISION

We all stood quietly in the shadow of the old oak.

Verbal phrases (gerund, infinitive, participle) should not be split off from their referents. (See **5h.**)

VERBAL PHRASE FRAGMENT

Citizens have a major responsibility. *Voting in each election.* (See gerund, **5h.**)

REVISION

Citizens have a major responsibility: voting in each election.

VERBAL PHRASE FRAGMENT

The troops had been sent to Grenada. *To rescue American medical students.* (See Infinitive, **5h.**)

REVISION

The troops had been sent to Grenada to rescue American medical students.

VERBAL PHRASE FRAGMENT

Lenore created quite a stir. *Wearing a scarlet cape.* (See Participle, **5h.**)

REVISION

Lenore created quite a stir wearing a scarlet cape.

frag **Dependent clauses should not be written as fragments (5i.)**

DEPENDENT CLAUSE FRAGMENT

Bankruptcy forced the closing of the newspaper. *Which had been published for ninety years.* (See Adjective clause, **5i.**)

REVISION

Bankruptcy forced the closing of the newspaper. It had been published for ninety years. [The fragment is revised by writing the second clause as a complete sentence.]

DEPENDENT CLAUSE FRAGMENT

Since I have been taking this class. My knowledge of physics has increased 100 percent. (See Adverb clause, **5i.**)

REVISION

Since I have been taking this class, my knowledge of physics has increased 100 percent. [The fragment is revised with punctuation.]

Appositives should not be split off from the words they identify. An appositive renames or re-identifies a preceding word. (See **21e.**)

APPOSITIVE FRAGMENT

Before the judge and jury he stood with his head down. *The defendant.*

REVISIONS

Before the judge and jury he, the defendant, stood with his head down. [The appositive is inserted into the preceding sentence and set off with punctuation.]

Before the judge and jury he stood with his head down, the defendant. [The appositive is attached at the end of the preceding sentence with punctuation.]

APPOSITIVE FRAGMENT

Young Sebastian was driven by some inner demon. *His raging passion for order.*

REVISIONS

Young Sebastian was driven by some inner demon—his raging passion for order. [The appositive is joined to its sentence with punctuation.]

Young Sebastian was driven by his raging passion for order, his inner demon. [The appositive is revised into an independent clause.]

Other word groups should not be written as fragments.

VERB PHRASE FRAGMENT (See **5h.**)

The author wanted to work with a photographer. *Searching for the best one available.*

REVISION

The author wanted to work with a photographer. She searched for the best one available. [The verb phrase is revised by writing the fragment as a complete sentence.]

COMPOUND PREDICATE FRAGMENT (See **5b.**)

The snowblower picked up the snow. *And kicked it out through its nozzle.* [The predicate is composed of the two verbs *picked up* and *kicked.*]

REVISION

The snowblower picked up the snow and kicked it out through its nozzle. [The predicate is revised by connecting the fragment to the independent clause.]

COMPOUND PREDICATE FRAGMENT

They sent all the packages by registered mail. *But got them back marked "Undeliverable."*

REVISIONS

They sent all the packages by registered mail but got them back marked "Undeliverable." [The fragment is attached to its sentence.]

They sent all the packages by registered mail. But they got them back marked "Undeliverable." [The fragment is revised by changing the predicate into an independent clause.]

frag

All the packages they had sent by registered mail were returned marked "Undeliverable." [The fragment becomes the main verb of the revised sentence.]

COMPOUND COMPLEMENT FRAGMENT (See **5c–g.**)

Naturally the suspicion fell on Butch Lashwell. *And his younger brother, Otto.* [The fragment is part of a compound direct object.] (See **5d.**)

REVISION

Naturally the suspicion fell on Butch Lashwell and his younger brother, Otto.

COMPOUND COMPLEMENT FRAGMENT

At the end of the election, Oona had become president. *And secretary too!* [The fragment is part of a compound predicate noun.] (See **5f.**)

REVISION

At the end of the election, Oona had become president—and secretary too!

COMPOUND COMPLEMENT FRAGMENT

Bettina knew herself to be clever. *And not at all shy with strangers.* [The fragment is a part of a compound predicate adjective.] (See **5g.**)

REVISION

Bettina knew herself to be clever and not at all shy with strangers.

ACTIVITY 1

Revise the following sentences; turn sentence fragments into complete sentences. Supply needed punctuation, change the wording, or supply additional words.

1. American automobile manufacturers have been complaining about cheap foreign imports. In the last few years.

frag

2. Since the cost of hospitalization and medical care can now be as much as several hundreds of dollars per day. Only the wealthy can afford to be sick.
3. Quietly, so that we would not awaken our sleeping teammates in the crowded dormitory provided by the Olympic committee as we attempted to leave for our morning workouts.
4. The clouds assume the faces of hermits or of nuns or sometimes look like sad dog acts. Hurrying off into the wings over the horizon.
5. Large pieces of broken cement falling from the medieval fretwork high above the entranceway where the King would soon make his appearance.
6. Another scene in *The Gold Rush*, which was invented on the same principle as the boot dinner, the one where the big gold miner, half crazed with hunger, suddenly sees Charlie as a fowl and tries to catch him and eat him.
7. From the magic wish catalog we each were allowed to select a gift for ourselves. And some small gift to be used as a present for a family member of our choice.
8. The youngsters on the team were exhausted from exertion. Too tired even to take showers and go home.
9. During prohibition, a large number of respectable, conservative Americans dutifully broke the law. In defense of what they called an inalienable human right.
10. Alfred was brought in. A frail young fellow, delicate, two wings fluttering behind his pale-blue shoulders, rippling with rosy light like two doves playing in heaven.

ACTIVITY 2

Read the following paragraph. Test each sentence by reading it aloud. Revise fragments with punctuation or by changing wording. You may revise any way you like as long as you don't produce any awkward sentences or leave any fragments.

Touch typing is an important skill. For those who plan to be writers. Although you may not intend to become a professional writer. You will probably need to type your papers in school. And perhaps in your work

frag

```
after you graduate. That you will have some experience
with a keyboard. Is almost certain. Nearly all students
today will learn to use computers. Whose keyboards are
very similar to a typwriter's. Unless your situation is
very unusual. You will almost certainly do some typing.
Or keyboarding. In your life. Therefore touch typing
can be very helpful to you. Looking at the keys while
typing. Slows down anyone. Even skilled typists. It is
worth the time it takes. To teach your fingers to do
the work. To strike the right keys automatically
without looking. Soon you will be able to type like a
professional. Without looking at the keys. And without
thinking about what you are typing! Once trained, your
fingers will fly over the keyboard. Faster than you can
say the words. That you are typing. You will have
become a skilled typist. A touch typist.
```

7b Some fragments are conventional and acceptable under certain conditions.

Fragments in dialogue can imitate informal speech:

"Hey, Jefferson!"
"What?"
"Going to the show?"
"What show?"
"At the Twin Cinema."
"Nope. Seen it."

Fragments are used in impressionistic style, emphasizing key elements of description (but this style is seldom used in formal, academic writing):

The evening sun slid into the trees. Red now. Glowing with fires of heaven or hell. The long fingers of pine stretching out. Grasping. Stroking. Gray bones of a life not quite human fondling the light. *cs, ro*

Fragments can be used to ask and answer rhetorical questions.

What is the end of life after all? The grave?

Should we, then, give up hope? Not very likely.

Fragments sometimes appear as transitional expressions:

So much for the background.

Now for an example.

A few fragments are familiar expressions:

The bigger the better.

Foiled again!

Thank you.

Fragments may be used for heavy emphasis:

We stared at the gauge in disbelief. Out of gas.

He vowed never to return. Nor did he. Not ever.

8 COMMA SPLICES AND RUN-ON SENTENCES

A comma splice is an error in formal writing. The comma splice is created by joining two independent ideas with a comma. A run-on sentence is always an error; it is created by fusing two complete ideas together with no punctuation between them. Edit your paper carefully to remove such problems.

cs, ro

COMMA SPLICE REVISED WITH COORDINATE CONJUNCTION

marsupial, and it
The kangaroo is the world's largest ~~marsupial, it~~ is native to Australia. (See Coordinate Conjunction, **4f.**)

COMMA SPLICE REVISED WITH SEMICOLON

rocks; no
Great Grandfather hid his money in trees and under ~~rocks, no~~ one has ever found any of it. (See Semicolon, **23a.**)

COMMA SPLICE REVISED WITH CONJUNCTIVE ADVERB

teeth; hence, his
George Washington wore ill-fitting wooden ~~teeth, his~~ lips protruded slightly. (See Conjunctive Adverb, **23b.**)

COMMA SPLICE REVISED WITH PERIOD

ships.
Columbus set out for the New World with his three little ~~ships,~~
They
~~they~~ were a gift from Queen Isabella of Spain.

COMMA SPLICE REVISED BY REWORDING

Hemingway wrote ~~several novels,~~ *A Farewell to Arms,* ~~is~~ one of
novels
his finest ^.

RUN-ON SENTENCE REVISED WITH A SEMICOLON

machine; just
It is easy to run the ~~machine just~~ turn the dial and hit the button. (See Semicolon, **23a.**)

RUN-ON REVISED WITH A COLON

uniform: they
Each of the girls was issued a rifle and a ~~uniform they~~ were marines now. (See Colon, **24c.**)

RUN-ON REVISED WITH A PERIOD

October was always the best ~~month the~~ month. The trees turned brilliant shades of yellow, gold, brown, and red.

RUN-ON REVISED BY REWORDING

~~Heavy~~ As the heavy wagons rumbled through the streets under cover of ~~darkness the~~ darkness, the dead bodies within jostled against each other at every thump.

ACTIVITY 3

Revise the following sentences to eliminate run-on sentences and comma splices.

1. Architects try to balance beauty and function against cost, homeowners must learn to accept compromises.
2. The old car was finally sold for a hundred dollars we got rid of it.
3. Sid finally quit singing "White Christmas" was not one of his better efforts.
4. Sadly we set the little cage on the windowsill where the bird was, no one knew.
5. After conducting the experiment, the chemist was sure that he had made an important discovery, he immediately phoned one of his colleagues with the results.
6. Estelle was a habitual liar, indeed, no one trusted her at all.
7. Dogs and little children brought out his tenderness about cats he maintained a different attitude.
8. The whole family conspired to send mother a ticket had been secretly purchased for her trip.
9. Rutherford, for whom we had worked so hard all night, failed to show up, he had evidently fallen in with a company of carousers.
10. He had taken the car to the shop three times to have the automatic choke repaired the mechanics still had not solved the problem.

ACTIVITY 4

Revise the following paragraph carefully. You may revise any way you like as long as you do not leave any comma splices or run-on sentences.

Odysseus was a clever man, he was renowned for his wit and ingenuity. It was his plan to fool the Trojans. The plan was to create a giant wooden horse it would be left on the beach. The Trojans, he said, would find the horse, they would assume it had been left as a peace offering. The Greek ships sailed away out of sight the great wooden horse was left behind. Into the city of Troy, behind their impenetrable walls, the Trojans pulled the wooden horse, its wooden wheels sank into the sand from its great weight. Late that night, as the Trojans slept, the Greeks came out of the horse Odysseus had hidden them within, they slew all the Trojans.

9 SUBJECT-VERB AGREEMENT

Any verb must match its subject in number and person.

The *sound* of the airplane *upsets* the dog.
Everyone wants his or her name to appear on the list.
He and she, the ones who are not present, *love* to create problems. (The dependent clause "who are not present" has its own subject, *who*, and verb, *are*. See **5i** and **9e.**)

Number refers to singular and plural.

Person refers to the speaker (first person), the person or thing spoken to (second person), and the person spoken about (third person). All nouns are third person and require third-person verbs. *agr*

Usually your own sense of language will tell you which verb form agrees with the subject of your sentence, but there are some special cases you may need to review.

9a In general, two or more subjects joined by *and* take a plural verb.

Football and baseball were his favorite sports.

Athletic ability and keen eyesight are necessary in sports.

Sheila and he are running for office.

Some subjects joined by *and* are considered a unit and take a singular verb, units such as *ham and eggs, horse and buggy.* Occasionally *and* indicates a single concept:

My secretary and friend, Jack, *is* going to the conference for me. (The individual has two roles.)

9b Two or more singular subjects joined by *or* or *nor* take a singular verb. Plural subjects joined by *or* or *nor* require a plural verb.

Nora or Ellen is available to take Mary's place.

Neither *he nor she* has been infected by the flu bug.

The *soldiers or* their *commanders were* expected to carry the plans.

Neither the *frogs nor* the *snakes are* able to withstand such low temperatures.

When *or, nor, either . . . or, neither . . . nor,* or *not . . . but* joins a singular subject to a plural subject, the verb should agree with the closer one.

agr *Neither* the dog *nor* the cats *were* responsible for the mess in the garage.

Not the daughters *but* the son *is* taking over the family business.

9c Collective nouns and certain other subjects take singular or plural verbs depending on meaning.

In general, use a singular verb when you refer to the whole group represented by a collective noun, such as *orchestra, class, family.*

The *family holds* its reunion every five years.

The *committee meets* on the first Tuesday of each month.

To suggest individual action of the members named by a collective noun, however, you may use a plural verb.

The *family want* Andrew to give up hang-gliding.

The *faculty have argued* among themselves for years over the issue of merit pay.

Some concepts may be either singular or plural.

The noise and confusion *was* unbearable. [*Noise and confusion* identifies a single concept: a general uproar.]

The noise and confusion *were* unbearable. [*Noise and confusion* identify two different things with a plural verb.]

In general, words like *all, half, any, more, part, none, some* require singular verbs when they refer to singular words, and they require plural verbs when they refer to plural words.

SINGULAR REFERENCE

Half of the team *has* the flu.

All the corn *was bought* on credit.

PLURAL REFERENCE

Half the contestants *are* sure they will win.

All of the children *were* excited about the picnic.

Certain subjects, plural in form but singular in meaning, take singular verbs:

Economics is required of all business students.

No *news is* good news.

9d *Each, every, everybody,* and most of the other indefinite pronouns require singular verbs. (See **4b.**)

Each of these men *was* given a different order.

Every student *thinks* his or her answer is best.

Everybody is concerned about the environment.

Neither of the boys *was* willing to admit the truth.

9e After *who, which,* or *that,* the verb agrees with the pronoun's antecedent.

A pronoun's antecedent is the word the pronoun identifies.

PLURAL ANTECEDENT — PLURAL VERB

He knows the *entertainers who sing* the old songs.

In California coastal waters, *great white sharks, which attack* more humans every year, have scientists as well as television reporters interested.

She is one of those *women who earn* high salaries. [Compare with: She is *the only one* of those women *who earns* a high salary.]

agr

9f Neither words that come between the subject and its verb nor inverted word order affect agreement.

The *books* as well as the author *were* on display in the library.

The President's *decisions* concerning the tax cut *surprise* me.

9g When a sentence begins with *here* or *there* followed by a verb, the subject comes after the verb.

Here are the book, the paper, and the blanket you asked me for.

There were only *two* of us who could continue.

9h The verb agrees with the subject rather than with a complement. (See 5c–5f.)

The winning *couple was* Ian and Loreen.

Ian and Loreen were the winning couple.

9i Noun clauses as subjects require singular verbs. (See 5h.)

That they still suspected us of cheating on tests seems unfair.

What we must give our laborers is recognition and a bonus for their effort.

9j Titles as subjects take singular verbs.

The Grapes of Wrath is Steinbeck's greatest novel.

"Three Blind Mice" has been a nursery tune for generations.

9k References to numbers as amounts usually take singular verbs.

The number of people at the game *is* ten thousand.
Three plus five *is* eight.
Three times five *is* fifteen.
Twenty acres *is* a lot of land for a lawn.

BUT

A number of people *are* coming to dinner tonight.
Three fives *are* fifteen.

ACTIVITY 5

Select the appropriate word in the following sentences.

1. Every child's desk (is/are) supposed to contain books, paper, and pencils.
2. *Fundamentals of Economics* (was/were) the textbook for our introductory course.
3. A trainload of nuclear wastes (is/are) expected through here in twenty-four hours.
4. Neither the library nor the English department (was/were) able to provide information about our poets.
5. It seemed that the students' behavior (was/were) a sign of their uncertainty about world events.
6. The horse and buggy (was/were) a main source of transportation in the last century.
7. There (was/were) a desk, a cot, and a bookshelf in the room.
8. The young actor in the lead, however, was one of those youths who (is/are) always in a hurry for success.
9. Each of them (was/were) certain the other (was/were) wrong.
10. The years dedicated to education (is/are) paid back with interest in later life.

case, ref

ACTIVITY 6

Revise any errors in subject-verb agreement in the following sentences. Be prepared to explain your answers.

1. That the Tigers were able to win so many games were hardly surprising to Detroit fans.
2. None of the bishops were prepared to argue with the Pope.
3. The prospect for many of our grandparents and other elderly relatives are that they will live long, healthy lives.
4. Neither poker nor bridge are allowed at church picnics.
5. Either the students or their professor are responsible for these poor test results.
6. The most enjoyable pair are a trusted friend and a loyal supporter.
7. What you must tell your friends and your parents are the truth and nothing but the truth.
8. General Motors this year are making an enormous profit at last.
9. Some of the tubes in our old TV set was replaced with new solid state resistors.
10. Each of the students in this room are soon to receive an unexpected reward.
11. The size of my father's sweaters are always too large.
12. Carlos and his brother is going to play music at our party.
13. We lost one of the new cars that was bought last year.
14. Not only the busses but also the train have stopped running.
15. There in the cellar is grandmother's wedding dress and grandfather's cane.

10 PRONOUN CASE AND REFERENCE

Pronoun case shows how pronouns are used in sentences. Pronouns can be used as subjects and objects, and they can be used to show possession.

If a sentence is written in "normal" order, that is, subject-verb-object, it is usually easy to determine a pronoun's proper case: *case, ref*

SUBJECT VERB OBJECT
The *pilot flew* the experimental *shuttles.*

The subject does the acting (**5a**), the verb names the action (**5b**), and the object receives the action (**5c**). If pronouns are substituted for the nouns in the sentence, a subjective pronoun must be chosen for *pilot* and an objective pronoun for *shuttles:* "*He* flew *them.*"

PRONOUN CASE

PERSONAL PRONOUN CASES

	FIRST PERSON		SECOND PERSON		THIRD PERSON	
	SINGULAR	PLURAL	SINGULAR	PLURAL	SINGULAR	PLURAL
SUBJECTIVE	I	we	you	you	he, she, it	they
POSESSIVE	my	our	your	your	his, her	their
	mine	ours	yours	yours	hers, its	theirs
OBJECTIVE	me	us	you	you	him, her, it	them

RELATIVE OR INTERROGATIVE PRONOUN CASES

SUBJECTIVE	who	whoever
POSSESSIVE	whose	whose
OBJECTIVE	whom	whomever

10a Use the subjective case for pronoun subjects and for pronouns that follow forms of the verb *to be.*

PRONOUN SUBJECTS

Gladys and *he* think alike.

We and *they* traveled in Mexico last summer.

We children stayed in our rooms and waited for Santa.

case, ref Forms of *to be* (*am, is, are, was, were, be, being, been*) do not take objects; in formal writing, use *subjective* pronouns after these verbs.

PRONOUNS AFTER *TO BE*

It is *I* [not *me*].

The one they wanted was *she* [not *her*].

10b Use the objective case for pronouns used as direct or indirect objects and after prepositions.

We all saw *him.* [*Him* is a direct object.]

The president has found *us* a home. [*Us* is an indirect object.]

There were no secrets *between him and me.* [*Him* and *me* are objects of the preposition *between.*]

ACTIVITY 7

Select the appropriate pronoun in the following sentences.

1. I finished my job application with: "Please send your answer directly to (I/me)."
2. (We/Us) men on the negotiating team hoped to finish early.
3. The letter said, "Let's keep this just between you and (I/me)."
4. When they announce the winner, do you think it will be (she/her)?
5. We all wondered whether (she/her) and her brother would soon leave.

10c Pronouns used as appositives take the same case as the word they refer to.

The job was offered to the two students on the left, *him* and *her.* [The pronouns refer to the "the two students," the object of a preposition; objective case is required.]

The class representatives, Lionel and *she,* have been invited to speak to the faculty. [The pronoun refers to the subject; subjective case is required.]

10d Before a gerund, pronouns require the possessive case.

case, ref

His playing the guitar is what started all the trouble.
The doctor was insulted by *my* questioning his bill.

See **5h** for the distinction between gerunds and participles.

ACTIVITY 8

Select the appropriate pronoun in each of these sentences.

1. Everyone knew Jose and (I/me) were to start the show.
2. (His/Him) writing that note started all this trouble.
3. The captain said the enemy might attack (we/us) marines in the night.
4. The rifle was aimed at the couple, (he/him) and (she/her).
5. Margo said she would divide the cake between Kyle and (I/me).
6. No one understood (him/his) leaving the cat out all weekend.
7. The person we need for this job is (he/him).
8. Someone saw the Joneses and (I/me) preparing to leave for Paris last summer.
9. Those two children, (he/him) and (she/her), will say the Pledge of Allegiance.
10. The one who needed it most was (she/her).

10e Distinguish between *who* and *whom*.

Whom is rapidly disappearing from oral English. But in formal writing, writers still maintain the distinction between *who* and *whom*.

Who and *whoever* are the subject forms; *whom* and *whomever* are the object forms; the proper case depends on how the pronoun is used in its clause.

case, ref

To test any who/whom question, mentally convert the question into a statement using some other pronoun. If a subject pronoun (like *he*) is appropriate, the sentence requires *who*. If an object pronoun (like *him*) is appropriate, the sentence requires *whom*.

Who/whom made that noise? [*He* made that noise. A subject pronoun is required; *who* is appropriate.]

Who/whom did you invite? [You did invite *her*. An object pronoun is required; *whom* is appropriate.]

Whom usually follows prepositions: To *whom* did you give the gift? But sometimes a preposition introduces a clause with *whoever* as its subject: *Give this message to* ***whoever*** *answers the door.*

ACTIVITY 9

Explain the pronoun choices in these sentences.

1. *Whom* shall I interrogate?
2. *Who* asks the questions here?
3. To *whom* is this addressed?
4. *Who* owns this car?
5. This letter is aimed at *whoever* owns a new car.

Reducing complicated sentences to basic ones in your mind can also help you to choose correct pronouns.

WHO/WHOM SENTENCE	ANALYSIS
The soldiers (who/whom) we thought were responsible have been punished.	The soldiers have been punished. We thought *they* were responsible. [A subject pronoun is required; *who* is appropriate.]
The students have identified the girl (who/whom) they want for president.	The students have identified the girl. They want *her* for president. [An object pronoun is required; *whom* is appropriate.]

It is often possible to substitute some other pronoun to determine whether *who* or *whom* is required. *case, ref*

I see (who/whom) is using the chainsaw. [*I see* **he** *is using the chainsaw.* A subject pronoun is required: ***who.***]

ACTIVITY 10

Select the appropriate word in the following sentences. Be prepared to explain your choices.

1. (Who/Whom) is supposed to be the favorite in this race?
2. (Who/Whom) do you trust?
3. Everyone knew (who/whom) the police would question.
4. (Who/Whom) we should elect is easy to see.
5. The surgeon we want to do the operation is the one (who/whom) will do the best job.
6. (Whoever/Whomever) needs the blood should report to the clinic.
7. We found the one (who/whom) had been doing the damage.
8. The winner will be (whoever/whomever) they select.
9. They tried to find the one (who/whom) they wanted to do the work.
10. This is the type of person (who/whom) we want for class treasurer.

PRONOUN REFERENCE

The *antecedent* of a pronoun is the word to which the pronoun refers. Make sure pronouns agree with their antecedents.

The *car* had *its* undercarriage lowered to within three inches of the ground. [*Car* is the antecedent of *its*].

Michael applied for the job, but *he* was turned down. [*Michael* is the antecedent of *he.*]

10f Collective nouns are singular and require singular pronouns.

Collective nouns identify groups: the *army*, the *band*, the *corporation*, the *faculty*, the *Ford Motor Company*, the *generation*, the *majority*, the *team*.

The *company* knows what *it* is doing.
The *navy* aims *its* recruitment campaign at high school graduates.

10g In general, use a singular pronoun to refer to indefinite singular pronouns.

Indefinite pronouns are words such as *one*, *anyone*, *everyone*, *anybody*, *everybody*, *each*, *neither*, *either*. (See **4b.**)

Everybody in the Boy Scouts earns *his* merit badges the hard way.
Neither of the girls was allowed to bring *her* pet to camp.

10h Avoid the use of masculine pronouns when *both* sexes are implied.

For example, when a team contains both men and women, you should indicate that fact.

Each player should bring *his* or *her* own towel.

To avoid awkwardness or too much repetition of *his/her*, write in the plural.

Players should bring *their* own towels.

10i Use a plural pronoun with antecedents joined by *and*.

Fred and Velma had a fine time on *their* vacation.

case, ref

10j Use a singular pronoun to refer to singular antecedents joined by *or* or *nor.*

Was it *Michigan or Illinois* that recalled *its* governor?

When *or* or *nor* joins a singular antecedent to another that is plural, the pronoun should agree with the closer one.

Neither *John nor the twins* had *their* applications in on time.
Neither *the twins nor John* had *his* application in on time.

It is often better to revise such sentences to get rid of the confusing pronoun problem entirely.

John did not have his application in on time, nor did the twins.

ACTIVITY 11

Select the appropriate word in the following sentences. Be prepared to explain your choices.

1. Each of the girls had (her/their) heart set on a career in government.
2. Our company is one of the leaders in (its/their) field.
3. The jury chose not to continue (its/their) deliberations.
4. Everybody has to make up (his/their) own mind.
5. Every girl who had seen the show offered (her/their) own interpretation.
6. Either Mom or the kids had to show (her/their) drawings.
7. Neither the garden nor the orchard showed (its/their) best after the drought.
8. Was it General Motors or AT&T that had (its/their) sharpest decline in years?
9. The team had (its/their) finest season in a long time.
10. He is one of those athletes who (drives/drive) (himself/themselves) too hard.

case, ref

ACTIVITY 12

Revise to eliminate problems in pronoun reference. It may be necessary to change verbs along with pronouns. You may revise any way you like as long as you do not create any awkward sentences or leave any pronoun problems.

1. Either of these computers can run their programs at ten megahertz.
2. Everyone who needs financial assistance should send in their application for a job listed on the job board.
3. Is it credible that General Motors could lose their customers to foreign competitors?
4. Each of the young men on the drill squad has their own ideas for winning the games.
5. Every student should develop his own study habits.
6. A good microcomputer and a big mainframe both do similar work for its users.
7. None of us want to have a party, but the date has been set.
8. Everybody in the house had their pajamas on when the fire alarm went off.
9. The faculty senate will announce their new guidelines in April.
10. Neither my brothers nor my sister wanted their rooms painted orange.

10k Avoid using ambiguous pronouns.

When a pronoun seems to refer to more than one antecedent, the reference is ambiguous.

AMBIGUOUS	REVISED
Don't put your feet into new boots when *they* smell bad.	Don't put on new boots when they smell bad.
	Don't put on new boots when your feet smell bad.

10l Avoid using vague pronouns.

A pronoun should refer to a single nearby antecedent—not to an implied idea or a group of words.

VAGUE (ANTECEDENT UNCLEAR)

We have to write Aunt Esther a thank-you letter, *which* is not easy for me.

REVISED

We have to write Aunt Esther a thank-you letter, but letter writing is not easy for me.

We have to write Aunt Esther a thank-you letter, but it is not easy for me to write to her.

VAGUE (ANTECEDENT NOT EXPRESSED)

My Labrador retriever is very intelligent, but she doesn't always show *it*. [*Intelligent* is an adjective and cannot be the antecedent of a pronoun.]

REVISED

My Labrador retriever is very intelligent, but she doesn't always show this quality.

My Labrador retriever has a great deal of *intelligence*, but she doesn't always show *it*.

10m Use *who, which,* and *that* to make appropriate reference to humans, animals, and objects.

Use *who, whom, whoever, whomever* to refer to humans.

Clyde is a young man *who* knows what he wants.

Mr. Edgars is the one *whom* we want for mayor.

The criminal must be *whoever* left the lights on.

case, ref

Occasionally it may be necessary to use *who* to refer to an animal: *My cat, Barney,* ***who*** *has been with me for ten years, is still the best mouser in town.*

Some writers use *whose* to avoid awkward or wordy pronoun constructions.

> This is an argument *whose* ending is certain. [*Whose* replaces *the ending of which.*]
>
> *Romeo and Juliet* is a drama *whose* love story is timeless. [*Whose* is more economical than the very formal *in which the.*]

Use *which* to refer to animals, objects, and ideas, especially in nonrestrictive clauses. (See **21e.**)

> The opossum, *which* is the only American marsupial, has a prehensile tail.
>
> We are studying nihilism, *which* is the theory that life has no purpose or meaning.

Use *that* to refer to animals and objects, especially in restrictive clauses. (See **21e.**)

> Any dog *that* barks at night may be picked up by the dog catcher.
>
> *Crime and Punishment* is a novel *that* presents the psychology of the criminal.

10n Avoid using an excessive number of pronouns.

Too many pronouns will sound repetitious and may produce an immature tone.

EXCESSIVE

> The boy knew *he* should go, and *he* thought *he* should say so, but *he* held back because *he* feared what might happen to *him*.

REVISED

Although *he* knew *he* should go and thought *he* should say so, the boy held back out of fear. ***case, ref***

ACTIVITY 13

Select the preferred sentence in the following pairs. Be prepared to explain your answers.

1. A. Louie's magic act was the main feature of the amateur show, but no one appreciated his tricks.
   B. Louie's magic act was the main feature of the amateur show, but no one appreciated it.
2. A. Aunt Wilma asked Mother whether she might wear a light-blue dress to the funeral.
   B. Aunt Wilma asked Mother whether it might be appropriate to wear a light-blue dress to the funeral.
3. A. The boys knew the girls had their keys.
   B. The boys knew their keys had been taken by the girls.
4. A. Science is a very difficult subject, which I realized almost immediately.
   B. Science is a very difficult subject, a fact which I realized almost immediately.
5. A. The fact that our entire family has inherited great grandfather's nose is considered a genetic accident.
   B. Our entire family has inherited great grandfather's nose, which is considered a genetic accident.

ACTIVITY 14

Revise the following sentences to remove pronoun case and reference problems. It may be necessary to change verbs when you change pronouns. You may revise any way you like as long as you do not create any awkward sentences or leave any pronoun problems.

1. Every young man in these classes hopes eventually they will make a million dollars.
2. It seems obvious that whoever we elect will have to serve for at least two terms.
3. Estelle is one of those beautiful young women who suffers because people assume she is unintelligent.

4. I was using my camera with a tripod to take a picture of our dog, but unfortunately it wiggled.
5. Aunt Beth is reluctant to put her teeth into containers until she has boiled them.
6. Make sure you speak firmly to whomever is making all the racket out there.
7. The class attempted to interrupt him lecturing in a monotone by asking questions.
8. You should never put braces on your teeth when they are rusty.
9. Someone will have to tell Ralph his dog has been killed, which is very unpleasant.
10. A monkey who wants a banana is likely to do anything you say.
11. After hearing legal precedent and argument, the grand jury announced that the guilty one was me.
12. The bank sent a letter saying that we had overdrawn our checking account, which was a great surprise to us.
13. Between she and I there is a long-standing friendship and trust.
14. Any dog which can fetch and do tricks is all right with me.
15. Each of these ten children have lost their mother.

11 VERB FORMS

Verbs have four forms: present, past, past participle, and present participle. Some have alternate forms; a few have repeated forms. Regular verbs form their past and past participle with *-d* or *-ed: seized, wanted, sailed.* Irregular verbs usually form their past and past participle with a spelling change; *swim, swam, swum.* Here are a few troublesome verb forms:

PRESENT	PAST	PAST PARTICIPLE	PRESENT PARTICIPLE
awake	awoke, awaked	awaked, awoke	awaking
awaken	awakened	awakened	awakening
begin	began	begun	beginning
break	broke	broken	breaking
bring	brought	brought	bringing
buy	bought	bought	buying
dive	dived, dove	dived	diving
draw	drew	drawn	drawing
drink	drank	drunk	drinking
freeze	froze	frozen	freezing
get	got	got, gotten	getting
go	went	gone	going
know	knew	known	knowing
lay	laid	laid	laying
lie (recline)	lay	lain	lying
lie (falsify)	lied	lied	lying
make	made	made	making
set	set	set	setting
sing	sang	sung	singing
sink	sank	sunk	sinking
take	took	taken	taking
wake	woke, waked	waked, woken	waking
wear	wore	worn	wearing

The past participle and present participle are used to form the *perfect* and *progressive* tenses. They are used with forms of *to be* (*am, is, are, was, were, be, being, been*) and with forms of *to have* (*have, has, had*).

Michael *is making* dinner.
The world *has known* about her secret for months.
I *have been sitting* here for hours.
You *will have worn* that coat ten times if you wear it again.

vb form

11a Avoid slang verbs in formal writing.

In informal writing, slang verbs can be appropriate, but for formal writing, slang should be avoided: *busted, rappin', frosted* (for *frozen*), *croaked* (for *died*), and so on.

11b Avoid nonstandard verb forms in formal writing.

Nonstandard verb forms are often acceptable in conversation or quoted dialogue but should be avoided in formal writing.

NONSTANDARD

The ship *had sank* in deep waters. The ship *sunk* in deep waters

REVISED

The ship *had sunk* in deep waters. The ship *sank* in deep waters.

NONSTANDARD

They *snuck* out of the house after curfew.

REVISED

They *sneaked* out of the house after curfew.

11c Use lie/lay and sit/set correctly.

Lie and *lay* have different meanings. *To lie* (lie, lay, lain, lying) means *to be at rest, to recline. To lay* (*lay, laid, laid, laying*) means *to put something somewhere. Sit* and *set* have different meanings. *To sit* (*sit, sat, sat, sitting*) means *to be seated. To set* (*set, set, set, setting*) means *to put* or *place in position.*

The pairs of words are also different in *grammar*. *Lie* and *sit* never take objects. They are usually followed by *place* expressions (lie *down*, lie *on the bed*, sit *up*, sit *on that chair*). *Lay* and *set* always take objects: lay *the book* down; lay *it* on the bed; set the *pencil* over there; set *it* on the counter. Note the past tense of *lie:* **vb form**

Today I *lie* down; yesterday I *lay* down [not *laid*].

ACTIVITY 15
Select the appropriate verb in the following sentences.

1. The Christmas decorations have (laid/lain) on the upper shelf all year.
2. She said our papers have been (sitting/setting) there all day.
3. (Set/Sit) the equipment out where we can see it clearly.
4. It's a good idea to (lay/lie) very still when you are overheated.
5. "It's no use (lying/laying) in bed pretending you are sick to avoid going to work," my father always said.
6. That dog has (sat/set) there all day.
7. If you're tired, you ought to (sit/set) down for a while.
8. The letter is (sitting/setting) right there in front of you.
9. They (lay/laid) in bed until noon yesterday.
10. They have (laid/lain) tracks right across our field.

ACTIVITY 16
Eliminate any verb problems in the following sentences.

1. It was my unpleasant duty to tell my father our speedboat sunk in ninety feet of water because I had been careless.
2. The girls thought no one ever saw them when they snuck out late at night.
3. "Don't you dare lay down in your bed until you have cleaned that room," Mother shouted.
4. Nona was very angry because her roommate had robbed her last pair of nylons.

5. It looked as if Father had drug out everything in the house for spring cleaning.
6. If we had stayed another few minutes, I could have drank my coffee.
7. I must have lain my glasses down somewhere, but I can't find them now.
8. "Sit that pitcher a little nearer to the center of the table, please," Mother said.
9. The boys were too wasted to answer the policeman's questions.
10. After the diamond was lain out in the dust, we started the ball game.

---

12 VERB TENSE

Verb tense indicates when an action takes place—past, present, or future.

The **past tense** indicates completed action or habitual action in the past.

The Premier *vetoed* the bill.

Festus *whistled* whenever he saw a pretty girl.

The **present tense** indicates action occurring in the present, generalizations, and habitual or continuing behavior.

Pollution *causes* acid rain.

Most humans *need* companionship.

John *clears* his throat before talking on the phone.

The **future tense** indicates that an action will occur in the future.

The space shuttle *will land* next week.

The distinction between *shall* and *will* is seldom observed today. Some writers still use *shall* when they want to be especially formal or emphatic: We *shall* surely die. But generally *shall* is no longer used except for formal requests: *Shall* we do it? *t*

The **past perfect tense** describes action completed prior to another action in the past.

> The government *had fallen* long before the truth was revealed.
>
> Jeff *had been asked* for the solution, but another student came up with the answer.

The **present perfect tense** describes action that began in the past and is continuing or action that took place at an indefinite time in the past.

> The Armed Services *have recruited* specialists in the field of electronics.
>
> He *has pondered* long and hard for many years.

The **future perfect tense** describes action that will be completed before another action.

> He *will have finished* before you.
>
> The protestors *will have spoken* for three hours by the time we get to the rally.

Verbs also have a **progressive** form (the *-ing* form) that indicates ongoing action.

> I *am writing* a letter.
>
> You *were working* very late last night.
>
> He *will be dancing* a new number in the show.

Any tense that fits your purpose is suitable; the key is to be consistent. The past tense is appropriate for most formal writing, but often a **literary present tense** is used to describe t what an author accomplishes in his or her works or to describe the actions of a character.

> Shakespeare *creates* a symbol of evil in the play *Othello.*
> Huck Finn eventually *escapes* from Pap.

12a Avoid unjustified shifts in tense.

The tense of the first verb in a sentence sets up a reference for the rest of the verbs; make sure the other verbs in the sentence conform.

REVISE FOR CONSISTENT TENSE

> The company's common stock *split* last December as production costs ~~decrease.~~ decreased

> In the play, Susan *is waiting* for the proper moment, but John suddenly *announces* he ~~was~~ is leaving.

12b Avoid inappropriate past tense.

Avoid using the simple past tense to indicate one event occurring before another. Use the past perfect tense for the earlier event:

REVISE INAPPROPRIATE PAST TENSE

> We knew the bird ~~escaped~~ had escaped when we saw that its cage door *was* ajar.

13 VERB MOOD

The mood of a verb suggests whether an action should be considered a statement of fact (indicative mood), a command (imperative mood), or a wish, a doubt, or a condition contrary to fact (subjunctive mood). The indicative mood is the most common, but the subjunctive mood is sometimes used in formal writing.

13a Use the subjunctive to express doubt, wishes, probability, conditions contrary to fact, or conditional statements.

The most common subjunctive forms are *be* and *were*. Others are formed from the plural present tense (without the *s*).

We insist that you *be* present.
If I *were* you, I would not get there too early.
He wished he *were* an astronaut.
She insisted that Henry *deliver* the manuscript.
Were it true, I would have told you so.

The subjunctive is appropriate for conditional statements.

If I *were* to do it, I would be penalized.

Avoid using a redundant conditional (If you *would* do it, you *would* be penalized). Use *will* or *would* only for the consequence, not the condition.

mood

13b Use the subjunctive for demands, preferences, or requests introduced by *that*.

He insists that she *do* it by herself.

We would prefer that he *sleep* in the garage.

ACTIVITY 17

Select the appropriate verb in each of the following sentences.

1. Tina wished she (was/were) a little taller and a lot thinner.
2. I quickly discovered that Mike had (drank/drunk) all of the milk.
3. If you break the window, you (would/will) have to pay for it.
4. It is the company's desire that Uncle Fred (attend/attends) the sales convention in Denver.
5. Would you lend him money if he (was/were) to ask you?
6. After the dance, the guests (lay/laid) around on the lawn.
7. The papers have been (lying/laying) on the floor since you left them there.
8. Their house (sits/sets) in the middle of their property.
9. Her fried chicken was the best we had ever (ate/eaten).
10. By twelve o'clock, they will (be/have been) flying across the Atlantic for six hours.

ACTIVITY 18

Eliminate any problems in verb tense or mood. You may need to change other words when you revise verbs. You may revise any way you like as long as you do not create any awkward sentences or leave any verb problems.

1. A neighbor finally found poor old Scout with his tongue froze to the pump handle.
2. Amazingly, the chorus had sang the entire number without a mistake.
3. The granite cracked with a loud report when we drive a wedge into its fault line.
4. Just as I begun to fall asleep the rooster crowed.

5. It seemed the burglars had took everything of value in the house.
6. Mom's cooling pies set precariously on the window ledge.
7. We yelled at Arfy to get out of the way, but he just laid there on the driveway.
8. Of course I wish I was wealthy, doesn't everyone?
9. Yesterday I just laid in bed all day thinking about my problem.
10. It looked like the canisters busted their seams when the temperature rose too high in the storage room.
11. Our surveyors had lain out the lot lines too close to the river bank.
12. Our dog likes to sleep in the house, but father prefers that it sleeps in the barn.
13. I knew that even if I would memorize all the words I would never be able to win the spelling contest.
14. When we examined the pictures, we realized immediately that Winnona drew them.
15. The cornered rat glared at us and gritched its teeth in anger.

14 ACTIVE AND PASSIVE VOICES

The voice of a verb indicates whether its subject acts or is acted upon. In a normal (active) sentence, the subject is the actor in the sentence. In a passive sentence, the subject is acted upon or receives the action of the verb, and the actor then appears in the object's place. See Transitive, **4c;** Direct Object, **5d.**

	ACTOR	ACTION	OBJECT
ACTIVE	The fish	took	the bait.
PASSIVE	The bait	was taken	by the fish.

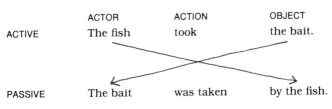

act/pass The *logical* subject in the passive sentence is *the fish* (the fish is the actor), but the *grammatical* subject is *the bait*. A passive verb acts upon its subject: ("My apartment has been robbed six times in three years"). It deemphasizes an actor: ("The experiment was conducted over a two-month period"). You may use the passive voice when writing about scientific subjects, but too much use creates a distant, depersonalized sound. Avoid the passive in nonscientific writing.

PASSIVE

Heavy books are seldom read by students.

ACTIVE

Students seldom read heavy books.

PASSIVE

That immunological activity is increased by raising the body's temperature is concluded by Smith.

ACTIVE

Smith concludes that raising the body's temperature increases immunological activity.

ACTIVITY 19

Revise each of the passives below to active.

1. A cancerous tumor was removed by the surgical team.
2. An angry letter had been sent by the President to Congress.
3. The doctor left his office after his last patient had been seen.
4. Several experiments were finished after the grant had been received by us.
5. Emergency procedures should be taken whenever gas is observed to be leaking.

ACTIVITY 20

Revise the following paragraph to eliminate any problems with verbs. It may be necessary to change other words when you revise the verbs. You may revise any way you like as long as you do not create any awkward sentences or leave any verb problems.

During President Carter's administration the Shah of Iran was ousted by conservative Moslems. After the Shah had been driven out, the leadership of the country was given to the Ayatollah Khomeini. One of the first acts of the new government under the Ayatollah was to nab the American embassy. Embassy workers and some civilians were held hostage by the Ayatollah's revolutionary guards. President Carter had gave orders to work patiently to free the hostages and not to hassle the Iranians too much. He felt that if we would treat the Iranians with respect, they would respond in kind. However, it finally dawned on him that the Iranians aren't going to release our people. He ordered that a helicopter raid was made on the embassy, but this plan fell through when sand gummed up the engines of the helicopters. The staging area for the helicopters laid out in the desert. An entire year of negotiations with the Iranians fails to release any prisoners. The Iranians are blaming America for the tyranny of the Shah, who had been supported by us. They imagined we are planning to sit him back on the throne. Then too, having America as the "enemy" allowed the revolution and control of Iran to be maintained by the Ayatollah; the people had been united with him against a common "threat" from America.

15 ADJECTIVES AND ADVERBS

Adjectives modify nouns and pronouns. Adverbs modify verbs, adjectives, and other adverbs. (See **4d, 4e.**)

Adjectives and adverbs have degrees of comparison, from least to most. The degrees of comparison are positive, comparative, superlative.

POSITIVE	COMPARATIVE	SUPERLATIVE
angry	angrier	angriest
angrily	more angrily	most angrily
bad	worse	worst
good	better	best
happily	more happily	most happily
well	better	best

A few modifiers are considered **absolute.** Words like *incomparable, total,* and *unique* suggest qualities that have no degrees of comparison: they are "absolute." Avoid expressions like *more unique,* or *most incomparable.*

Use the comparative degree, not the superlative, for comparisons between the two things: "He is the *younger* [not the *youngest*] of the two boys."

15a Avoid redundant, invented, or otherwise faulty comparatives and superlatives.

REDUNDANT OR FAULTY SUPERLATIVES

Alicia is the *most prettiest* girl I have ever seen.

Professor Glade is the *bestest* teacher I know.

REVISED

Alicia is the *prettiest* girl I have ever seen.

Professor Glade is the *best* teacher I know.

15b Avoid dropping *-ly* from adverbs.

Most words ending in *-ly* are adverbs, especially when the *-ly* is a suffix added to a root word. The suffix *-ly* added to the adjective *quick* produces the adverb *quickly.* (Not all words ending in *-ly* are adverbs: *motherly, priestly,* and *scholarly* are not adverbs. See **4e.**)

The car rides very *smoothly* [not *smooth*].

Walk *quietly* [not *quiet*] so you don't disturb anyone.

15c Use adjectives after linking verbs, adverbs after action verbs.

These apples *taste delicious.* [The predicate adjective describes the subject.]

We *tasted* the wines *carefully.* [The adverb describes the verb.]

Your new haircut *looks youthful.* [predicate adjective]

Everyone *looked intently* at the insects. [adverb]

15d Use adjectives to modify objects, adverbs to modify verbs.

They found their new puppy *clever.* [The adjective, *clever,* describes the direct object, *puppy.*]

They found their new puppy *cleverly.* [The adverb, *cleverly,* describes the verb, *found.*]

15e Use *bad, badly, good, well* appropriately.

Bad is an adjective.

This is a *bad* day for swimming.

The doctor felt *bad.* [Linking verbs take predicate adjectives; *bad* describes *doctor.*]

Fish and guests smell *bad* after three days.

adj/adv

Badly is an adverb.

The car was *badly* damaged in the accident.
She fell *badly* on the ice.

Good is an adjective.

Mother makes *good* desserts.
The flowers look *good* in that old pot.

Well is both an adjective and an adverb.

I hope we all remain *well* during the flu season. [*Well* is a predicate adjective after the linking verb *remain.*]
She paints *well* for such a young child. [*Well* is an adverb after the action verb *paints.*]

ACTIVITY 21

Revise the following sentences to remove any problems with adjectives and adverbs. You may need to change other words when you revise modifiers. You may revise any way you like as long as you do not create any awkward sentences or leave any faulty adjectives or adverbs.

1. The troops had orders to move quick or be left behind.
2. The punishment is more worse than anything you can possibly imagine.
3. Sid tied the boat good, so it should still be there.
4. I felt badly about losing the lottery.
5. You have to do your work quick if you want to have any time for fun.
6. Benny is the most coolest teenager in our class.
7. It will be more better for you to have the milk than coffee.
8. Between Felicia and Dawn, I think Dawn is the prettiest name.
9. "The Windhover" is the most unique poem I have ever heard.
10. Our dog was hurt bad when the car struck it a glancing blow.

ACTIVITY 22

Section review: Select the appropriate word in the following sentences. Be prepared to explain your answers.

1. Every memo we get from these committees (describes/describe) problems we do not have the resources to solve.
2. A long memory and a certain skill with words (is/are) required for success in education.
3. Neither the citizens nor their President (was/were) surprised when Congress levied a new tax.
4. This spaniel is one of those dogs that (remains/remain) loyal to their owner throughout life.
5. The man most likely to win is (he/him), Mr. Farley.
6. Just between you and (I/me), the army may have made a mistake when it replaced the old Colt .45.
7. (Who/Whom) we intend to give the award to is a secret.
8. We thought (him/his) playing the violin might cheer you.
9. If I (was/were) you, I would resign immediately.
10. The Chinese abacus works as (good/well) as an electric calculator.
11. She had written in the last page of her diary, "It is (they/them) who will be sorry."
12. We found one of those trashy novels that (is/are) full of romantic nonsense.
13. The note said the police insist that he (come/comes) to the station immediately.
14. She knew this was a message for (whoever/whomever) would feel guilty about it.
15. The expensive wine will be (drank/drunk) by all the guests at the main table.
16. Cyril and Deliah—the latter was the (stronger/strongest) of the two.
17. The President asked whether he was one of those aides who (tell/tells) everything you say to them.
18. Each of the young marines (was/were) going to be tested for the first time under fire.
19. Everyone will be (more better/better) off with a little exercise.
20. You have to work extra (slow/slowly) if you want your work to be perfect.

21. Long after the exam was over, he (lay/laid) in bed for hours wondering whether he had passed.
22. *Time* magazine writes (its/their) stories for maximum reader interest.
23. We were told that she had a mad aunt (who/whom) it was not easy to get to know.
24. They boasted that they could have (swum/swam) all night.
25. The police insisted that he had (laid/lain) the luger there purposely to mislead them.

REVISION PRACTICE

ACTIVITY 23

Revise each of the following sentences.

1. Telegrams can now be sent to whomever has a mailing address anywhere on the planet.
2. Riesa wished with all her might that Evan was a member of her religious group so that they could be married.
3. The pigeons laid somewhat left of the oak, out of range.
4. There, just beyond the parking lot, go the wealthiest group of young people in the country.
5. Who are you trying to identify as "the phantom"?
6. Neither the city nor the town were ready to raise taxes.
7. The reward was that if we would cross the finish line first we would gain a point.
8. It is a mistake to put the dog near the cat if it is excited.
9. He is one of those men who has a good time no matter what.
10. You cannot get the thread through the needle when it is wet.
11. News that the Russians' new weapons were more powerful than our rockets were disturbing to our leaders.
12. Either their materials or their craftsmanship are the reason for the high quality of the work.

13. The children were given to their grandparents, although they had wet their pants. ***adj/adv***
14. My brother was the only one of those applicants who were qualified for the job.
15. When they asked her who had done it, she said that it was her.

Sentence Structure

coord, sub A primary consideration in writing is *readability*, the ease with which readers can get information from your sentences. Readability does not, however, imply merely the ability to "decode" a sentence. After all, elementary books are "readable" in their childish simplicity: "See Dick run. Run Dick. Run, run, run." But the *effect* on a mature reader of this kind of simplicity is tiresome and possibly insulting. You must balance simplicity with other sentence structures for effective sentences.

16 COORDINATION AND SUBORDINATION

Coordination and subordination refer to the balance between clauses in a sentence. Clauses of equal emphasis are connected by coordinating words (see **4f**) or punctuation. When one clause is given less emphasis than another, the lesser clause is *dependent* and is introduced with a subordinating word. (See **4f.**)

COORDINATE CLAUSES

The plumber soldered the pipes, but he forgot to turn the water back on. [The two clauses share equal emphasis and are joined by the coordinating conjunction *but.*]

The gourmet restaurant served only the finest food; however, the owners had misjudged their market and were forced to close. [Two clauses are given equal emphasis and are joined with a semicolon and a conjunctive adverb. See **23b.**]

Coordinate clauses can also be joined with a semicolon (see **23a**) or a colon (see **24c**).

SUBORDINATE CLAUSES

Since the race was to be run over a longer track, the filly was now considered the favorite. [The first clause is dependent and is introduced by the subordinating conjunction *since.*]

Every tree *that we plant today* may one day provide fuel, paper, or shelter for our children. [The dependent clause begins with the relative pronoun *that* (see **4b**) and is embedded in the main clause.]

16a Avoid excessive coordination.

Mere length by itself is not the goal. By stringing together phrases and clauses with *and, but,* or *or,* you will succeed in producing a long sentence, but it may become unreadable. Avoid the overuse of coordinating words.

EXCESSIVE COORDINATION

My car is a Chevrolet, *and* it has a six-cylinder engine, *and* it gets twenty miles to the gallon, *and* it is a hot rod.

REVISED FOR BETTER COORDINATION

My car, a hot-rod Chevrolet, has a six-cylinder engine *and* gets twenty miles to the gallon.

Excessively coordinated sentences sound immature. Readers perceive such strings as separate sentences tacked together with *and*'s.

16b Avoid faulty coordination.

In informal English, the additive conjunction (*and*) is frequently used to join coordinate clauses, even when the clauses are contrastive.

CONFUSING COORDINATION

He drank the poison, *and* he didn't die.

REVISED FOR CONTRAST

He drank the poison, *but* he didn't die.

sub

16c Avoid excessive subordination.

Too many words indicating subordination or relationship can make a sentence hard to read.

EXCESSIVE SUBORDINATION

When they opened the package *after* it arrived, they knew it was dangerous *even though* they weren't afraid of it *although* they should have been.

REVISED FOR CLARITY

They opened the package when it arrived. Although they knew it was dangerous, they weren't afraid of it.

16d Avoid faulty subordination.

Avoid sentences in which your reader may feel that you have subordinated the wrong idea, that the relationship is unnatural, or that the connecting word is inappropriate.

FAULTY SUBORDINATION

The oil well exploded in flames when thousands of gallons of fuel were lost.

SUBORDINATION REVERSED

When the oil well exploded in flames, thousands of gallons of fuel were lost.

FAULTY SUBORDINATION

The storekeepers put up security shutters as the citizens threatened to riot.

CONNECTIVE IMPROVED

The storekeepers put up security shutters after [or *because*] the citizens threatened to riot.

flty

comp

ACTIVITY 1

Revise for clarity. Edit the sentences to eliminate errors of coordination and subordination. In some cases you may wish to create more than one sentence.

1. As no one lived there now, we were disturbed to hear noise coming from the apartment upstairs.
2. Until the engines of the plane are started by the man who is to be the pilot until the real pilot arrives, the man that is standing by must wait until it is ready.
3. The red hint of dawn was showing a pale line, and it was below the clouds, and they were at the horizon, and it was just beyond the dark string of islands.
4. We saw the snake crawling toward the baby until we were frightened.
5. After two men had died there while they were trying to cross the swamps that were full of traps that you couldn't get out of because they had quicksand in them that most people just sank down and died in, a warning sign was put up.

17 ILLOGICAL SENTENCES

17a Revise faulty comparisons.

Avoid inexact use of *than*.

ILLOGICAL

She is *stronger than any* swimmer in the meet. [Acceptable only if she is not in the meet or if she is not a swimmer.]

REVISED

She is the *strongest* swimmer in the meet. [Or] She is *stronger than any other* swimmer in the meet.

flty comp

ILLOGICAL

The smell of cigarette smoke is more disgusting than a cigar. [The sentence makes an illogical comparison of an odor with an object.]

REVISED

The smell of cigarette smoke is more disgusting than *the smell of cigar smoke.* [Or] The smell of cigarette smoke is more disgusting than *that of a cigar.*

Avoid faulty interruption of comparisons.

ILLOGICAL

Steel is as strong, *if not stronger,* than iron. [If the interrupter is removed, the remaining statement is not grammatically acceptable: "Steel is as strong . . . than iron."]

REVISED

Steel is as strong **as,** *if not stronger than,* iron. [The interrupter can be removed, leaving a grammatically acceptable statement: "Steel is as strong **as** . . . iron."]

17b Revise faulty apposition.

An appositive renames or reidentifies its referent.

ILLOGICAL

All week he had received only one job offer, a clerk. [*A clerk* is not a job offer.]

REVISED

All week he had received only one job offer, a clerk's job.

17c Revise faulty predication.

Be sure your predicates agree with their subjects. (See Agreement, **9.**)

flty pred

ILLOGICAL

The design of the building was too close to the street. [The sentence says the design, not the building, was too close to the street.]

REVISED

The design of the building *placed it* too close to the street.

ILLOGICAL

The little trees were knocked over and the large oak damaged. [Plural *trees* and singular *oak* cannot both be subjects of the plural verb *were.*]

REVISED

The little trees *were* knocked over, and the large oak *was* damaged.

Avoid illogical predicate nouns. (See **5f.**)

ILLOGICAL

Lifting weights is where you strengthen your muscles. [Clauses beginning with *where* should be used only when they refer to a *place.*]

REVISED

Lifting weights strengthens your muscles.

ILLOGICAL

Argumentation is when you try to convince someone of your point of view. [Clauses beginning with *when* should be used only when they refer to *time.*]

REVISED

Argumentation is an attempt to convince someone of your point of view.

ILLOGICAL

The *reason* the campaign was such a success was *because* of the many contributions. [*Because* is redundant when used as a predicate noun for *reason.*]

flty
prep

REVISED

The campaign was such a success because of the many contributions.

The reason the campaign was such a success was *that* there were so many contributions.

17d Revise illogical prepositions.

You must make sure that your prepositions match both elements of a compound prepositional phrase.

ILLOGICAL

She said she had been simultaneously worried and delighted *with* her new neighbor.

REVISED

She said she had been simultaneously worried *about* and delighted *with* her new neighbor.

ACTIVITY 2

Revise each of the following sentences.

1. Granny Dearborn was one of the oldest, if not the oldest, resident in the retirement village.
2. Professors enjoy lectures more than students.
3. The boys in her class all had only one career in mind, an investment broker.
4. In a few minutes we had with the help of our field glasses spotted standing near a cave an old grizzly in the face of the cliff just below the plateau above.
5. The new teacher was as young, if not younger, than some of her students.
6. The meaning of the book was a love story between an older woman and a young man.
7. She said Bobo was as tall, if not taller, than Ernie.
8. I think Tolstoi's *War and Peace* is longer than any book in the library.
9. Clarissa had the best costume at Halloween, a witch.
10. One kind of poetry is when the words rhyme.

---

18 MODIFIERS

18a Revise dangling and misplaced modifiers.

Dangling modifiers have nothing to modify; misplaced modifiers are attached to the wrong word. Move modifiers next to the word you intend to modify, or supply a suitable subject to avoid the problem.

DANGLING MODIFIER

Swinging the axe with all my strength, the old tree fell toward me. [There is no actor here to swing the axe, unless the old tree has a murderous intent.]

REVISED

Swinging the axe with all my strength, *I* realized the tree was falling toward me. While *I* was swinging the axe with all my strength, the tree began falling toward me. [An appropriate subject has been supplied.]

MISPLACED MODIFIER

We all brought gifts with us for the orphan children *in our cars*. [The sentence says the children were "in our cars."]

REVISED

We all brought gifts with us *in our cars* for the orphan children.

18b Revise ambiguous modifiers.

Avoid ambiguity with movable modifiers (*almost, just, only*, and so on). For example, "I only washed the cups" can be interpreted "I merely washed them, I didn't dry the cups," or "I washed only the cups, the saucers I left for you." Place the modifier next to the word it modifies and, when neces-

mm sary, give the reader additional information to make your meaning clear:

AMBIGUOUS	REVISED FOR CLARITY
I just rented a summer cottage.	I rented a summer cottage just now.
	I just rented a summer cottage; I didn't buy one.
Everyone doesn't become senile in old age.	Not everyone becomes senile in old age.

Squinting modifiers seem to modify two words at once. Move the modifier next to the word you intend to modify.

SQUINTING	REVISED FOR CLARITY
The professor asked them *frequently* to review Homer's work.	The professor frequently asked them to review Homer's work.
	OR
	The professor asked them to review Homer's work frequently.

18c Revise split infinitives.

An infinitive is the word *to* plus a verb (*to miss, to go, to understand*). Putting a modifier between *to* and its verb is called splitting the infinitive (*to easily miss, to quickly go, to really understand*). In formal writing, the split infinitive is usually a mistake; it is always a mistake when it sounds unnatural.

SPLIT INFINITIVE	REVISED
You have *to usually work* hard in college.	You usually have to work hard in college.
You need *to slowly develop* your stamina.	You need to develop your stamina slowly.

ACTIVITY 3

Revise the following sentences to eliminate errors in modification.

1. Barking furiously as he approached, our veterinarian tried to hold Fluffy with one hand.
2. Bert opened the box with a bright red geranium design.
3. Tall, willowy, and highly intelligent, her hair glistened in the afternoon sun.
4. We just told them to leave their shoes outside.
5. Too tired to work anymore, the office suddenly looked hostile and uninviting.
6. She swore she had, just where you and I are standing now under this old willow, seen grandfather's ghost.
7. Everybody isn't too young to remember Elvis.
8. Hooking him with my best fly, the fish proved quite a catch.
9. The window faced a brick wall through which the sunlight streamed.
10. Racing down the street and shouting for the driver to stop, the midtown bus slowly moved away from me.

ACTIVITY 4

Revise the following paragraph for clarity. Combine sentences, add and delete words, shift words around, change the forms of words, and change punctuation. You may revise any way you like as long as you do not produce any garbled, illogical, or ineffective sentences. Revise so that the paragraph contains several sentences; avoid overusing *and* to string words together.

The Platypus

The platypus is a unique animal and it is a mammal and it is a primitive creature. It has a bill like a duck's which is like leather and it has a body which is covered by hair which is brown. It has a tail which is as flat, if not flatter, than a beaver's, although it does not have teeth since it only has short claws. The male has a spur that is made of material which is *shift*

```
similar to a horn that is near each foot. It uses this
spur to only defend itself. This spur contains poison.
The poison is from a sac although it will not kill
human beings. Being scratched by a platypus is when you
will get ill. The reason the poison will not kill a
person is because it is not strong enough. However,
everyone doesn't react the same way to platypus poison.
Since they are used for swimming, there are webs on its
feet. Being a mammal, its milk feeds their young
although they do not have real nipples. Oozing from a
gland, the hair of the platypus becomes wet with milk.
Because it is different from other mammals, it lays
eggs. The platypus lives in a burrow and it eats bugs
and it eats small shell fish and it eats worms. This
animal is stranger than any living creature. Being
about two feet long, its head is part duck. Its tail is
more like a beaver. Its burrow protects it like a mole,
Truly the unique parts of this creature puzzle for
science that lives on despite comic mismatch of
features may be nature's joke on it.
```

19 SENTENCE CONSISTENCY

19a Avoid shifts in voice, mood, person, number.

Avoid shifting conditional verbs. Avoid mixing *can* with conditionals: *might, could, should, would.*

SHIFTING CONDITIONAL

The silk *might* be purchased for less if you *can* go directly to the manufacturer.

REVISED

The silk *might* be purchased for less if you *could* go directly to the manufacturer.

Avoid shifting voice.

SHIFT FROM ACTIVE TO PASSIVE

He first *writes* his essay, and then it *is revised.*

REVISED

He first *writes* his essay, and then he *revises* it.

Avoid shifting mood of verbs. (See **13.**)

SHIFT FROM IMPERATIVE TO INDICATIVE

Now *read* your books, and then you *will write* an essay.

REVISED

Now *read* your books and then *write* an essay.

SHIFT FROM SUBJUNCTIVE TO INDICATIVE

It is necessary that he first *clean* his boat and then *paints* it.

REVISED

It is necessary that he first *clean* his boat and then *paint* it.

SHIFT FROM INDICATIVE TO INTERROGATIVE

They *said* he *was* a respectable citizen and *why would* we *think* otherwise?

REVISED

They said he was a respectable citizen, and *they wondered* why we would think otherwise.

shift

19b Avoid shifting level of formality.

Choose words consistent with your stance, and avoid shifting unnecessarily from one level to another.

SHIFT FROM FORMAL TO INFORMAL

The psychologist's profile and the evaluation of Harry's analyst established conclusively that he was a nut case.

REVISED

The psychologist's profile and the evaluation of Harry's analyst established conclusively that he had severe mental problems.

SHIFT FROM INFORMAL TO FORMAL

It was a complete turn-on—out-of-sight jams, foxy-looking women, and stimulating beverages.

REVISED

It was a complete turn-on—out-of-sight jams, foxy-looking women, and good juice.

19c Avoid shifting point of view.

Keep your point of view consistent. A less formal approach is to use *I* or *you;* more formal is the third person *she, he, they,* or *one.* Most formal is not using personal pronouns at all. Consistency is the key: if you begin writing from the point of view of *I*, stick to it.

SHIFT FROM FIRST PERSON TO THIRD

I have difficulty writing a paper when *one* does not understand the assignment.

REVISED

I have difficulty writing a paper when *I* do not understand the assignment.

SHIFT FROM INDEFINITE PRONOUN TO PERSONAL PRONOUN

One should be extra careful when *he* drives with bald tires.

REVISED

One should be extra careful when *one* drives with bald tires.

Drivers should be extra careful when their tires are bald.

19d Avoid shifting pronoun number.

SHIFT

Nursing is a challenging career, and *they* receive good wages.

REVISED

Nursing is a challenging career, and *it* pays good wages.

19e Avoid shifting conjunctions.

Keep subordinate conjunctions in compound expressions consistent.

SHIFT

Because we had paid in advance, and *since* we couldn't get our money back, we decided we had better go.

REVISED

Since we had paid in advance, and *since* we couldn't get our money back, we decided we had better go.

ACTIVITY 5

Revise for consistency.

1. I enjoy a good detective story when the author lets you solve the case.
2. It is imperative that Louis win the long jump and then runs the 100-yard dash.
3. After he had finished typing and since he had proofread the paper, Michael handed it in.
4. Computers might be the best buy if you can increase its memory storage.
5. The lobster is considered a delicacy, but I know many people who won't eat them.

ACTIVITY 6

Revise the following paragraph for consistent sentences. Combine sentences, add and delete words, shift words around, change the forms of words, and change punctuation. You may revise any way you like as long as you do not produce any garbled, illogical, or ineffective sentences. Revise so that the paragraph contains several sentences; avoid overusing *and* to string words together.

The Jester

The fool was known in ancient times. The fool was an entertainer. If someone could be clever then they can pretend to be stupid in a way that will amuse people. Playing the fool is hard work, and they are respected by their audiences. The professional fool is called a jester, and sometimes they were a musician, sometimes poets and philosophers. Some jesters became famous. They are remembered in history. Because some jesters were dwarfs, and since people thought dwarfs brought good luck, there is a long tradition of dwarf jesters. European fools wore a cap with bells on it. They dressed in a suit of many colors. In France there was a Feast of Fools. It was celebrated at Christmas.

Church members behaved like buffoons at the Feast; they flapped around like ninnies. Wealthy people and royalty kept fools. Some fools became wealthy themselves. Some famous fools appear in literature. The most famous appear in Shakespeare's plays. They are As You Like It, Twelfth Night, and King Lear. The fool in literature represents someone who sees the truth; they can see through pretenses. Most people try to live with dignity. They overlook or deny things that make life undignified. One is reminded by the fool that they are humiliated by life.

20 EMPHASIS AND VARIETY

Avoid monotonous, dull sentences. Give your sentences emphasis and variety.

20a Make writing emphatic by being economical.

In rough drafts, sentences may be unclear, illogical, or rambling because of the *extra* words in them. However, even short sentences can be wordy: *Her hair was blond* ***in color.*** *The tile was rectangular* ***in shape.*** During revision, make your sentence emphatic; edit wordy, redundant language.

WORDY

Our determination of the situation has been that in the matter of the death of the rat, it was the dog that should be blamed or credited as the case may be.

EDITED

The dog killed the rat.

REDUNDANT

The authors have managed to condense all this information into a two-page article which is straight to the point and wastes no words!

EDITED

The authors have managed to condense all this information into a concise two-page article.

ACTIVITY 7

Edit to make the following sentences economical.

1. The injury which had been suffered by the youthful young knight turned out to be a mortal wound and so then he died from it.
2. We must read our past history to learn from the words on the printed page those events that happened long ago.
3. After she said her name orally, I asked her the question if she would please repeat it again.
4. In the consequence of a terminal sequence having been reached it is advisable if not altogether necessary that there be a cessation of forward progress.
5. The car came into view; it was a red Corvette; it was going flat out; it came over the hill; it was leading a police car by half a mile.

ACTIVITY 8

Revise each of the following sets of short sentences to produce a longer, more effective sentence. You may add and delete words, shift words around, change the forms of words, and change punctuation. You may combine sentences any way you like as long as the result is a *single,* effective sentence. Avoid overusing *and* to string words together.

1. Commander Lucifer took a long puff. He was smoking his pipe. He blew out the smoke. The smoke made a dense cloud. He turned to stare. His manner was absent-minded. He saw the young sailor. The sailor steered the ship.

2. Gregor woke up suddenly. He was lying on his back. He looked down at his body. He saw dozens of tiny legs. They were wiggling. They were waving in many directions. Gregor had been changed. He was a bug.
3. The tank is an armored vehicle. The tank's armor is heavy. The tank's armor will stop a bullet. The tank was used in World War I. The tank revolutionized warfare.

20b Make sentences emphatic by subordinating material.

Subordinate means "lower in order"; it means a complete idea or complete sentence has been reduced to a dependent clause. Connect lesser ideas with subordinate conjunctions (**4f**) or relative pronouns (**4b**).

> *Although the fire destroyed the house,* we managed to save our business records.

Though it might seem to us that saving the records is less important than loss of the house, only the writer can make this judgment. Perhaps the writer thinks that the house can be replaced but business records cannot.

> *Although we saved our business records,* the fire destroyed the house.

Here the writer has decided that the loss of the house is the more important idea. Note that the independent clause comes last when the writer is trying to emphasize the most important idea.

Avoid faulty subordination.

SUBORDINATE CLAUSE IN EMPHATIC POSITION

The fire destroyed the house, *although we saved our business records.*

emph Putting business records in the subordinate clause is a signal that this is the lesser idea, but putting it last, in the most emphatic position makes an ambivalent effect. Ambivalence and ambiguity are usually errors; however, occasionally the writer may wish to create a deliberately ambivalent effect:

> Melvina lost the contest, although she was the most beautiful girl in it.

ACTIVITY 9

Revise the following sentences to produce greater emphasis and rhythm. Connect some or all of them any way that produces more readable, less choppy writing.

1. The men of the *USS Stark* were prepared for anything. But they were not prepared for something. It was the possibility. The possibility was an Iraqi jet. It might actually fire on them.
2. That was the first day. My mother dressed me. I was neat-as-a-pin. I was in a starched shirt. I was in creased trousers. She had brushed my hair. She sent me off to school. It was in a taxi.
3. We slept in the sand. It was close to the water's edge. It was between two protecting boulders. They took care of the stormy night winds for us.
4. I must have been asleep. All of a sudden there was the moon. It was a huge moon. It was framed in the window.
5. Eva was shy. She was chinless. She would be straining her upper lip. It would be over two teeth. They were enormous. She would sit in corners. She would be watching her mother.

20c Use effective repetition for emphasis.

Repetition is one way to achieve emphasis, as long as you don't become redundant.

UNEMPHATIC

In every time, tongue, lonely, troubled corner on earth, this bewilderment has been uttered.

REVISED

In every time, in every tongue, in every lonely, troubled corner of the earth, this bewilderment has been uttered.

Benjamin Kogan, *Health*

UNEMPHATIC

Society is sustained by communication, which makes human life possible.

REVISED

Society is sustained by communication: communication makes life possible.

Peterson, Goldhaber, Pace, *Communication Probes*

ACTIVITY 10

Revise the following paragraph for clarity. Combine sentences, add and delete words, shift words around, change the forms of words, and change punctuation. You may revise any way you like as long as you do not produce any garbled, illogical, or ineffective sentences. Revise so that the paragraph contains several sentences; avoid overusing *and* to string words together.

Quebec

Quebec is a province of Canada, and it is the largest one. There are ten provinces in Canada although the capital of Quebec is Quebec City, although Montreal is Quebec's largest city. Most people in Quebec speak a language which is French because it shares a boundary with Maine, New Hampshire, Vermont, and New York. It is popular with hunters. It is popular with fishing enthusiasts. It is popular with tourists. Since it was called New France, Quebec was originally a French possession. In the eighteenth century France ceded it to England. The reason was because of the French and Indian War. This was where the French Canadian farmers kept their farms. They held much of the land. Being merchants, England supplied many new people. Others came from Scotland when they became merchants. They controlled most of the trade. The language and customs of Quebec remained French conflict which between French Canadians and English Canadians warfare. The French Canadians mostly were Catholic. They were farmers; they speak French. The English Canadians were mostly Protestant. They were merchants. They spoke English. In 1867 French Canadians won the right to survival as a culture; their language and religion had been protected. They were higher than a kite about it. Today you can see Quebec has become much more industrial. Its people now live primarily in, if not entirely, the cities.

20d Use parallelism for emphasis.

Similar concepts should be written in similar forms; that is, they should be parallel. Parallelism is a form of repetition.

NONPARALLEL
I like *fishing and to ski.*

REVISED
I like *fishing and skiing.*

NONPARALLEL
We selected plants that were *tall and that were full of strength.*

REVISED

We selected plants that were *tall and strong.*

Avoid problems with parallelism. Incorrectly parallel expressions are confusing for readers.

CONFUSING

The short-order cook had to be *a fryer and baker* of bread. [Is he frying and baking the bread?]

REVISED

The short-order cook had to *fry hamburgers and bake bread.* [The two actions have been separated.]

CONFUSING

They showed their appreciation *by eating and washing* the dishes.

REVISED

They showed their appreciation *by eating dinner and washing the dishes.*

Avoid problems with *who, which,* and *that.* Clauses beginning with *and which, and who,* or *and that* require a preceding *who, which,* or *that* clause to achieve proper parallelism.

CONFUSING

We ordered a powerful new sports car with an overhead cam, *and which* would go 200 miles an hour.

REVISED

We ordered a powerful new sports car, *which* had an overhead cam *and which* would go 200 miles an hour. [Or] We ordered a powerful new sports car with an overhead cam and a 200-mile-an-hour top speed.

ACTIVITY 11

Revise the following sentences for effective parallelism.

1. The men paid for their night in the barn by hoeing and helping grandma in the garden.
2. The mail order house has sent us a set of wrenches we can't use, and which we didn't order.
3. They were sent to prison for stealing and shooting a policeman.
3. We hired ourselves out that summer as trash haulers, lawn mowers, and guys to paint houses.
5. In less than two weeks we had covered neural, epidermal, and intestine disorders.

20e Use contrast for emphasis.

WITHOUT CONTRAST

The black-eyed ermine stole seemed to suggest that Etka had arrived directly from Minsk so that the fact that she had actually made many moves was concealed.

REVISED

Etka from Minsk had arrived *not* directly from Minsk, as the black-eyed ermine stole seemed to suggest, *but* after many moves.

Laura Cunningham, "The Girls' Room"

20f Vary sentence beginnings.

Begin with absolute constructions. Absolutes look like sentences with deleted verbs. (See **5h.**)

His hands in his pockets, the boy stood shyly waiting for her. [His hands *were* in his pockets; the boy stood shyly waiting for her.]

The first plan failing, she tried an alternative. [The first plan *failed;* she tried an alternative.]

His rod lying out on the logs, Nick tied a new hook on the leader, pulling the gut tight until it grimped into itself in a hard knot. *var*

Ernest Hemingway, "Big Two-Hearted River: Part II"

Begin with adjectives or adverbs.

Red and glowing mysteriously, the evening sun sank into the ocean.

Small, dirty, and *pathetic*—the puppy was irresistible.

Swiftly, silently the hawk dived on the pigeon.

Begin with appositives. The appositive is a synonym, an identifying name or label for a noun or pronoun. It can come before or after its referent: *A bluish green haze,* oxidation, gradually transforms copper exposed to air. Oxidation, *a bluish green haze,* gradually transforms copper exposed to air. (See **21e.**)

Begin with infinitives.

To be or not *to be,* that is the question.

To save his house was his only thought.

Begin with modifying clauses. A clause (unlike a phrase) must have both a subject and a verb. Start adverb clauses with a subordinate conjunction. (See **5i.**)

After the guns had stopped, we found soldiers everywhere.

Before the fire reached the barrels, we had connected the second hose.

Begin with noun clauses. The noun clause (with its own subject and a verb) is used like a noun. (See **5i.**)

Why they would do such a thing was the mystery.

Who we were was her biggest worry.

That such a crime could be committed here baffled our local police.

var **Begin with prepositional phrases.** The prepositional phrase contains a preposition and its object, with optional modifiers for the object. (See **4g.**)

> *At dawn*, we turned the dogs loose in the yard.
>
> *Near the bank of the river*, a great old willow had stood for fifty years.

Begin with participles. The present and past participles are the *-ing* and *-ed* forms of regular verbs. (See **5h.**)

> *Tilting* heavily towards the shore, our raft began moving off into the current.
>
> *Twice elected* to the Presidency, the second time in a record landslide, Mr. Nixon seemed immune from serious challenge.
>
> Staff of the *New York Times, The End of a Presidency*

Begin with similes. A simile is a comparison using the words *like* or *as*.

> *Like a badly rusted hinge*, the huge rocket groaned ominously and slowly leaned off perpendicular.

ACTIVITY 12

Revise the following paragraph for emphasis and variety. Combine sentences, add and delete words, shift words around, change the forms of words, and change punctuation. You may revise any way you like as long as you do not produce any garbled, illogical, or ineffective sentences. Revise so that the paragraph contains several sentences; avoid overusing *and* to string words together.

Plastic

Plastic is not a natural substance. It is made by humans. It is a remarkable substance. Its products will have strength. It can be formed into any shape. It is used in toys. It is used in household goods. It is used in industrial products. It can be found, too, in

```
clothing and all kinds of packaging. It is used in just
about everything. Ballpoint pens are made of plastic.
Plastic is in false teeth. It is used for photographic
film. Billiard balls and plumbing pipe have plastic in
them. Plastic is in paint and thread and even in things
that make you healthy and for grooming. Plastic is
lighter, if not the lightest, of many natural
materials. It is stronger. It does not rust like metal
or wood. And it seldom deteriorates as rubber does. And
its conductivity of electricity is as low, if not
lower, than anything. Plastic does not absorb water.
Plastic can be molded. It can be cut. It can be fused
together. It can be made stiff and hard. It can be made
soft and pliable. Some plastic will not burn. It can be
produced in long sheets and which are as thin as paper.
It can be produced in liquid form. It is used for
lacquer. It can be produced in any color. It can also
be transparent like glass. It resists wear. It is
relatively inexpensive. Without plastic the modern
world could not exist.
```

20g Vary sentence types.

Avoid writing the same type of sentence over and over again. Use simple, compound, complex, or compound-complex structures for variety.

SIMPLE SENTENCE

The simple sentence is "simple" only in a grammatical sense: it has only one subject-predicate relationship. But there are several options for variety with simple sentences.

var **Use compound subjects.** Two sentences expressing similar ideas can often be revised into one sentence with a compound subject:

TWO SENTENCES

The motorcycle is a noisy road vehicle. Old cars with faulty mufflers are also noisy road vehicles.

REVISED

Motorcycles and old cars with faulty mufflers are noisy road vehicles.

Use compound predicates. Two sentences about the same subject can often be revised into one sentence with a compound predicate:

TWO SENTENCES

The boys designed their own clubhouse. Then they built it.

REVISED

The boys *designed and built their own clubhouse.*

Use compound complements. Sentences with the same verb can often be revised as one sentence with a compound complement:

TWO SENTENCES

The youths painted the old house. Then they painted its garage.

REVISED

The youths painted *the old house and its garage.*

Use other compounds. Other possibilities for compound elements within the simple sentence include compound adjectives, compound adverbs, compound prepositional phrases, and so on.

SIMPLE SENTENCE WITH COMPOUND APPOSITIVE, DIRECT OBJECT

The old horse and its companions, a dog and a cat, hauled paper, junk, and sometimes furniture.

COMPOUND SENTENCE

The compound sentence looks like two sentences joined with one of the coordinate conjunctions: *and, but, or, nor, so, for, yet.* It is composed of two independent clauses—each with its own subject-predicate relationship, and each of which could be written as a separate sentence.

TWO INDEPENDENT CLAUSES

The planes landed. [and] The passengers got off.

REVISED

The planes landed, *and* the passengers got off.

Note the difference between a compound sentence and a simple sentence with compound predicate:

COMPOUND SENTENCE

SUBJECT + PREDICATE + SUBJECT + PREDICATE

The planes landed, and they taxied down the runway.

SIMPLE SENTENCE WITH A COMPOUND PREDICATE

SUBJECT + PREDICATE

VERB + VERB

The planes landed and taxied down the runway.

ACTIVITY 13

Identify the following sentences as either *compound* or *simple.*

1. Rolf decided he probably would not get a date that night, for he had just won the stegosaurus look-alike contest.
2. We had planned to stay all night, but the furnace quit at 7:00.
3. The boys were playing basketball, and the girls were playing football.
4. Mimi drove into the parking lot at top speed and stopped just short of the mailbox.
5. Two captains and their general hopped in a jeep and headed for town, but only after evening prayers.

---

var

COMPLEX SENTENCE

The complex sentence has only one independent clause but at least one dependent clause.

INDEPENDENT

They bought plain white dishes

DEPENDENT

because they planned to serve very simple dinners.

Dependent clauses start with subordinate conjunctions—*after, because, since* and so on—or one of the relative pronouns—*who, which, that.* (See **4b, 4f.**)

SUBORDINATE CLAUSE FIRST

After the cease-fire had been declared, they worked to sabotage plans for the peace talks. [Note comma.]

SUBORDINATE CLAUSE LAST

They worked to sabotage plans for the peace talks *after the cease-fire had been declared.*

COMPOUND-COMPLEX SENTENCE

The compound-complex sentence contains two or more independent clauses and at least one dependent clause.

INDEPENDENT

The puppy chased its tail awhile,

DEPENDENT

and *when it tired of that,*

INDEPENDENT

it tried to wriggle into an old slipper.

ACTIVITY 14

Using a variety of sentence structures, revise the following paragraph. Combine sentences, add and delete words, shift words around, change the forms of words, and change punctuation. You may revise any way you like as long as you do not produce any garbled, illogical, or ineffective sentences. Revise so that the paragraph contains several sentences; avoid overusing *and* to string words together. *var*

The Eye

The eye is nature's triumph. It is one of the great works of nature. It works like a camera. The outer cover of the eye is the cornea. It is transparent. Between the cornea and the iris is a liquid. It is called aqueous humor. The iris surrounds the pupil. The pupil is the opening of the eye. The rest of the eye is filled with another liquid. It is called vitreous humor. There is a lens right behind the pupil. This lens is focused by muscle action. This action allows us to focus on near and far objects. This lens gets less flexible as we grow older. It also becomes less transparent. Light enters the eye. The amount of light is controlled by the colored part of the eye. It is called the iris. The light falls on the back of the eye. This is called the retina. The lens of the eye reflects light from above on the lower part of the retina. It reflects light from below upon the upper part of the retina. Then objects on the retina are upside down. The retina is stimulated by the light. This is transmitted to the optic nerve. It has nearly a million fibres in it. The nerve transmits the message to the brain. The brain interprets the message from the eye. Then we see things properly. They appear right side up in the brain.

var

20h Vary sentence patterns.

Avoid monotonous sentence patterns. Use loose (cumulative), periodic, and balanced patterns for variety.

Use loose sentences. The typical English sentence is called the loose or cumulative sentence. It begins with a subject and verb, adding modifiers and qualifiers at the end. The sentence develops in "normal" or "natural" order.

> The grasshopper took hold of the hook with his front feet, *spitting tobacco juice on it.*
>
> Ernest Hemingway, "Big Two-Hearted River: Part II"

> Our old rowboat rested on the beach, *bobbing gently with the incoming tide, its new paint shining faintly in the moonlight.*

ACTIVITY 15

Combine the following short sentences.

EXAMPLE

The house became ominous at night. It creaked. It popped. It moaned softly.

REVISED

The house became ominous at night, creaking, popping, moaning softly.

1. Mother's apple pie sat on the window ledge. It dared us to lift it.
2. They laughed. They joked. They jostled each other. The boys made their way toward the store.
3. The car was full of possibilities. It was a 1970 Pontiac. It was rusted. It was dented. It was sagging on its springs.
4. She was tall. She was stern. She was intimidating. Miss Marsh waited for the class to settle.
5. Miss Heilman fired the .45. The bullet struck her father's antique clock. It nicked the autographed picture of Woodrow Wilson. It lodged in the armrest of the sofa.

Create variety with periodic sentences. The periodic sentence is an inverted structure; its main clause or its predicate is withheld until the end. *var*

STRING OF LOOSE SENTENCES

I had left home late in the afternoon to go for a walk along the banks of the river. I had no real plans for getting home in time for dinner. I began to think of food more and more as the day wore on.

REVISED TO A PERIODIC SENTENCE

Having left home late in the afternoon to go for a walk along the banks of the river and having no real plans for getting home in time for dinner, I began to think of food more and more as the day wore on.

Periodic sentences can be constructed in a number of ways:

MAIN CLAUSE AT END

After a decade of heavy losses, labor troubles, and mediocre management that almost drove it into the ground, *Italian auto giant Fiat is once again on the fast track in the European auto market.*

"Fiat Slims Down to Get Back into the Black,"
Business Week, 4 July 1983

PREDICATE WITHHELD UNTIL THE END

The minister, worried about the souls of his parish and fearful that many of them might already have been lost to the forces of temptation, *gave a sermon on the return to faith.*

Create variety with balanced sentences. The balanced sentence has a formal elegance; for this reason it is often used in public oratory. The balanced sentence is crafted by balancing similar ideas in similar language.

var

WEAK

And so my fellow Americans when you want to know what your country can do for you, just ask yourself that question the other way around.

REVISED AS BALANCED SENTENCE

And so my fellow Americans, ask not what your country can do for you; ask what you can do for your country.

John F. Kennedy, Inaugural Address

WEAK

The only way to win is through perseverance; however, if you quit, obviously the victory will not be yours.

REVISED AS BALANCED SENTENCE

Winners never quit; quitters never win.

ACTIVITY 16

Revise the following weak sentences as balanced sentences.

EXAMPLE

Life is not long enough for all the things we do, but then there isn't much reward in taking the time to do most of the things anyway.

REVISED AS BALANCED SENTENCE

Life is not long enough for all the things we do, and the things we do are not reward enough for all the time they take.

1. Learning is the price of wisdom, but then if there is any profit in learning, wisdom is it.
2. The truth never diminishes the strong, and strong people don't try to cut down things that are true.
3. Curiosity begets understanding, and the more you learn the more curious you will be.
4. It doesn't do much good to say how many problems you have that might overcome you; it's better to say if you can overcome your problems.
5. America must defend her children, but then they have a duty to do the same for their country.

Create emphasis by inversion. Changing the usual order (subject-verb-object) of sentences can provide emphasis. *var*

> Gone was the sweeping mandate Mr. Nixon had won from the American electorate in November, 1972. . . .
>
> Staff of the *New York Times, The End of a Presidency*

ACTIVITY 17

Revise the following paragraph for variety and emphasis. Combine sentences, add and delete words, shift words around, change the forms of words, and change punctuation. You may revise any way you like as long as you do not produce any garbled, illogical, or ineffective sentences. Revise so that the paragraph contains several sentences; avoid overusing *and* to string words together.

The Death of Socrates

Socrates was a great man. He was a philosopher. He lived in Greece. He was born about 469 BC. He was the wisest man of his time, probably. He was physically unattractive. Some people called him ugly. He was fat. He was bald. He liked to read. He was also a teacher. He taught by questioning. He would ask people what they believed. Then he would ask why they believed it. Then he would ask how it was possible to believe such a thing. Then he would ask if they could believe things that were contradictions. This way he made people understand. His questions caused them to examine their beliefs. It also caused them to analyze their logic. Many people were unhappy with his methods. They did not like to be forced to analyze themselves. They did not like to be forced to change their minds. The people of Athens decided to get rid of Socrates. They said he was not a religious man. They said he corrupted his

var

```
students. They said he should be put to death for this.
He went to trial. There were 501 jurors. Socrates was
his own lawyer. He said none of his students were
corrupted. No student testified against him. The jury
convicted him anyway. He mocked the jury. He said his
punishment should be a lifetime pension. It should be a
gift from the state for his good work. He was sentenced
to die. He was forced to drink poison. It was hemlock.
```

20i Vary sentence lengths.

If all your sentences are the same length, you may produce a monotonous rhythm that suggests all the sentences are of the same importance, as in a list. Furthermore, it is true that professional writers tend—on the average—to write longer sentences than students do. For example:

> When he was done shaking hands with me, the Judge smoothed back his thick black mane, cut off square at the collar, like a senator's, put one hand in his pocket, played with the half-dozen emblems and charms on his watch chain with the other, teetered from his heels to his toes two or three times, lifted his head, smiled at me like I was the biggest pleasure he'd had in years, and drew a great, deep breath, like he was about to start an oration. I'd seen him go through all that when all he finally said was, "How-do-you-do?" to some lady he wasn't sure he hadn't met before. The judge had a lot of public manner.
>
> Walter Van Tilburg Clark, *The Ox-Bow Incident*

Clark's first sentence is eighty-five words long. The unusual length was achieved almost entirely through the use of compound predicates and similes. Here the author is trying to create an image, building suspense with his long sentence. His second sentence is twenty-six words long, and the third is eight. The final, very short sentence is emphatic by contrast.

The interplay among long, medium, and short sentences sets up a rhythm that helps to make the writer's point. *var*

Avoid rambling sentences. A sentence "rambles" when the writer strings ideas together in an unplanned stream, usually with too many coordinators or subordinators. Sometimes these rambling sentences can be revised by deleting irrelevant details, sometimes by breaking the sentence into smaller sentences. But frequently it is necessary to rethink and start anew with a more controlled *idea*. Unless you are deliberately trying to create an image, as Clark did in *The Ox-Bow Incident*, revise excessively long sentences.

RAMBLING (TOO MANY COORDINATORS AND SUBORDINATORS)

We went to the pond to do some fishing *because* we knew there were lots of good brim there *and* we didn't have much else to do *so* we decided just to take some time off *and* try to relax *and* have some fun for a few hours *until* we had to go home *and* get ready for work that night at the new factory *where* they were building the experimental car the government had promised last year in its budget proposal for restoration of small towns like ours *that* were in need of assistance to get out of the recession *and* put people back to work *so* they could have something to do besides go fishing all the time.

REVISED FOR EFFECTIVE LENGTH

As part of the government's small-town-restoration proposal last year, the experimental car was being built at the new factory where we worked. There was a small pond near the factory, and since we had a few hours before work with not much to do, we went fishing for brim.

Do not pad your sentences. It is possible (but not advisable) to lengthen sentences artificially simply by padding them. *Padding* means sticking in detail after detail, modifiers, phrases, and so on, in a mechanical fashion—whether they fit the context or not. Revise your sentences to create the effect you want to have on your reader. For example:

PADDED

Our dear little gray goose, whose feathers shine so sleekly when they are wet, runs waddling fatly and honking brazenly *var* around and about the yard until its poor frail webbed feet become shredded quite beyond repair on the sharp old fieldstones lying carelessly strewn here and there in the outback without regard for the simple bird's comfort.

REVISIONS

We have a gray goose running free in our yard. [The emphasis is on the act.]

With feathers that shine sleekly when wet, our little gray goose waddles fatly about the yard, honking brazenly. [The emphasis is on appearance.]

We had strewn fieldstones here and there in the yard without regard to the little goose's webbed feet, which were soon shredded by the sharp stones. [The emphasis is on cause.]

Waddling about on the sharp fieldstones in the yard, our little gray goose has shredded her frail webbed feet beyond repair. [The emphasis is on consequence.]

ACTIVITY 18

Revise these sentences. Edit out any padding (but try not to lose the central meaning).

1. There is an idea and it is about animals, namely that they have their own languages, and this idea is an old notion.
2. It is probably true that the reason that we have not really conquered nature is because of the fact that we have not conquered ourselves.
3. Our fine old adorable-looking cocker spaniel whose name is Hero and who had big round brown eyes and long silky blond fur and great floppy ears was accustomed to giving furious pursuit to the sneaky gray and black striped cat which belonged to our neighbor.
4. Our monument to Joe Louis, who was one of the world's great heavyweight boxing champions, is an art work which is in Detroit that is simply a great bronzed arm with no body attached to it but ending in a fist, which could stand for boxing.
5. His father got up into the seat where the older brother already was sitting at and then he struck out at the two very thin-looking mules with two blows which were savage with the peeled willow stick but he didn't really put any heat into it.

Avoid too many short choppy sentences. Too many long sentences may put the reader to sleep. Too many short ones may irritate the reader. For example: *var*

CHOPPY

Our cat is a Persian. Its hair is long. It is pure white. It has unusual blue eyes.

REVISED

Our cat, a long-haired Persian, is pure white and has unusual blue eyes.

The revised sentence not only has more mature rhythm, it actually contains fewer words than the four original sentences. Thus, while it is longer, it is more concise.

ACTIVITY 19

Revise the following passage for effective sentence structure. Combine sentences, add information, delete redundant words, change the wording of the passage but try not to change the main ideas. Use this exercise to show how well you understand sentence structure.

Making False Teeth

The dentist first takes an impression. It is of the patient's bite line. The dentist does this with a pair of things that are shaped like the letter U made of rubber. They are impression trays. Once this activity of the dentist has been brought to a completion the models can be made and it is the usual thing for the dentist to pour the models. Or an assistant can. But usually the dentist does it. Sometimes they are sent to the technician since this is when the technician can construct them. A model is a replica of something. It is the patient's upper palate. Or it could be the lower palate. The model is made of plaster. First, there is

var

excess rubber which is extra and must be trimmed away from the tray and this makes it easier to work with it. Mixing this stuff to a medium consistency, is a bowl of plaster. Plaster which is watery is difficult to work with because plaster which is stiff sets up too fast. The plaster must be thoroughly blended. Then the bowl of plaster must be tapped. Firmly. It is done on a hard surface. This is to force the air bubbles out or it will be ruined by air bubbles. The impression tray is filled with plaster by one using a small knife. Or you could do it with a spatula. Next a patty is made. This is done with the remaining plaster. The patty should be about the size of a hamburger. Next the tray is set upside down on the patty. It is wiggled into the patty. Gently. It is done just so all the plaster in the tray is making contact with the patty. The tray should not be buried in the plaster. This would be a disaster. This has to dry completely. Then the tray can be pried off to carefully expose the model. Then the model is finished. Then the technician's work begins.

Punctuation

^,

21 COMMA

In written English, the comma separates one grammatical structure from another.

21a Use commas to separate sentences joined by the coordinate conjunctions: *and, or, nor, for, but, yet, so.*

Thousands of teenagers packed the concert, but they made hardly a sound as she finished the song.

The questions became more and more embarrassing, so he abruptly terminated the press conference.

If the sentences are very short, and there is no possibility of confusion, the comma is sometimes eliminated.

It rained and it rained.

Using only a comma to join two sentences is an error—called a *comma splice,*—unless the sentences are very short and similarly constructed.

COMMA SPLICE

The opponents of the new tax legislation were aggressive and bad mannered, they screamed obscenities and jammed their placards into the faces of the congressmen.

ACCEPTABLE

I came, I saw, I conquered. [The sentences are short and similarly constructed.]

A comma splice can be corrected by replacing the comma with a semicolon, a colon, or a period or by adding a coordinating conjunction immediately after the comma. (See **8.**)

ACTIVITY 1

Edit the following sentences: insert the proper punctuation and appropriate words; delete unnecessary punctuation.

1. Expanding rapidly, the star glowed brighter and brighter, it dominated its portion of the sky.
2. Bacon and ham sizzled on the grill, the rich smell of coffee floated into the room.
3. Granger slowly lifted his head but he still could not see the buck.
4. Although Picasso had studied classical art, he grew tired of its predictable subject matter and slick style and he began to experiment with modern art.
5. His ego was shattered and his mind was a blur.

21b Use a comma after most introductory elements.

First, we must organize a committee of volunteers.

Besides John, there were three who refused to participate.

Near a great blue spruce, they set up a salt lick for the deer.

The comma may be omitted if the introductory material is very short. The effect of leaving the comma out is to deemphasize the beginning. Be careful to use the comma if its omission makes the sentence ambiguous.

AMBIGUOUS

In time capsules accounted for 50 percent of sales.

CLEAR

In time, capsules accounted for 50 percent of sales.

If the sentence begins with a long introductory phrase or series of phrases, use the comma.

In the old barn across from the Smithers' rebuilt farmhouse, Jeremy sat and contemplated his future.

If the introductory material contains a verb or verb form, use the comma.

> Until the welders had secured the beams, no one was allowed near the scaffolding.
>
> Stumbling down the long hallway, Ruth kept muttering about staying up all night to study for a test that was canceled.

ACTIVITY 2

Edit the following sentences: insert commas where appropriate.

1. They understand that you enjoy donating and apologizing for your small gift is not necessary.
2. Having carved the roast expertly Cynthia began to serve her guests.
3. Slipping quietly into the back of the room the student slid noiselessly into his seat.
4. In addition to Mary Jane was also added to the list.
5. To run an effective business inventories must be closely monitored.

21c Use commas to separate items in a series.

> Jojo lost his glasses, his wallet, and his sunny disposition when the sailboat capsized.

Some writers treat the comma before the *and* as optional when there is no possibility of misreading the series. However, retaining the comma is never wrong, and sometimes it is necessary for clarity. Students should mark each item in a series with a comma. For example:

> Dan's favorite breakfast was coffee, orange juice, corn flakes and beer.

To make clear that Dan did not put beer in his corn flakes, use a comma before *and*.

When the series is the subject of the sentence, do not insert a comma after the last item—do not separate the subject from its verb.

> Dates, places, and the names of presidents were all he could think of.

21d Use commas between movable adjectives.

If adjectives describe the same word and can be rearranged without loss of meaning, separate them with commas. A good test is to ask whether the word *and* could be inserted between them; if so, use commas.

> It was a long, arduous, depressing exam. (It was a long [and] arduous [and] depressing exam.)

Often the adjective closest to the noun forms the meaning of the noun, such as *short story, business major, Victorian mansion.* In such cases, preceding adjectives describe the whole idea, and the final comma must be eliminated.

> She was an inquisitive but dedicated business major.
>
> Jean reluctantly rapped on the door of the old, dilapidated Victorian mansion.

21e Use commas to set off "nonessential" elements in a sentence.

Nonessential here means an element which can be eliminated without altering the meaning of the base sentence. These elements are usually called *nonrestrictive;* they can be words, phrases, or clauses. They can be contrasted with *restrictive* elements, which are necessary to preserve the meaning of the base sentence. Nonrestrictive modifiers should be set off from the essential parts of the sentence with commas.

^, **Set off nonrestrictive appositives.** An appositive "renames" a preceding noun or pronoun. A nonrestrictive appositive provides added information but does not limit or restrict its noun or pronoun. Most appositives that follow full proper names should be set off; the appositives are nonrestrictive because usually a proper name is the most specific limiting information there is.

Herman Melville, author of *Moby Dick*, spent many years at sea.

A standing ovation was given to Jimmy Carter, former President of the United States.

The next two examples show the difference between a nonrestrictive appositive and a restrictive one that identifies its noun or pronoun.

Mike's brother Bob lives in California.

Mike's brother, Bob, lives in California.

Without the commas, the writer is saying that Mike has more than one brother, and the one named Bob lives in California. With commas, the next sentence says there is only one brother.

Set off nonrestrictive modifying phrases and clauses. The meaning of the sentences changes if the commas are left out. These examples assume the reader knows which group and which young man are being discussed.

The rock group, playing its final number, had been arrested in London last summer.

The young man, who had just turned eighteen, entered the university instead of working for his father.

Set off contrastive elements.

The issue is one of people, not of politics.

A number of shareholders voted for the merger, while others wanted to maintain the status quo.

Set off explanatory and parenthetic material.

The decision, it seems to me, was arbitrary and rash.

The plan, or at least the latest version of it, was not well received by the group.

Set off transitional words and phrases.

The harp seal, however, has been threatened for years.

On the other hand, Sally is admirably suited to her job.

ACTIVITY 3

Edit the following sentences: insert or delete commas where appropriate.

1. Maple oak walnut and cherry were all possibilities.
2. The women who joined the action crusade represented a cross-section of society.
3. Mrs. Stanhope-White denied the cat was hers, she didn't like pets of any kind.
4. Ardently devoted to his wife Mary Lou telephoned every night when he was on the road.
5. The experiment by the way will be run three times not twice.
6. By the time we were allowed to see the animal cages hadn't been cleaned for weeks.
7. The breakfast orders called for an omelet waffles and ham and eggs.
8. John Renquist a minister in a local church wrote the article about boxing.
9. The lawn or what passed for one hadn't been mowed all summer.
10. Because Halloween October 31 marked the end of the Celtic summer and the beginning of the "barren" season it came to be thought of as a dark sinister festival.

21f Use commas to separate dialogue from the rest of the sentence.

He asked, "How can you distinguish between the dancer and the dance?"

"It's not who wins," he commented bitterly, "but how much you get paid."

When quoted matter ends with an exclamation point or question mark, the comma is redundant.

REDUNDANT

"Is everyone ready to go?", she asked.

CORRECT

"Is everyone ready to go?" she asked.

21g Use commas to set off names and titles in direct address.

Direct address means speaking to a person (directly addressing) and calling him or her by name, descriptive phrase, or title. It occurs in dialogue, in letter writing, and sometimes in essays when the writer addresses the reader.

You see, Jill, losing your job doesn't mean the end of the world.

Doctor, how bad is it?

"Say, man, what're you doing here?"

So once again, citizens of America, the future lies in our own hands.

21h Use commas correctly in dates and addresses.

He was born on November 16, 1939, at Letterman General Hospital.

San Francisco, California, is still his permanent residence. [Notice especially the commas after *1939* and *California*.]

When the day precedes the month, military style, no commas are required:

He was born 16 November 1939.

No comma is used for a month-day combination:

He was born on November 16 in San Francisco.

Some writers omit commas for month-year combinations:

January 1985 is the date we expect the bill to come before the committee.

21i Use a comma after the salutation of informal letters and after the closing of any letter.

Dear Marcia, Dear Dad, Hi, Babe,
Sincerely yours, Love, With best wishes,

21j Use a comma with a short interrogative at the end of a declarative sentence.

You're not going to go out with me, are you?
The Magna Carta was signed in 1215, right?

21k Use commas correctly with *too*.

When *too* is used to mean "also" and falls at the beginning or end of a sentence, most writers set it off with a comma.

Willie wondered if his mother was going, too.
Too, an abstract must be submitted with the paper.

If *too* falls in the middle of the sentence, the use of commas depends on the emphasis you want to provide.

His mother, too, was going.
His mother too was going.

21l Use commas correctly with mild interjections and words like *yes* and *no*.

Yes, the cells have duplicated themselves.

Well, I'm not sure if that's true.

21m Use commas for clarity.

Sometimes, even if there is no specific "rule" for using a comma, one might be needed to prevent ambiguity or misreading.

Those who can teach the rest of us.

Those who can, teach the rest of us.

Eight months before I had taken the class.

Eight months before, I had taken the class.

ACTIVITY 4

Edit the following sentences: insert or delete commas where necessary.

1. We bought the old railroad tracks and all.
2. Henry you're going to have to start coming to class more often.
3. The package was addressed to Mr. Daryl Groutt 5002 Chipwall Drive Weidman Michigan.
4. "That combination" Rachel said knowingly "will never work."
5. "Was Halley the name of the comet or the name of the astronomer?", the test question asked.
6. The children were covered by the policy too.
7. In November 1988 Father wrote "Until we got the new monkey business was slow."
8. Stalley replied "I'm not sure sir. I thought I was only going fifty-five."
9. Attendance too was one of the requirements.
10. Yes quantities of oil have been limited by the embargo.

22 OVERUSE OF COMMAS

22a Do not separate a subject from its verb, nor a verb from its complement or direct object.

MISUSED

The well-educated but naive attorney, could not understand why anyone would commit such a crime.

REVISED

The well-educated but naive attorney could not understand why anyone would commit such a crime.

MISUSED

The astronaut gave, fully detailed instructions to the ground crew.

REVISED

The astronaut gave fully detailed instructions to the ground crew.

22b Do not use a comma before the first or after the last item in a series.

MISUSED

Aunt Anne gave him, good advice, $300, and a sloppy kiss.

REVISED

Aunt Anne gave him good advice, $300, and a sloppy kiss.

MISUSED

They liked athletic, ambitious, intelligent, students.

REVISED

They liked athletic, ambitious, intelligent students.

no ,

22c Do not use a comma to signal a series or list after *such as* or *like.*

MISUSED

They were known to give tests such as, multiple choice, true/false, and essay.

REVISED

They were known to give tests such as multiple choice, true/false, and essay.

MISUSED

From a distance the birds looked like, children, flowers, and ornaments.

REVISED

From a distance the birds looked like children, flowers, and ornaments.

22d Do not separate compound elements.

Many sentence elements can be joined (compounded) with conjunctions like *and* or *or.* No comma should be used with such compounds.

MISUSED

We read essays by Lamb, and Montaigne.

REVISED

We read essays by Lamb and Montaigne.

MISUSED

The student typed her paper carefully, and handed it in two weeks late.

REVISED

The student typed her paper carefully and handed it in two weeks late.

23 SEMICOLON

23a Use a semicolon to connect two closely related sentences.

Quantities of the material were missing; only about one third remained in the warehouse.

You must pay attention to detail; you must count the variations.

23b Use a semicolon to separate two sentences joined with conjunctive adverbs like these:

also	incidentally	next
anyway	indeed	otherwise
besides	in fact	still
consequently	instead	then
finally	likewise	therefore
furthermore	meanwhile	thus
hence	moreover	
however	nevertheless	

The spacecraft was sighted by several different stations; moreover, it was headed straight for earth.

Johnson refused the transfer; indeed, he quit the company.

The comma after the conjunctive adverb may be omitted for less emphasis.

We found no difference in the rats; hence we abandoned the experiment.

;

23c Use a semicolon to separate two main clauses joined with transitional phrases, such as *as a result, on the other hand, for example, in fact, on the contrary.*

The experiment failed; as a result, the research grant was canceled.

Mary Jane has always been fortunate; for example, she won $10,000 in the lottery last year.

23d Use a semicolon to separate items in a series if the items are long or have internal punctuation.

The following were some of the guests: John Markham, president of United Endeavors; Fred Slasher, vice-president of Consolidated Shipping; Paula Zunkel, chairperson of the board, Products Unlimited.

23e Use a semicolon to separate multiple references in footnotes and endnotes.

[1] Chap. II, pp. 6-13; chap. IV, pp. 78–81; chap. IX, pp. 231–35.

2. See Flint 1980; Whetlock 1982; Pangborne 1985.

ACTIVITY 5

Edit the following sentences: insert semicolons where appropriate; delete or change errors in punctuation.

1. The typewriter finally stopped working the keys were bent beyond hope.
2. W. C. Handy was a black composer who popularized the blues, for example, he wrote "Memphis Blues" and "St. Louis Blues."

3. He subscribed to three newspapers: the *Times*, which was conservative, the *Post*, which was extremely liberal in its views, and the *Standard*, which never took a firm stand either way.
4. Claudia got to her feet trembling inside, nevertheless, she spoke confidently and knowledgeably.
5. The reaction took place just as expected, in fact the result surpassed everyone's hopes.

24 COLON

24a Use a colon to introduce a series.

The following students must report to the office: Baines, Rhydall, Stelling, and Johnson.

The project demanded specific attributes: intelligence, endurance, adaptability, and courage.

In the first example the series is clearly signaled by the words *the following*. Other such signals are words like *as follows* and *namely these*. In the second example, the signal for a series is implied; the colon itself means *such as the following*.

Do not use a colon after forms of the verb *to be* or after prepositions.

MISUSED

My classes this semester are: math, history, Spanish, accounting, and English.

REVISED

My classes this semester are math, history, Spanish, accounting, and English.

MISUSED

I am enrolled in: math, history, Spanish, accounting, and English.

REVISED

I am enrolled in math, history, Spanish, accounting, and English.

Do not use a colon to separate a verb from its object.

MISUSED

We initiated: Estelle, Irving, Denise, and Frank.

REVISED

We initiated Estelle, Irving, Denise, and Frank.

24b Use a colon to emphasize an appositive at the end of a sentence.

We said that in America we are proud of our ex-President's former career: acting.

24c A colon may be used between sentences when the second explains, illustrates, summarizes, or complements the first.

The photograph is unique: it is the only proof of the animal's existence.

There are serious side effects of the drug: we may be curing the disease at the cost of the patient's sanity.

24d Use a colon to introduce long or formal quotations without speaker tags.

He reminded me of Patrick Henry's words: "Give me liberty, or give me death." [No speaker tag present.]

:

He reminded me that Patrick Henry said, "Give me liberty or give me death." [Speaker tag, *Patrick Henry said*, is present.]

Note that the first word of a quotation following either a colon or a comma is capitalized. For rules on long prose quotations, see **29c.**

24e Use a colon after the salutation of a formal letter.

Dear Ms. Atkins: Dear Sir: Doctor Charles:

24f Use colons between chapter and verse of Biblical references and between hours and minutes (and seconds) in precise time references.

Luke 4:12 10:30 P.M. 1:06:32

ACTIVITY 6

Edit the following sentences: insert colons where appropriate; delete incorrect punctuation.

1. The librarian indicated several areas where I might find information on my question, zoology, biology, ethology, and morphology.
2. The small dog was absolutely ferocious, it bit seven people between January and March.
3. She said that one requirement was absolutely necessary for working with the children, enthusiasm.
4. The winners of the spelling contest for the sixth grade are: Mary Jean Arch, Nancy Arbor, and George Johnson.
5. At 12 15 P.M. the following athletes should report to the starter Higgins, Roman, Hay, McClintock.

ACTIVITY 7

Combine the following sets of sentences using colons. You may add to, delete, or change the words in the sentences, but be sure to use a colon in your answer.

1. Hannibal crossed the Alps into Italy with his surprise weapons. They were elephants.
2. Fort Sumter holds a unique position in American history. It was the site of the first shot in our Civil War.
3. There are several U.S. Presidents few people know very much about. Some of them are James Knox Polk, Zachary Taylor, Millard Fillmore, Franklin Pierce, and James Buchanan.
4. Many dangerous drugs are abused by large numbers of people. Some of them are LSD and heroin. Others include cocaine and amphetamines. Alcohol, too, is abused.
5. Robert Goodloe Harper is the author of the stirring American challenge to the French. He said, "Millions for defense, but not one cent for tribute."

25 DASH

Too frequent use of the dash can be bothersome to the reader, but proper use can bring emphasis to your writing.

In typing, a dash is indicated by two hyphens with no space before, between, or after (--).

25a Use a dash to indicate a sudden interruption in thought.

Let me explain my situation—but you don't care about that.

If the police found out—they were bound to find out—I would be a candidate for the mallard mortuary.

25b Use a dash for emphasis or clarification.

Each of the following could be punctuated with commas, but the dash adds emphasis.

There was only one thing Michael wanted in his life—love.

The mist stole eerily—remorselessly—into the blackened streets.

25c Use a dash after an introductory series.

Furniture, the stereo, the television, the kitchen appliances—the burglar took them all.

To produce a less formal tone, the dash can be used instead of a colon before a series.

The prosecutor tried everything—intimidation, friendliness, cajolery, humor.

25d Use a dash to indicate faltering or abruptly ending speech.

"Will you m—, m—, mar—, marry me?"

"You stop that right now or I'll—." Tom had already run out of the house.

25e Words between dashes may take question marks or exclamation points but not periods.

The young princess—have you met her?—is having a party.

Sexually transmitted AIDS—the disease may become a plague!—has already killed thousands of people.

--

ACTIVITY 8

Edit the following sentences: insert dashes where appropriate.

1. Valhalla was that happy place in Norse mythology where slain warriors, but that's another story.
2. Five dollars, ten, twenty, a hundred any amount would help.
3. His life was devoted to the pursuit of the one thing he thought would make him happy money.
4. "The life span of the mayfly is." The professor stopped; Emily had fallen asleep again.
5. The chihuahua who called a dog man's best friend? chewed up my term paper and slobbered all over my pillow.

ACTIVITY 9

Combine the following sets of sentences using dashes. You may add to, delete, or change the wording of the sentences if necessary. Make sure your answer uses a dash.

1. Uranium has only one really important use. It is atomic energy.
2. Let me show you how. Watch out for the acid!
3. Sydney looked sadly at his brother. Sydney was the wiser twin.
4. Cheesecake, butter cookies, quarts of ice cream were the main ingredients. These were mainly our diet.
5. Captain Peabody showed up wearing a handlebar mustache. He was the one who had insisted on strict military dress.

26 PERIOD

26a Use a period at the end of a complete statement.

> The quality of life is affected by the quality of one's natural environment.

A sentence embedded within another (set off with dashes or enclosed by parentheses) does not require a capital letter or a period:

> We experimented foolishly—government regulations meant nothing to us then—with all sorts of dangerous substances.

But embedded questions and exclamations retain their marks:

> We spent a fortune—doesn't everyone?—on our vacation.

SENTENCE FRAGMENTS

A sentence fragment is a group of words punctuated like a sentence but not expressing a complete idea. Although professional writers occasionally write fragments in fiction or informal writing, students are advised not to use them in academic writing. (See section **7** for a complete discussion of sentence fragments.)

RUN-ON SENTENCES

Run-on or fused sentences are those that have been joined with no mark of punctuation; they are not necessarily long or "rambling." They can result from a failure to recognize sentence boundaries, from faulty punctuation, or from not analyzing the relationship of one idea to another. (See section **8** for a complete discussion.)

26b Use a period after an indirect question.

She asked why she had to supply everybody in the dorm with deodorant. [Compare: *She asked, "Why do I have to supply everybody in the dorm with deodorant?"*]

26c Use periods after most commands and after requests expressed as questions.

Please sit down.

Will you please reply as soon as possible.

Emphatic commands may use exclamation marks to convey tone of voice: *Shut up! Drop that immediately!* But writers may omit exclamation marks when no extraordinary emphasis is intended: *She looked him in the eye and said, "Shut up."*

26d Use a period for each item in a sentence outline or list of full sentences.

The employees had only a few minor complaints.

1. The working hours were too long.
2. The pay was too low.
3. The working conditions were too uncomfortable.
4. The boss was too arrogant.

In a list or outline of words or phrases rather than sentences, do not use periods.

26e Use periods with most abbreviations and initials.

e.g. Inc. Co. km. pp. J.F.K. Ms. Dr.

Do not add an additional period when an abbreviation or initial comes at the end of a sentence.

After eight years of postgraduate study, John finally earned his Ph.D.

We were set to go at 8:00 P.M.

Many abbreviations of well-known organizations do not require periods. Less well-known names can be given as initials without periods after you have once spelled out the full name: CIA, NCAA, NAACP, FBI, UNESCO, NHL.

The Government Printing Office (GPO) has published everything from menu-planning guides to instruction manuals for building nuclear bombs; the President was eager to cut back on the GPO's activities.

26f Use a period to express a decimal number.

.01 .20 16.05 .007 3.14159

ACTIVITY 10

Insert periods where appropriate. If necessary, add material to create full sentences.

1. Professor Oren asked whether Ms Lloyd and Mr Cordoba knew which Canadian university was the oldest
2. The deadline was 10:30 A M
3. The quarterly report gave an optimistic account the company looked healthy at last
4. Stepping carefully on the line of rocks across the stream, which was gurgling quietly
5. The bus, which was usually overcrowded with schoolchildren that were bursting with laughter after a long day of classes

---

ACTIVITY 11

Edit the following paragraph to eliminate problems with punctuation. Add any needed punctuation; delete unnecessary marks. Combine word groups and add words if necessary.

!

Aida

Written to celebrate the opening of the Suez Canal, Verdi's Aida remains one of the most popular operas in 1871 the premiere performance was held in Cairo Egypt. Aida, an Ethiopian slave loved by Radames captain of the Egyptian army. However, Radames is loved by Amneris Princess of Egypt, she knows he loves Aida. Love jealousy, honor and death, the motifs of Aida. The Egyptians defeat the Ethiopians, and to reward Radames, the King of Egypt announces that Amneris will marry Radames how the lovers, Aida and Radames, will deal with this development is the plot of the opera. Among the captured Ethiopians, is Aida's father the king, Amonsaro. His plan to attack the Egyptians again depending on secret knowledge of the Egyptian battle plans. Torn between love of her country and Radames Aida tricks him as he tells her the secret, Amneris arrives and denounces him as a traitor to Egypt. Radames is condemned to be buried alive in his tomb he discovers Aida waiting for him the two lovers perish together.

---

27 EXCLAMATION POINT

Exclamation marks signal strong emotion. Use these marks infrequently and, for the most part, only with dialogue. Using more than one exclamation mark at a time is not appropriate in formal writing. *!!!!* is not more emphatic than *!*.

Wow! Did you see what that guy did?
What a disgusting thing to say!

Avoid the use of exclamation marks for sarcasm. *The government's experts (!) have declared that tobacco smoking may have hidden benefits.* The sentence would be better without the exclamation mark's heavy-handed irony.

28 QUESTION MARK

28a Use a question mark after a direct question.

What are you doing here?
Can anyone tell me where the stadium is?

Notice the difference between direct questions and indirect questions (no question mark):

She wondered why nobody liked her.
She wondered, "Why doesn't anyone like me?"

Any statement can be made into a question with a question mark: *Go now? You're passing English?* But this use is more common in oral English than in formal writing.

A question inserted into a statement retains its question mark.

Hawthorne wrote *The Marble Faun*—was that his last novel?—while he was living in England.

?

28b Use a question mark for each item in a series of short questions.

Are you going to accept the manuscript? reject it? sit on it?
Is the body affected after one drink? two? five?

28c Use a question mark within parentheses to indicate uncertain information.

Quintilian was born in AD 35 (?) in Spain.

Avoid the sarcastic use of question marks to challenge an author's words or ideas: *Carstair's data (?) indicate that infantile paralysis is almost unknown in India.*

28d Use a question mark with an embedded question.

An embedded question is one set off by dashes or enclosed by parentheses within another sentence.

The novel *The Right Stuff*—have you read it?—is a good example of the new journalism.

29 QUOTATION MARKS

Quotation marks signal spoken words or words copied from a written source. Use quotation marks carefully to make clear to the reader which words belong to whom.

Don't use quotation marks with indirect quotes, rhetorical questions, or thoughts and conversations one has with oneself.

What I want to know is how can we survive this way? [Rhetorical question.]

Why me, I thought, as the ball bounced off my glove and rolled to the wall. [Internal thought.]

I asked myself, as Joan prepared dinner, how could anyone be happier? [Internal conversation]

Refusing to accept the transfer, Phil said he would rather quit. [Indirect quote. Compare: *Refusing to accept the transfer, Phil said, "I would rather quit."*]

29a Use quotation marks correctly with direct quotations.

Direct quotations are the spoken or written words of others that you "quote" in your writing.

Direct quote begins sentence.	"We have enough nukes," Marny shouted.
Direct quote ends sentence.	He said, "A white dwarf is the corpse of a star."
Direct quote interrupted.	"Not me," Mary screamed, "not in a hundred years."
Quotation marks withheld until speaker finishes.	"The question," Congressman Fields asserted, "is not only irrelevant but also impertinent. "We cannot dictate our morality to nations receiving our aid."
Direct quote ends; speaker resumes.	"Small rockets can carry enough power to sink a large ship," I argued. "Our experiences in the Persian Gulf showed how vulnerable ships can be."

If closely related, two sentences like these last could be separated with a semicolon instead of a period.

Use quotation marks for four or fewer lines of poetry, drama, or prose. Such short quotations are not displayed;

that is, they are not set off from your words by space and indentations. They *are* enclosed in quotation marks.

> In his poem "Peter Quince at the Clavier," for example, Wallace Stevens writes, "She felt, among the leaves, / The dew / Of old devotions."

The slash (/) shows line divisions; use a space before and after it.

The quotation of fewer than four lines of prose is handled in the same way, except that line divisions are not shown.

> Thoreau states, "Old shoes will serve a hero longer than they have served his valet—if a hero has a valet—bare feet are older than shoes, and he can make them do."

29b Use quotation marks to indicate dialogue.

Paragraph indentation shows changes of speakers in dialogue.

> "Seven."
> "Naw, couldn't be more than five."
> "Seven. I counted 'em twice."
> "Get your eyes checked, man."
> "Say, listen, there's seven of 'em," Hedley said, with some heat, "an' don't you tell me not."
> I was in no mood to argue, so I allowed, "O.K. Seven."
> "Right."

29c Use quotation marks around source material incorporated into your own sentences.

> Calling her "guilty as Jezebel," the judge sentenced her to twenty years.

An incorporated quote does not create the need for a comma or a colon. Also, the incorporated quote usually does not require an ellipsis unless you think it is important to tell the reader that you have incorporated less than a full sentence.

29d Use quotation marks within quotation marks correctly.

Singleton said, "Have you read Melville's 'Bartleby the Scrivener'?"

"Amanda's really being difficult," Lori complained. "She said, 'Do it yourself' when I asked her to help me clean the room."

If something you want to quote is already in quotation marks, you must indicate that you are quoting a quote.

ORIGINAL

Huttenlocher says, "Six seems to be a critical period, a time when the brain is especially receptive."

AS IT MIGHT APPEAR IN YOUR PAPER

```
Huttenlocher states that "six seems to be a critical
period, a time when the brain is especially receptive"
(qtd. in Campbell 143).
```

On rare occasions it may be necessary to use a third set of quotation marks. Quotations must always begin with double quotation marks; thereafter you may alternate single and double marks as often as needed.

ORIGINAL

"How dare you say, 'Horse tails,' to me," Lady Small cried.

AS IT MIGHT APPEAR IN YOUR PAPER

```
"'How dare you say, "Horse tails," to me,' Lady Small
cried."
```

29e Display long quotations correctly.

When typing prose, poetry, or drama quotations of more than four lines, do not add quotation marks. Indent all the lines of the quotation ten spaces from the left margin and double space the material. Do not indicate the beginning of a single quoted paragraph with indentation. However, if you display two or more full paragraphs, indent the first line of each paragraph an additional three spaces.

Last summer Jim was reading Robert Pirsig's Zen and the Art of Motorcycle Maintenance, and one paragraph really struck home:

> The real cycle you're working on is a cycle called yourself. The machine that appears to be "out there" and the person that appears to be "in here" are not two separate things. They grow toward Quality or fall away from Quality together. (209)

If there are quotation marks in the original, you should copy them, but do not supply any additional marks.

ORIGINAL

At the same time, the brain of a six-year-old has a slower and more irregular activity than that of an adult, and this, too, increases the child's capacity to acquire and remember knowledge. Huttenlocher says, "One of the most interesting aspects of the six-year-old brain is that a child who has had little educational experience in this crucial year has tremendous difficulty in catching up later, even with a very good effort. Six seems to be a critical period, a time when the brain is especially receptive."

AS IT MIGHT APPEAR IN YOUR PAPER

Another cause of learning disabilities as cited by Huttenlocher, can be traced to delaying education until after the child's sixth birthday:

> "One of the most interesting aspects of the six-year-old brain is that a child who has had little educational experience in this crucial year has tremendous difficulty in catching up later, even with a very good effort. Six seems to be a critical period, a time when the brain is especially receptive." (qtd. in Campbell, 142-43)

29f Use quotation marks with titles of short works.

Short stories, magazine and newspaper articles, most poems, book chapters, specific episodes of radio or television series, and short musical works require quotation marks.

"The Fog" is a Sandburg poem popular with our class.

Books of the Bible are written without quotation marks.

Michael was told to go to his room and read Leviticus.

29g Use quotation marks with words used with special meaning and with invented words.

His "forecast" had no relation to what eventually occurred.

Al called them "quiffs," and it wasn't complimentary.

“/”

29h Quotation marks may be used with words referred to as words and with letters and numerals referred to as symbols.

He called her “madam,” not knowing how right he was.
“Mississippi” has four “s” ’s and four “i” ’s.

See **36** for optional use of underlining here.

29i Use other punctuation correctly with quotation marks.

Commas and periods always go inside quotation marks.

“The Beatles,” Tom said, “were just lucky.”
Thomas responded, “The first poem I memorized was ‘The Highwayman.’ ”

Colons and semicolons always go outside quotation marks.

“The book was called *The Brave*”; it was less than a commercial success.

Question marks and exclamation marks go either inside or outside the quotation marks. If the quoted matter is a question or exclamation, the mark goes inside, regardless of the rest of the sentence; if not, the mark goes outside.

How can you say, “The Beatles were just lucky”?
Her only response was, “Horse manure!”

ACTIVITY 12

Revise the following sentences: supply quotation marks and appropriate punctuation where required.

1. He called his brief poem Jasmine; it was delicate and beautiful.
2. Miss Rowhard screeched I don't want to hear another person in this class use the word puke!
3. James Joyce's short story Araby served as the basis for Jack's paper.
4. He's about as sensitive said Amy sarcastically as an armadillo.
5. Receive was misspelled fourteen times in the essay.
6. I wonder said Steve to himself how I got myself into this mess.
7. What do you think of Emerson's essay Gifts? I asked.
8. We were suddenly reminded by the biblical aphorism that the wages of sin is death.
9. Did you enjoy Hammond's song A New Love asked Barb.
10. Aunt Sally asked why did you say Miss Evans can't spell Mississippi?

30 SLASH

30a Use a slash to mark the division between run-in lines of poetry or drama.

Run-in lines of poetry or drama are those you quote but do not display (do not set them off as an indented quote).

Hughes concludes his poem, "The Lovepat": "It went far away, they could not speak, / Only their tears moved."

/

30b Use a slash to indicate fractions.

4/5 3/7

30c Use a slash to indicate a choice between terms.

pass/fail either/or and/or

31 ELLIPSIS

31a Use an ellipsis to show that material has been omitted from quoted material.

An ellipsis signifies omission. The omission may be material deliberately excluded from a quotation, or it may be the missing words of an unfinished statement. To show an ellipsis, type three periods with equal space before and after each (. . .).

> The Secretary of the Interior stated: "It is my intention to see that . . . the wetlands be incorporated into our National Park systems."

If the omitted material is at the end of a sentence, use four periods, placing the first as you would a sentence-ending period.

ORIGINAL

> Watching him, the boy remarked the absolutely undeviating course which his father held and saw the stiff foot come squarely down in a pile of fresh droppings where a horse had stood in the drive and which his father could have avoided by a simple change of stride.

From William Faulkner, "Barn Burning"

AS IT MIGHT APPEAR IN YOUR PAPER

```
Watching him, the boy remarked the absolutely
undeviating course which his father held and saw the
stiff foot come squarely down in a pile of fresh
droppings. . . .
```

If whole lines of poetry or prose have been omitted, indicate this with four periods (but remember that four periods must appear only at the end of a sentence, never within a sentence).

ORIGINAL

Out walking in the frozen swamp one gray day,
I paused and said, "I will turn back from here.
No, I will go on farther—and we shall see."
The hard snow held me, save now and then
One foot went through.

From Robert Frost, "The Wood-Pile"

AS IT MIGHT APPEAR IN YOUR PAPER

```
Frost's "The Wood-Pile" uses many winter images:
          Out walking in the frozen swamp one gray
          day. . . .
          The hard snow held me, save now and then
          One foot went through.
```

31b Use an ellipsis to indicate a pause or an unfinished statement.

John began to count the money. "Let's see now . . . ."
The name was . . . . He was unable to remember.

Do not permit any of the ellipsis points to wrap to the next line or separate from the word they follow.

If necessary for clarity, you may use other punctuation with an ellipsis.

ORIGINAL

She said, but don't tell her I told you, "Rip out their eyes!"

WITH ELLIPSIS

She said, . . . "Rip out their eyes!"

ORIGINAL

His speaking style was full of shouts, whistles, laughter, animal noises, giggles, and obscene gestures.

WITH ELLIPSIS

His speaking style was full of shouts, whistles, . . . and obscene gestures.

32 BRACKETS

If your typewriter doesn't have brackets, leave spaces for them as you type and draw them in later with a pen.

32a Use brackets around clarifying material you insert into quotations.

They [Lewis and Clark] opened up the Northwest to the white man.

ORIGINAL

The tornado ripped through the village, destroying seventeen houses.

IN YOUR PAPER

```
The tornado ripped through [Quentenville], destroying
seventeen houses.
```

32b Use brackets with *sic* to indicate errors in quoted material.

To point out errors in fact, logic, grammar or spelling in source material, insert *sic* in brackets [sic] directly after the error. *Sic* means "thus" in Latin and tells the reader that you recognize the error. (You may correct minor typographical mistakes without using *sic.*)

> In 1982 [sic], Soviet athletes stayed away from the Summer Olympics, turning some of the American gold to brass.

Notice that *sic* is not followed by a period; it is not underlined, according to the new *MLA Style Manual.*

32c Use brackets for parenthetical material within parentheses.

> The defendants (Elsworth and Petry [Sommers was being tried separately]) were brought into court chained and handcuffed.

As you can see, this is an awkward construction; and when you find yourself needing it, you should revise the sentence, if possible.

33 PARENTHESES

Parenthetic material can usually also be set off with commas, but the parentheses give greater emphasis to such material.

(/)

33a Use parentheses to set off incidental or explanatory material and material not grammatically connected to the sentence.

Before the Civil War (1861–1865) was fought, the South relied heavily on slave labor.

The breakdown of the figures (see the chart on p. 17) shows population increasing exponentially.

33b Use parentheses to label items in a list.

In order to score well, you must (1) line up your shot, (2) assume the correct stance, and (3) execute the mechanics of the swing.

It is informal usage (not recommended) to use a half parenthesis: 1), 2), 3).

33c Use other punctuation correctly with parentheses.

The end mark (period, question mark, exclamation point) falls outside the parenthesis. Even if the parenthetic material embedded within a sentence is a full sentence, a capital letter to begin or a period to end is not required.

The veteran thought about his struggle (it was too painful to speak), but he tried not to be bitter.

If the parenthetic material is a question or exclamation, you need both the appropriate mark within the parentheses and a period outside.

Kyle kept telling the same story over and over (talk about boredom!).

If the parenthetic material begins after an end mark and is not part of another sentence, final punctuation goes within the parentheses. (/)

Many professionals are in the top ten percent of the income scale. (Teachers are another story.)

A comma is not used before an opening parenthesis, but one may be required after a closing parenthesis.

Because the house was built on sand (poor choice, builders), it had a tendency to shift. [The parenthetical material is part of a long introductory clause, which must be set off from the rest of the sentence.]

ACTIVITY 13

Revise the following sentences: add parentheses and other punctuation where appropriate.

1. The smallest Scandinavian country, Denmark is a constitutional monarchy (Queen Margrethe II, 1972).
2. To assemble the swingset, you should 1 read the instructions carefully 2 try to follow the instructions exactly 3 call a professional 4 take an aspirin.
3. America's involvement in World War II 1941–1945 was costly in money and human life.
4. During the early part of the year Jan.–Mar. the gross national product rose four percent.
5. The Parthenon on the Acropolis in Athens 438 BC? was a temple for the goddess Athena.

Mechanics

34 APOSTROPHE

34a Use apostrophes correctly to show possession.

Singular nouns, add **'s**	*a tiger's claws* *our ambassador's mistakes*
Singular nouns ending in **s**, add only the apostrophe	*Mr. Jones' house* *the goddess' hair*

An exception to this rule: if you want the possessive to be pronounced as a separate syllable, you may add an extra *s*: Mr. Jones's house, the goddess's hair.

Singular indefinite pronouns, add **'s**	*one's options* *anyone's problem*
Joint possession: add **'s** to the last owner named	*Joan and Dean's computer*
Individual ownership, add **'s** to each owner mentioned	*Joan's and Dean's computers*

Notice the plural *computers*, indicating each owns a machine.

Plural nouns ending in *s*, add only the apostrophe	*the animals' habitats* *the newspapers' headlines*
Plural nouns not ending in *s*, add **'s**	*women's responsibilities* *children's toys*
Abstract or inanimate nouns and familiar expressions follow the normal rules	*a day's work* *five dollars' worth* *life's difficulties*

34b Do not use apostrophes in possessive pronouns.

Do not use the apostrophe with possessive pronouns: *its, hers, theirs, yours, whose,* and so on. Note carefully that there is no word *its'* in the language. See **34c** for *it's*.

34c Use apostrophes to show the omission of letters in contractions.

In contractions the apostrophe takes the place of any missing letters. Contractions give a less formal tone to your writing; they are generally acceptable except in the most formal writing situations: *we're, he'll, I'm, you're, haven't, didn't, they're, who's, doesn't, it's* (*it is*).

34d Words referred to as words, abbreviations, and letters and numerals referred to as symbols form their plurals by adding 's.

p's and *q*'s	C.P.A.'s
rpm's	*if*'s, *and*'s, or *but*'s
M.A.'s	I used to think *3*'s were erased *8*'s.

Modern practice often drops the apostrophe when dates are treated as collective nouns: *1900s, 1980s.*

ACTIVITY 1

Proofread the following sentences: insert or delete apostrophes where appropriate.

1. Sherlock Holmes stories are narrated by his companion, Dr. Watson.
2. Its been approximately sixty years since television was invented.
3. Youre not serious, are you?
4. The entertainment world was saddened by Fred Astaires' death in 1987.
5. James laughter echoed through the halls.
6. You have too many Is in you paper.
7. Its going to be a great summer if Kathy and Jims pool gets finished.
8. Everyones reputation is threatened by the tapes.
9. The two mens car was in for repairs.
10. He doesnt have a nickels worth of sense.

hyph

35 HYPHEN

35a Use correct forms for compound words.

Many compound words are spelled as two words, others as one word, and still others as hyphenated words. Look up in the dictionary any compound word you are unsure of.

handlebar mustache	dogtrot	hand-me-down
kiss of death	happenstance	mother-in-law

Compound-word modifiers before a noun should be hyphenated. This guideline does not apply to *-ly* words, which are never hyphenated.

UNHYPHENATED -LY COMPOUND	HYPHENATED COMPOUND
quickly dried material	quick-dried material
loosely packed fibers	loose-packed fibers

Compound-word modifiers after a noun are not hyphenated. Modifiers that are hyphenated when they precede the noun do not need hyphens when they come after the noun.

This essay was *well written.*
Their dog was *bad tempered.*

Plurals of compound words may be irregular. The plural is formed on the most significant word in the compound: *mothers-in-law, sergeants-at-arms.* In some cases you must use your own judgment: *Johnnies-come-lately* or *Johnny-come-latelies.*

Possessives of compound words are usually regular. The possessive of a compound word is usually formed at the end of the word: *pig in a poke's, mother-in-law's, standard-bearer's.*

35b Hyphenate words formed with certain prefixes and suffixes.

hyph

Words that use the prefixes *all-*, *cross-*, *ex-*, *half-*, *ill-*, *well-*, and *self-* and the suffix *-elect* are usually hyphenated.

all-knowing	ex-President
self-sacrifice	governor-elect

When *self* is a word's root rather than a prefix, it is not hyphenated.

selfhood *selfish*

The prefixes and suffixes listed below form words that are spelled without hyphens (*antiballistic*, *counterrevolution*, *nonfattening*, *twofold*, *underrated*):

anti	intra	pro	super
co	like	pseudo	supra
counter	non	re	ultra
extra	over	semi	un
fold	post	sub	under
infra	pre		

But use the hyphen when one of these is attached to a proper noun:

un-American anti-Communist ex-New Yorker

Two-word numbers are hyphenated. Spelled-out numbers from twenty-one to ninety-nine are hyphenated, as are spelled-out fractions.

twenty-one three-fifths

hyph

35c Use a hyphen to signal a common root for two or more words or prefixes.

Nineteenth- and twentieth-century art is on display.
We have to write a 10- to 20-page paper.

35d Use a hyphen to avoid ambiguity, confusion, or an awkward combination of letters.

He was excited about the re-creation.

The hyphen is needed to distinguish between *re-creation*, a reenactment, and *recreation*, a diversion of some kind.

The hill-like effect was created with globs of paint.

The hyphen is needed here to avoid running three *l*'s together.

35e Use a hyphen to divide a word at the end of a line.

Insert the hyphen only between syllables of two or more letters. Dictionaries show syllable division.

It was not a sound of his own superiority but an exclamation of surprise.

 (See also the beginning of section **40**.)

ACTIVITY 2

Proofread the following sentences: add or delete hyphens.

1. A well designed house should last at least a hundred years.
2. The report was well received by the committee.
3. Lee's preoccupation with food was mere selfindulgence.
4. Uncle Bono served lightly-salted butter on crystal plates.
5. There were thirty three different wines on the restaurant's menu.
6. At the present time, the plans for the reorganiza tion of the league have been shelved.
7. The flowers were cross pollinated to produce a new variety.
8. Manufacturers claimed the yoghurt was non-fattening.
9. At the last minute, our counter-offer was rejected.
10. Somebody ought to do something about my brother's in law car.

36 UNDERLINING (ITALICS)

Typesetters use italic type (*type that looks like this: slanted*) for any words that are underlined in manuscripts. Underlining takes the place of italics in typed and handwritten papers. Of course, if you have a typewriter or word processor that has both italic and roman (regular, unslanted) type, you may want to use italics rather than underlining.

36a Use underlining (*italics*) for the titles of long works.

Titles of books, booklets, magazines, newspapers, long poems, plays, record albums, operas, films, works of art, radio and television series (the name of the series, not the titles of individual segments), require underlining.

ital Have you read Shakespeare's *Titus Andronicus*?

Masterpiece Theatre is one of the most popular offerings on PBS.

The titles of court cases should not be underlined nor quoted, according to the new MLA guidelines.

In the 1830s, Freelink v. Bishoff created a precedent that is still cited.

36b Use underlining (*italics*) for the names of airplanes, trains, ships, and other vehicles.

the *Orient Express* the *Nina*, *Pinta*, and *Santa Maria*

36c Use underlining (*italics*) for emphasis.

"What's *your* problem?" asked Bevins as I raised my hand.

In general, let your word choice and syntax carry the emphasis. Too much underlining for emphasis distracts readers and gives writing an informal look.

36d Use underlining (*italics*) to indicate words from other languages.

If a word or phrase from another language becomes widely used by and generally familiar to speakers of English, the special treatment is dropped. When in doubt, check your dictionary.

The first part of the piece is played *vivace*, fast and light. *ital*

How are things going, amigo? [No underlining; although *amigo* is Spanish, it has become so familiar to Americans that it is accepted as part of our language.]

36e Underlining (*italics*) may be used with words referred to as words and with letters and numerals referred to as symbols.

Our assignment is to trace the history of the word *aromatic*.

Professors complain when students make *f*'s look like *t*'s.

See **29h** for use of quotation marks here. When there are many references to words, underlining is preferred.

36f Use underlining (*italics*) for the scientific (*genus and species*) names for animals and plants.

The doctor announced that I had been in contact with *Rhus radicans*, poison ivy.

Chemicals (sodium chloride), diseases (glaucoma), astronomical terms (nebula), geological (pliocene), and most other scientific terms are not usually underlined, except when being introduced. (See **36g**.)

36g Use underlining (*italics*) to introduce key words and special or technical terms.

The *hypothalamus*, one of whose functions is to regulate body temperature, is a region in the forebrain.

ACTIVITY 3

Proofread the following sentences: underline where necessary.

1. We spent an hour discussing words like whey and whir and whoa.
2. His Excellency smiled and murmured, "Benedicté," as he passed.
3. Poison ivy (Rhus toxicodendron) causes a skin rash and intense itching on contact.
4. The space shuttle program suffered a severe loss when the Challenger exploded, killing the entire crew in full view of the TV cameras.
5. The Hasslebergs had purchased tickets to sail on the Titanic but changed their plans just before departure time.
6. When I asked Julio where the fish were biting, he smiled and said, "Quien sabe?"
7. Sports Illustrated features an article on the New York Islanders this week.
8. Steinbeck's book East of Eden was banned by the school board.
9. The jury in Maxwell v. Carmody deliberated for twelve days.
10. Two famous sixteenth-century comedies are Gammer Gurton's Needle and Ralph Roister Doister.

37 CAPITALIZATION

37a Capitalize the first word of a sentence and first word of a direct quotation.

Looking out over the crowd, she said, "Let us pray for world peace."

Do not capitalize the first word of an incorporated quotation. *cap*

The government report cited "repeated violations of Health Code Regulation 145-G" as the reason for closing the factory.

Capitalize only the first word of an interrupted quotation.

"The country you know as Iran," she said, "was once known as the Persian Empire."

Capitalize the first word after a colon if it begins a quotation, a speech in dialogue, a formal statement, a question, or material of more than one sentence.

Patrick Henry stated: "Give me liberty, or give me death."

This is the question: Where will we get the money?

Capitalize the first word of a line of verse. (Some modern poets ignore this convention.)

Some say the world will end in fire,
Some say in ice.
From what I've tasted of desire
I hold with those who favor fire.

From Robert Frost's "Fire and Ice"

37b Capitalize names, nicknames, and descriptive names.

Clara	Virginia Woolf
Snooky	the Wizard of Menlo Park

Descriptive names following a given name are usually set off with quotation marks: *Babe Ruth, "the Sultan of Swat."*

cap **Capitalize words formed from proper nouns.**

Alaskan peninsula	American oil fields
Shakespearean sonnet	Victorian household

Do not capitalize derivatives of proper names that have a special meaning.

brazil nut	brussels sprouts	french dressing
india ink	panama hat	roman numerals
morocco leather		

Capitalize names identifying nationalities and ethnic groups.

Irish	Indian

Black and *White* as racial designations may be capitalized or not; whichever practice you follow, use it for both words.

Capitalize the names of awards, brand names, structures, and historical, cultural, and other events.

Congressional Medal of Honor	April
the Tony Award	April Fool's Day
Izod shirt	Rosh Hashanah
the Holland Tunnel	the Battle of Hastings
the *USS Arizona* Memorial	the French Revolution
Thursday	the Great Depression

Do not capitalize popular names for, or informal references to, periods of history.

the seventeenth century	nuclear age
the classical period	information age

Capitalize the names of geographic features and places. *cap*

the Badlands	Detroit
Carlsbad Caverns	Maple Street
Great Bear Lake	Yellowstone National Park
the Mojave Desert	the North

Do not capitalize the names of seasons.

autumn   fall   spring   summer   winter

Capitalize *north, south, east, west,* and their derivatives only when they refer to specific geographical areas, not when they refer to directions.

From Canada we drove southeast to Bismarck.

The United States cannot afford to mistake the motives of Western Europe's peace activists.

Do not capitalize terms like *city, county, state* when written without a name or when written before the name:

Workers in the city often live in its suburbs.

The village of Logansport has a population of ninety-seven.

Capitalize the names of military groups, battles, and wars.

the Battle of Bull Run	United States Air Force
the Coldstream Guards	War of the Roses

Do not capitalize informal references to the armed services:

Lester is going into the army, but I chose the marines.

Capitalize names of institutions and organizations.

the Bureau of Indian Affairs	Exxon Corporation
the Democratic Party	the Politburo
Department of the Treasury	United States Congress

cap Do not capitalize nouns and adjectives formed from names of political parties unless you are referring to the party or a member of a party.

He said that *communism* was a failed experiment.
They were promised *democratic* elections.
He is a Libertarian [party member].

Capitalize the names of religious groups, books, deities, events, figures, and holidays.

Hindu	Allah
Methodist	Hera
Islam	He (God)
the Bible	Jehovah
the Torah	Yom Kippur
God	Ramadan

Do not capitalize the names of religious objects.

crucifix   mezuzah   rosary   stations of the cross

Capitalize such school-related terms as languages, specific courses, and degrees (with names) and their abbreviations.

English   History 300   Karen Siegle, Ph.D.   B.A.   M.A.

Do not capitalize subjects other than languages.

chemistry   physical education   computer sciences

Do not capitalize school years.

freshman   sophomore   junior   senior

Do not capitalize academic degrees except after a name:

associate of arts   bachelor's   master of arts   doctorate

cap

Capitalize scientific names.

Tyrannosaurus rex (genus only)	Orion
the Andromeda Constellation	Earth

Do not capitalize the common names of most plants and animals:

maple tree	blue jay
rose	dachshund

Do not capitalize generic terms without names.

asteroid	moon
meteor	quasar

Do not capitalize the generic term when it comes before the name.

the comet Kohoutek   the asteroid Ceres

Do not capitalize the names of diseases or medical conditions:

arthritis   jaundice

Capitalize the names of ships, planes, and trains.

the *Spirit of St. Louis*	the *Orient Express*
the *Merrimac*	*Viking* II

Note: Use underlining to indicate italic print. See **36b.**

37c Capitalize titles of address, position, and rank.

Mr. and Mrs. Kester	the Pope
Ms. Kwan [married or single]	Empress Josephine
Uncle Rex	President Truman
Her Excellency	the Queen

cap The title *President* is often capitalized even without a specific name.

Do not capitalize labels signifying family members unless the labels are used in place of names or with names.

> Both my mother and my grandmother were physicians in Anchorage. [Compare: *Both Mother and Grandmother were physicians in Anchorage.*]

Do not capitalize most titles without names or when the name precedes.

the lieutenant	Martha L. Collins, governor of Kentucky
a congressman	the senator

37d Capitalize significant words in the titles of publications.

Capitalize the first word and the last word and all words in between except articles, coordinate conjunctions, and short prepositions. Capitalize the first word of a subtitle following a colon.

> *Great River: The Rio Grande in North American History*

Do not capitalize *the* as part of a newspaper title:

> Her interview was in the *Wall Street Journal.*

In footnote and bibliographic references, omit *The* as a first word in titles of newspapers and journals.

Capitalize both elements of a hyphenated word in a title.

The Ballad of the Harp-Weaver
Hell-Bent Fer Heaven

Capitalize divisions of a book or paper.

Preface Conclusion Bibliography
Chapter Seven: Red Giants

Capitalize the important words in the titles of government documents, acts, and policy statements. Such documents do not require quotation marks or italics.

the Declaration of Independence
the Lend-Lease Act
the United Nations Charter

37e Capitalize the pronoun *I* and the exclamation *O*.

"Lurch on, lurch on, O skateboard of fools," I muttered.

37f Capitalize significant words in the greeting and the first word only in the closing of a letter.

Dear Mr. Chekzikksy: Respectfully,
My Dear Friend, Sincerely yours,

ACTIVITY 4

Revise the following sentences for capitalization.

1. archbishop frankendorf turned and said, "mr. president, the prime minister will see us now."
2. professor logan had been a rhodes scholar in the thirties and had written his dissertation, "extinction of the grizzly bear," while studying in a tibetan village high in the himalayas.
3. After surveying homes on lakes superior and huron, we decided to move farther west.

4. Jane had a choice between majoring in history or english.
5. the president will address the nation on the subject of the equal rights amendment.
6. While the north was suffering a bitter winter, most of the south was clear and warm.
7. His study of the bible required him to learn hebrew.
8. The Scotch Terrier chewed up chapter one of charlotte's new book.
9. each tuesday the visitors to the lincoln park zoo were treated to a fine display by bushman and the other gorillas.
10. using only a radio shack trs-80 and a simple random access program, two high school students tried to break into the computer at chase manhattan bank.

---

38 ABBREVIATIONS AND NUMBERS

38a Abbreviate titles and honorifics before and after names.

Dr. Carter	Gov. William P. Harrison	Ms. Piazza
Helen L. Montgomery, Ph.D.		Mark S. Donnaly, Jr.

38b Abbreviate institutions, companies, agencies, organizations.

Wellington Corp. YMCA CIA UNESCO CBS

38c Abbreviate time, dates, measures, etc. with specific numbers.

12:00 A.M. 1066 BC 12 qts. 9 mm.

ab/nos

Note: Both BC and AD are given without periods in the new *MLA Style Manual.*

38d Abbreviate bibliographic references.

p. (for page, pp. for pages) vol. (for volume)
ed. (for editor or edition) no. (for number)

38e Use numerals for numbers that are expressed as more than two words.

1,568 7,120,000 3 1/2

38f Spell out numbers expressed as one or two words.

twelve seventy-seven forty billion

38g Spell out numbers that start sentences.

One hundred and forty-three students graduated.

39 SPELLING

Most readers will forgive one spelling mistake, and many will forgive two. But readers who recognize more than two errors may begin to develop a prejudice against the writer. Even if you are a good speller, the chances are high that you will still miss some words or make some typing errors. If you sp have a spelling problem, you need to memorize the words that cause you difficulty. In either case, learn to proofread carefully.

39a Proofread thoroughly.

Proofread your work several times because your eyes are likely to miss errors. A quick reading does not work; force yourself to look at each word, one letter at a time.

Seek help. Unless your instructor says otherwise, seek help in proofreading. The more important the paper is, the more sense it makes to seek help in proofreading. (Check with your instructor for your school's proofreading policy.)

Create objective distance for more effective proofreading. Writers fail to see errors because they are "too close" to their work. You need some objective distance on your writing—time enough to allow objectivity. Finish your paper at least a day before it's due. A day later you will have a more critical view of everything in your writing—including mistakes.

Memorize the correct spelling of words you habitually misspell. Though English is largely phonetic (spelled by sound), there are many exceptions to the sound system. Only memorization is foolproof.

39b Watch for troublesome letters and letter combinations.

The greatest difficulty is not obviously misspelled words, but words about which you are not quite sure. Many of these have built-in trouble spots, like the *-able/-ible* and the *ei/ie* combinations. Familiarize yourself with this list:

-able/-ible These two suffixes sound alike. More words end with *-able*, but *-ible* frequently follows an s sound: *forcible, plausible, visible.* (But note *kissable, passable.*)

-age/-edge/-ege/-idge These letter combinations all sound similar: *sp*

suffrage	knowledge	college	abridge
sewage	pledge	privilege	partridge
mileage	dredge		

-ant, -ance/-ent, -ence These endings are generally pronounced alike: *redundant, insistent; redundance, insistence.*

-ceed/-cede/-sede Most of the words with the sound of *eed* are spelled *-cede: accede, concede, precede, recede, secede.* Only *exceed, proceed,* and *succeed* end in *ceed.* Only *supersede* ends in *sede.*

Double consonants Many words double a final consonant before adding a suffix: *scar: scar r ing; bar: bar r ing.* Words containing a long-vowel sound before the final consonant (*scare, bare*) do not double the final consonant: *sca(r)ing, ba(r)ing.*

ei/ie Most cases are covered by

> "*I* before *e*
> except after *c*
> or when pronounced as *a*,
> as in *neighbor* and *weigh*."

That is, the combination is usually *ie* (*believe, die, fiend, friend*), but after *c* the combination is *ei* (*ceiling, receive, deceive*), and it is also *ei* when the combination is pronounced with a long *a* sound (as in *freight* and *sleigh*). However, there are a number of exceptions (*leisure, seize,* and so on).

-ery/-ary Most words end with *-ary;* only a few words end with *-ery: cemetery, stationery* (paper).

Final e Final *e* is usually dropped before a suffix beginning with a vowel: *hop[e]ing, scrap[e]ing.* But in some cases it is sp kept: *changeable, peaceable.* And it is nearly always kept when the suffix begins with a consonant: *hopeful, boredom* (but note some common exceptions: *argument, judgment, truly*). Check doubtful words; some words are spelled either way (*livable, liveable*).

-ful Words formed with *-ful* always end with one *l: cupful, eyeful.*

-ly Add *-ly* to a word that already ends with an *l: accidental(ly), real(ly).* Words ending in double *l* add only the *-y: fully, hilly.*

-or/-er/-ar All these endings sound alike (*author, grammar, painter*). When in doubt, check your dictionary.

-o Words ending in *-o* usually become plural by adding *es: tomatoes, potatoes, mosquitoes, zeroes.* But words related to music add only *s: solos, sopranos, pianos, radios.* A few words can be spelled either way.

pre-/per-/pro- Check words with these prefixes: *perspiration, performance, prepare, protect.* Don't count on sound here. Many people pronounce them all alike; others interchange them (*prespiration* for *perspiration*, or *pertect* for *protect*).

Silent letters A number of words contain silent (unpronounced) letters: *clim(b), hon(e), Conne(c)ticut, (k)nife, (p)syc(h)ology.*

-y words Change *-y* to *i* before all suffixes (endings) except *-ing: beauty, beautiful; noisy, noisily; buy, buying.*

-y words Change *-y* to *i* and add *es* for the plural: *babies, families.* But note that proper names do not follow this rule: *Kennedys, Sheltys.* When the *y* follows a vowel (*monkey*) the plural is formed by adding *s* only (*monkeys*).

39c Distinguish between homonyms.

sp

Many words, though spelled differently, sound alike or very similar. Homonyms are often hard to detect because they don't *look* misspelled.

LIST OF COMMON HOMONYMS

bare/bear
been/bin
board/bored
cite/site
complement/compliment
for/fore/four
groan/grown
hear/here
higher/hire
rain/reign
right/rite/write
rote/wrote
sea/see
sail/sale
stake/steak
stair/stare
steal/steel
tail/tale
their/there/they're
threw/through
to/too/two
wail/whale
weak/week
your/you're/yore

39d Learn the correct spelling of irregular plurals.

SINGULAR	PLURAL
alumna	alumnae (f)
alumnus	alumni (m)
analysis	analyses
appendix	appendixes, appendices
bacterium	bacteria
cactus	cactuses, cacti
crisis	crises
criterion	criteria
curriculum	curriculums, curricula
datum	data
die	dice

sp

formula	formulas, formulae
index	indexes, indices
medium	media
memorandum	memoranda
nucleus	nuclei
octopus	octopuses, octopi
parenthesis	parentheses
stimulus	stimuli
stratum	strata
thesis	theses

ACTIVITY 5

Proofread these sentences and correct spelling errors you find.

1. Though the revolutionary leaders were first percieved as liberators, they were soon revealed as terrorists and murders.
2. Because of her fluant Spanish she was a competant translater.
3. Advisors to the King reminded him of his soveriegn duty to pertect the nation.
4. Painters, authers, and sculpters share a common interest in the fine arts.
5. *Sorgum*, *Arkansaw*, and *neumonia* all contain spelling surprises.
6. The biggest, burliest Marine sergent D.I. (drill instructor) has just turned away and clicked his heels.
7. We were lounging around the pool side of a local racket ball club, gazing up into the sky.
8. Most people, being somewhat apprehensive about anything with more than four legs, do not appreciate spiders—much less tarantellas.
9. I realize there are problems and inconvenences in voting: the weather's bad, you have to work, your going out of town, you don't trust the government, you don't like the choice of candadates, and so on.

10. My instincts rallied together and introdused the thought that later led me to my decision of a drastic hairstyle change. *sp*
11. When I see you on the street or catcht a glimpse of you, I get the weirdest sensation inside, like falling through a pit with no bottom.
12. "From a public health perspective it is quite clear that this increase in the drinking age is in the interest of that (18–20-year-old) population," stated Richard Douglass, assistent research scientist at the University of Michigan's Highway Safety Reserch Institute.
13. Reserchers claim that by using a large number of animals per experiement, they are more certain of their results and can also predict the percentage of people who will be effected.
14. The morning went by quickly with the tempeture rising to a humid 96 degrees at noon.
15. Now the only lights noticable are ocasional cigerretes casting minute red sparks like fireflies blinking in the night.

Diction

diction

Diction refers to word choice. Effective word choice shows a writer's feeling for language distinctions; and it depends on purpose, audience, subject. *Effective* means not just "good" but "having an effect on the reader," the effect you intend.

40 THE DICTIONARY

Read your dictionary's introductory pages to see how to interpret its entries. Here is a sample entry from *Webster's New Collegiate Dictionary:*

> **im·bro·glio** \im-'brōl-(,)yō\ *n, pl* **-glios** [It, fr. *imbrogliare* to entangle, fr. MF *embrouiller* — more at EMBROIL] (1750) **1 :** a confused mass **2 a :** an intricate or complicated situation (as in a drama or novel) **b :** an acutely painful or embarrassing misunderstanding **c :** a violently confused or bitterly complicated altercation : EMBROILMENT

This entry shows the syllabication of the word (for word division in typing) and the pronunciation of the word; note that the syllables for pronunciation are slightly different from those for printing. Note that the *g* is silent and there is an optional secondary accent on the last syllable. The dictionary shows the part of speech (noun), giving you a clue to its use.

ACTIVITY 1

Use a college dictionary to look up the following words. Write sentences using each word appropriately. In what kind of writing situations might you use these words?

ablate	lacunae	rapprochement
casuistry	penultimate	sesquipedalian
infra dig	obviate	synoptic

ACTIVITY 2

Revise the following sentences by replacing incorrect words with correct diction.

1. For dessert the waiter brought us a peach flambeau.
2. At the top of each column the architect had placed an ornate corniche.
3. They had finally become lovelorn from kissing so often.
4. From my hours of studying, I had found the history of the Punic Wars very edificing.
5. For Christmas we all chipped in to buy grandmother a ruby pendent.

40a Use standard English appropriately.

Avoid oral English in formal writing situations. We all speak a dialect of English, largely depending on what region of America we live in—North, South, East, West—and whether we live in a city or in a rural area.

I reckon y'all heard the news.

We be back after a while.

They ain't nobody here.

Many expressions that we all use and accept in oral English should be avoided in formal writing. Slang, regional words, "dialects," and other oral expressions are appropriate in formal writing only to imitate speech, as in realistic dialogue.

40b Understand the difference between denotations and connotations.

DENOTATION

The denotation of a word is its dictionary definition. Many words have several denotations, a fact that can sometimes cause problems. For example, the word *grave* means "burial diction site," but it also means "serious," and no writer can afford to use the word as if it meant only one thing and not the other. Many readers will "hear" the other meaning, despite the writer, often with comic effect:

DENOTATION PROBLEM

Washington considers the death of the Russian ambassador a very grave matter.

REVISED

Washington considers the death of the Russian ambassador a very serious matter.

GENERAL CONNOTATIONS

Connotations are clues to the way a word is actually used by speakers and writers. For example, *to pretend* means "to fake or falsify"; *pretense* is a claim not supported by fact. We can pretend to be sick, pretend to be someone else, make a pretense of doing homework. But we do not usually say, "The builders pretended the girders were steel." Nor are we likely to say, "The counterfeiter pretended his money was real." *Pretend* denotes "fake" or "false," but it generally connotes "fakery without serious consequences," the pretense of children. For more serious kinds of falsification we are likely to select more serious-sounding words: *allege, dissemble, simulate, fraud,* and so on.

SPECIAL CONNOTATIONS

In addition to general connotations, many words also have special connotations. These often suggest a positive or negative quality and evoke emotional responses from readers. They can also be private reactions: for example, different readers might respond differently to each of the following: *law-enforcement officer, police, cop, fuzz, smokey.* All the terms could identify the same individual, but each term carries a different emotional meaning.

People often try to change labels in order to get away from negative connotations, and this can led to pretentious or deceptive writing. *Garbage dumps* become *sanitary landfills*, *janitors* become *maintenance engineers*, *toilets* become *lavatories or bathrooms*, military *attacks* become *preemptive strikes*. Knowing denotative meanings is not sufficient; you must also have an ear for connotations.

ACTIVITY 3

Read the following sentences carefully. Replace any words that interfere with the meaning of the sentence.

1. Those who cannot speak may nevertheless answer dumb questions.
2. In the kindergarten play, all the girls were elves and all the boys were fairies.
3. Ollie is a pig farmer and a terrible bore.
4. Though he was a famous ventriloquist, the critics felt he had given a very wooden performance.
5. The directions said to force the spit through the mouth of the chicken.

40c Use synonyms carefully.

The dictionary lists synonyms for most terms. A special dictionary for this purpose is called a *thesaurus*. But care must be taken with synonyms. They too have connotations; few synonyms are *exact* replacements for other words. Here you need a writer's ear; you must think about the context of the word before selecting a synonym: *wastebasket* and *trash can* may be synonyms, but there are subtle differences between the words. Some words are different only because they have different language histories: while *ice box* and *refrigerator* both denote the same thing, *ice box* now sounds dated, old fashioned. You may make an unintended statement about yourself if you refer to your *ice box*.

ACTIVITY 4

Revise the following sentences so that their use of denotation and connotation becomes more effective.

1. Asa proudly announced that she had a new infantile brother at home.
2. We soon learned that VD was a very healthy disease, one not easily controlled.
3. Everyone had been working for ten hours without rest, and we were all suffering from fugue.
4. Of all those huge tomes on ancient history, the epitome was the biggest one of all.
5. All the boys were laughing and clowning around and being as supercilious as they could to try to get her attention.

40d Use idioms appropriately.

An idiom is an expression that has become conventional despite its logic or grammar. When English speakers say they will "take a train," they do not mean that they will take it away with them. Similarly, expressions like *catch fire, do a good turn, give someone a hand,* and so forth are idioms that mean something different from what they literally say.

While native speakers have little difficulty using and understanding such expressions, occasionally they do have trouble with another kind of idiom called *prepositional idioms,* those expressions that conventionally link a word and a specific preposition.

abide by
abstain from
acquiesce in (an injustice)
adhere to
agree to (a proposal)
agree with (a person)
alarmed at (the news)
aspire to
assent to
avail oneself of
capable of
concur in (an opinion)
concur with (someone)
confer with (someone)
confer about (a problem)
conform to (specifications)

contend with (a person)
contend for (a principle)
die of
differ about (an issue)
differ from (in appearance)
differ with (a person)
different from
disappointed in (a performance)
discuss with (someone)
divest of
identical with
in accordance with
independent of
indifferent to
oblivious of (warnings)
plan to
prevail on (or upon)
refrain from
required of (people)
resolve on (an action)
succeed in
superior to
try to
wait at (a place)
wait for (a person)
wait on (a customer)

SLANG

Slang is street-English, the latest "in" words by which individuals establish their relationship to a group. Only those in the group ("in the know") know the slang, until it begins to creep into the general language. In the early 1980s, "grody to the max" and "gag me with a spoon" were new slang terms.

In most formal writing, slang should be avoided. Imagine writing about a President's reaction to Congress's overriding a veto: "The President was really bummed, but he decided to cool it and go to his ranch and kick back for a while." Though such use of slang may be effective in less formal writing, particularly in dialogue, it is inappropriate in formal writing.

ACTIVITY 5

Revise for correct use of prepositional idiom and to eliminate slang.

1. Our engineers are working overtime to make sure the building will conform with the new safety regulations.
2. The archeologist flew to Egypt to try and discover whether the dates of the pottery shards were different than those in Israel.
3. The efficiency expert began to scope out the copying procedures to see if they were in accordance to those he had suggested.

lang

41 EFFECTIVE LANGUAGE

41a Clarify general concepts with specific language.

General language identifies groups or classes of things; specific language identifies individual members of a class. *Games* is a general term, *football* is specific; *literature* is general, *novel* more specific, *The Grapes of Wrath* most specific. General statements without specific examples can produce dullness, ambiguity, and confusion. Readers need specific details in order to make precise meaning from generalities.

GENERAL

People say the economy is their biggest worry.

REVISED WITH SPECIFIC LANGUAGE

On the news last night, four patrons of city soup kitchens said they wanted jobs, not charity.

GENERAL

He was a cute guy.

REVISED WITH SPECIFIC LANGUAGE

He was six feet one, built like Sean Penn, had blond, curly hair, baby blue eyes, and a smile that made him look like a mischievous little boy.

The specific details here allow the reader to understand what you mean by *people*, *economy*, and *cute*.

Specific language is greatly preferred to general. It takes study, observation, and thought to produce the specific details that constitute real information.

GENERAL

Changing Places is a fine movie that lives up to the reputations of its stars. The acting is superior in this film, and the plot is very good. Those who see this interesting new film will have an enjoyable experience.

REVISED WITH SPECIFIC LANGUAGE

The film *Changing Places* stars the comic actors Eddie Murphy and Dan Akroyd. Together the two young comedians are first the victims and then the winners in a plot set in motion by aging actors Don Ameche and Ralph Bellamy, two evil stockbrokers who set out to manipulate the younger men for the sake of a one-dollar bet. The bet is that a penniless, low-grade street shyster (Murphy pretends to be blind and legless) can successfully take over the job of a rising young Wall Street analyst and that the analyst, when reduced to poverty, will soon resort to crime.

Except for the title of the film, there is no information in the general paragraph; it offers only a set of unsupported and imprecise evaluations.

Writers cannot separate the general from the specific in a mechanical way. The two must work together so that readers have both facts and ideas. While everyone prefers specific language to concrete *most* of the time, there are times when general language will be appropriate. The purpose of your writing determines the level of specification you need. For example, if you were tracing the history of a study carried out by a cost-control group, you might say at one point:

EXCESSIVE SPECIFICATION

The energetic and intelligent committee, comprised of six men and two women (one of whom had just been divorced), accepted by a vote of five to three the report.

USEFUL GENERAL LANGUAGE

The committee accepted the report.

If you want to indicate only that the report was accepted, details about the committee and the vote may not be relevant.

lang

41b Clarify abstract concepts with concrete language.

Tie intangible concepts to physical reality. Abstractions are qualities and ideas removed from physical reality. Many writers consider generalizations and abstractions to be the same. But although generalizations may have physical referents, abstractions don't. For example, "beauty" is an abstraction; beauty does not exist in the environment; it is an idea. We can find people we think *have* beauty, but beauty itself exists only in the mind. We cannot show people *freedom*, nor can we touch *democracy, socialism, purity, perfection*, and other abstract concepts. Abstractions are intangible: not observable by the senses.

The writer's challenge is to tie abstractions to reality, to illustrate the intangible idea with concrete examples. You may have your own idea of what *communism* means, but if you compare your definition with those of the people of the USSR, the People's Republic of China, Albania, Cambodia, France, and so forth, you will discover many different concepts of what the word means. To assist your reader, you must supply concrete terms that will illustrate abstract concepts.

ABSTRACT

He lost the election because of accusations of dishonesty.

REVISED WITH MORE CONCRETE TERMS

He lost the election because he was accused of taking a $10,000 bribe.

Dishonesty is a vague abstraction; the specific charge gives readers a much clearer sense of the accusations.

Concrete means physical. If you kick a concrete block, you will get sharp information from your foot. Something similar happens with concrete language; it gives the reader information at the physical level. When people say, "Give me an example," they are asking for concrete information. The more intangible or abstract writing becomes, the harder it is for readers to know what you are talking about. "Liquidating my assets to increase cash flow" can mean several things, one of which could be "selling my old Ford because I'm short of money." *lang*

While abstractions have their uses, readers need to visualize what you are writing about. Examples, illustrations, and details help sharpen pictures, and concrete words help to clarify the impression.

ABSTRACT

The presence of deciduous windbreaks may produce less effective results than similar establishment of conifers.

REVISED WITH CONCRETE LANGUAGE

Pines and spruces make better windbreaks than do trees that lose their leaves.

ACTIVITY 6

Revise each of the following sentences by replacing abstract language with concrete wherever possible.

1. Law-enforcement officials announced the recovery of a cache of merchandise illegally sequestered by criminal accomplices.
2. Presidential advisors at the highest levels proffered recommendations that recently expounded commitments be jettisoned.
3. Upon termination of normal chronological development, mortal remains are customarily interred in a sepulcher.
4. Individual liberties such as those governing oral communication are guaranteed by governmental documents.
5. The official military prediction with regard to the optimal transportation implementation to the targeted destination relative to the present cite of origin projects a negative realization of goal attainment.

Use effective modifiers. Some modifiers carry only vague meanings, often just a hazy positive or negative suggestion. Use precise modifiers to gain clarity and effectiveness.

WEAK

It was an interesting film.

REVISED

The way the film created the effect of space ships speeding around the buildings of the city nearly brought me out of my seat.

The word *interesting* carries only a shadowy meaning, that something in the film caught your attention. Most readers won't respond to such a sentence; they need more specific information.

ACTIVITY 7

Add effective modifiers to these sentences. Imagine they are sentences for essays in your composition class.

1. The children were frightened by the strange behavior of the wino.
2. A lot of work was involved in writing the program.
3. Because of its violence, the storm's effects were terrible.
4. The alligator is a fairly long and ugly creature.
5. The performance of the symphony was nice.

Use effective nouns. Using the most specific, concrete nouns can add power to your writing and can also save you from excessive use of modifiers to describe more general nouns. Selecting accurate nouns will also make your writing more economical.

WEAK

They planted a tree between the bushes and the flowers.

REVISED WITH ACCURATE NOUNS

They planted a red oak between the lilacs and the rose garden.

Particularly important to effective writing is the noun in the subject position of any sentence. Well-chosen nouns will add strength to your writing and may help to eliminate the colorless verbs that often accompany general and abstract nouns. Avoid starting sentences with "empty" language like *It is* and *There are.* *lang*

WEAK

It is the belief of most Americans that their taxes are too high.

REVISED WITH SPECIFIC SUBJECT NOUN

Americans believe that their taxes are too high.

Some relatively empty nouns that often produce dull sentences are words like *situation, facet, aspect, factor,* and *elements.*

WEAK

A factor that should be taken into consideration is class attendance.

REVISIONS WITH SPECIFIC NOUN

The professor should count class attendance as part of the grade.

Empty or abstract subjects cannot *do* anything, so choosing them limits the verbs you can use. Often the verbs must be passive or a form of *to be,* both relatively weak choices. (See p. 238.)

ACTIVITY 8

Revise the following sentences by restructuring them or supplying specific nouns.

1. In the area of household finance, Lena was sure too much was being spent on junk food, entertainment, and clothing.
2. The guards were told to be on the alert for any conflict situations.
3. We knew the aspect of greatest importance was the cost of medicine.

4. With the practiced eye of a determined shopper, he selected various foodstuffs and household supplies in quick succession.
5. A promise was made to her by the army concerning her becoming a soldier and learning the provisions of weaponry care.

Use effective verbs. Weak verbs sap your writing's strength. Use the most specific verb appropriate to your context. In general, look for direct, one-word, active, concrete verbs. Avoid overusing the passive voice and forms of the verb *to be*.

The passive voice can be effective now and then, but overuse dulls your writing. (See **14.**)

WEAK PASSIVE

The grapes were crushed by the peasants' feet.

REVISIONS TO ACTIVE

The peasants' feet crushed the grapes.

The peasants crushed the grapes with their feet.

Forms of the verb *to be* are central to our language, but since they merely tell the reader that something "is" or "was," they are not strong verbs.

WEAK *TO BE*

The man *was* a scavenger; he was often seen picking through the trash left by the roadside.

REVISED

The scavenger often *picked* through the trash left by the roadside.

The man, a scavenger, often *rummaged* through the trash left by the roadside.

Precise verbs give your writing power, as do exact nouns; meaning is condensed and writing becomes efficient. For example, read this simple sentence:

Jean went down the hall.

Maybe that is all you wish to say, but there is much you could reveal about Jean and the way she moved by selecting a more specific verb:

Jean tiptoed down the hall	Jean wandered
Jean staggered	Jean swaggered
Jean marched	Jean crept
Jean strutted	Jean ambled
Jean reeled	Jean stomped

There are many possibilities. Writing loses strength when writers fail to select the most effective verbs, but it loses both strength and interest when they select the most common, the most predictable, and the least informative.

41c Avoid archaic words and neologisms.

Archaic words have passed out of common usage but may appear in older texts or in special contexts. The dictionary labels such words as *obsolete*. Archaic words should be avoided unless you have a specific purpose for using them. Examples are words like *erst* (formerly), *anent* (about), *anon* (soon), and *fain* (gladly).

Words that have been created too recently to have come into common use are called *neologisms*. Some will become permanent parts of our language; some will not. *Brunch, fall-out*, and *space shuttle* are examples of ones that have. Whether words like *palimony* and *computerese* will become generally accepted remains to be seen. Use new words only if you are sure your audience will understand them easily and accept them in a particular writing situation.

In coining your own words, exercise extreme caution. It is usually better to use an existing word than to try to invent a new one.

41d Learn when jargon is appropriate and when it is not.

Jargon is the specialized vocabulary of a particular profession or discipline, but the word has come to mean the inappropriate use of such vocabulary with general audiences. Used with specialized readers, jargon is efficient and helpful. But when you are writing to an audience of nonexperts, the use of such language can be irritating, confusing, even incomprehensible. Technical terms might be fine for your physics professor, but for another audience, those same terms might be confusing. If it is necessary to use technical terms in papers for general audiences, you should define those terms.

UNNECESSARY JARGON

From a military point of view, your destination does not seem logistically accessible.

REVISED

The army doesn't think you can get where you want to go from here.

41e Avoid inflated diction.

Students often think their own language is inferior, that their vocabulary is insufficient, or that teachers will be impressed with long, obscure words. As a result, they turn to a thesaurus or dictionary and pick out impressive-sounding words. *Predict* turns into *prognosticate, use* becomes *utilization, rich* changes to *opulent, rank* is transformed into *prioritize.* In general, it is better to select the simple words. Pretentious words call attention to themselves. We do not suggest that you neglect adding to your vocabulary—just the opposite. But additions should become part of your working language, not just borrowed to impress an audience.

41f Avoid euphemism.

Euphemisms are inoffensive words substituted for offensive ones. In daily conversations we may wish to spare our own or others' feelings when discussing sensitive subjects like death, sex, or bodily functions. People *pass on* or *pass away* instead of *die* or *croak;* people *make love;* children *tinkle* or *have a bowel movement.* However, a problem arises when euphemisms are used to cloud the truth or mislead the reader. For example, during the Vietnam War government sources spoke of "pacification programs," which, in reality, meant the wholesale destruction of villages. Recently the MX missile was referred to as a "peacekeeper." You have an obligation to your readers to deal directly and honestly with your topic.

41g Avoid wordiness.

Unnecessary words make your writing sound loose and weak. Avoid adding extra words to reach an assigned paper length. Most instructors would prefer a shorter, concise and economical paper to a padded one. Condense expressions like the following:

WORDY	REVISED
at this point in time	now
for the reason that	because
due to the fact that	because
in American society today	in America

Loosely written sentences can almost always be condensed. Much depends on your purpose, of course: in other contexts *the President of the United States* could be shortened to *the President,* but in some contexts that change might produce an unwanted effect. The rule is not to cut every possible word but to cut every unnecessary word. In general, loosely written *wordy* sentences can be tightened with the following kinds of deletions:

LOOSE

Uncle Billy Bob was a man who liked to smoke cigars.

REVISED BY REDUCING A CLAUSE

Uncle Billy Bob was a cigar smoker.

Uncle Billy Bob smoked cigars.

LOOSE

We had a date for a movie at twelve o'clock P.M.

REVISED BY REDUCING PHRASES

We had a movie date at noon.

LOOSE

All of a sudden there was this great big explosion that scared the heck out of us.

REVISED WITH SINGLE-WORD SUBSTITUTES

Suddenly there was a huge, terrifying explosion.

REDUNDANCY

Redundancy is another kind of wordiness, stemming from the use of different words to say the same thing. It is redundant, for example, to write *past history*, since history is by definition "past." Other redundant expressions include:

rectangular in shape	disappear from view
orange in color	disregard altogether
basic essentials	revert back
separate and distinct	advance planning

WORD REPETITION

Sometimes writers unnecessarily repeat words within a sentence or in adjoining sentences. Avoid unnecessary repetition by finding adequate synonyms, using pronouns, or combining sentences.

REPETITIOUS

Charmain wanted to study ecology. Ecology is the study of the relationship between organisms and their environment.

REVISED

Charmain wanted to learn about ecology, the study of the relationship between organisms and their environment.

UNNECESSARY PASSIVE

The passive voice contributes to wordiness. It often takes more words to write a passive sentence than an active one.

PASSIVE

It was decided by the group to close shop. [nine words]

REVISED

The group decided to close shop. [six words]

ACTIVITY 9

Revise to eliminate wordiness.

1. Due to the fact that hang gliding gave him a sense of freedom, Ralph escaped from the city every weekend to go hang gliding.
2. At just about approximately 12 o'clock noon in the P.M. there was all of a sudden this enormous vehicle type of flying device thing which was huge in size and a round spheroid in shape which was seen by a small group of several people who were onlookers hovering over the Renaissance Center in Detroit.
3. The game of basketball is a game that is becoming more and more popular in Europe at this point in time.
4. The record was recorded by Michael Jackson, and it was a unique and different rendition of a song that had never been done before.
5. It was Professor Edwards who insisted that we stick to the basic essentials for the reason that the command which we had of more sophisticated material was less than expert.

---

cliché

41h Avoid clichés.

A cliché is a trite, overused expression that has lost its freshness and force, a ready-made phrase that requires little thought from you or your reader. Clichés are predictable: readers can usually complete the expression after hearing the first word or two. "Blind as a bat," "straight from the shoulder," "out of the blue"—these and other expressions like them ought to be "avoided like the plague."

Here is a partial list of clichés:

a chip off the old block
all walks of life
as happy as a lark
at the crack of dawn
better late than never
burn the midnight oil
conspicuous by its absence
crying shame
dire straits
easier said than done
few and far between
fine and dandy
good time was had by all
goes without saying
last straw
like water off a duck's back
makes my blood boil
nipped in the bud
off the beaten track
proud owner
rude awakening
selling like hotcakes
sink or swim
sneaking suspicion
straight and narrow
strike while the iron is hot
truer words were never spoken
truth is stranger than fiction

42 FIGURATIVE LANGUAGE

Figurative language makes a "figure," an "image" for the reader. Literal language is direct: it means exactly what it says; figurative language, on the other hand, stretches meaning to make a comparison. For example, a translation of "That guy eats like a pig" would be something like "That guy eats sloppily." The comparison, "like a pig," does not literally mean that he sticks his snout into the food, roots around, and grunts while ingesting huge amounts; but the comparison does suggest that his eating habits are very sloppy, like those of a pig. *fig lang*

42a Create effective metaphors.

A metaphor is an implied comparison. If you said, "The meeting was a zoo," the comparison is implied: it does not say the meeting is *like* a zoo, but the meeting *is* a zoo.

EFFECTIVE METAPHORS

The parking meters, urban pelicans, gulp quarters instead of fish.

The television set, a drug that lulls and pacifies, sapped her vitality.

42b Create effective similes.

A simile expresses a comparison directly, using the words *like* or *as*.

EFFECTIVE SIMILE

Aunt Mary's coffee pot, like a fountain of youth, brought movement back to aged limbs, activity back to her tired mind.

Max was attracted to the gambling table like a lemming to the sea.

42c Use effective personification.

Personification is a kind of comparison in which human qualities are attributed to animals, objects, or abstractions.

EFFECTIVE PERSONIFICATION

The video games called to him invitingly.

Don't fool with Mother Nature.

fig lang In general, make figurative language blend with your meaning; avoid overused comparisons, but use restraint. A simile or a metaphor should not call such attention to itself that it would distract the reader from your purpose.

EXCESSIVE FIGURE

The pencil slipped from his hand just as a soul slips from a dead body.

REVISED FOR RESTRAINT

The pencil slipped from his hand like a falling leaf.

42d Avoid using overstatement to make a strong impression on your reader.

Avoid overemphasis. Beware of writing in absolute terms, overemphasizing, and making dogmatic statements. Words like *always, never, most, least, best, worst,* and so forth should be used with caution.

It was a day I'll never forget. [How do you know what you will remember thirty years from now?]

She was the best woman who ever lived. [Do you know all the women who ever lived?]

Create emphasis with understatement. Sometimes it is better to use understatement than to overstate the obvious.

OVERSTATED

Poor old Mr. Ditters was laid out stone cold dead as a mackerel in his coffin, stiff as a board and ready for the grave.

UNDERSTATED

Mr. Ditters lay unnaturally quiet and unresponsive, a manikin in a box.

Avoid overusing intensifiers. Intensifiers are modifiers indicating degree. Intensifiers like *very, really, certainly, rather,* and so on, should be used with care. Overuse can give your writing an excessive, insincere tone. Often they suggest you have a limited vocabulary. *fig lang*

UNNECESSARY INTENSIFIERS

I felt really alive.

Are you perfectly sure?

INTENSIFIERS DELETED

I felt vigorous.

Are you positive?

Avoid overly dramatic modifiers. Sometimes writers try to force an impression on their readers by using excessively dramatic modifiers.

He had *incredible* strength and a *terrific* personality.

Her success was *fabulous* and her future *marvelous*.

Other words to avoid or use with care are *good, nice, wonderful, stupendous, fantastic, terrible, devastating, ghastly*, and the like. These overused words have been nearly drained of meaning; they indicate only positive or negative emotions.

WEAK

It was a terrible day.

She had this ghastly dress on.

REVISED WITH SPECIFIC MODIFIERS

The day was cold, rainy, bleak.

She was wearing an electric-green silk dress covered with little pink and yellow baby chicks.

ACTIVITY 10

Revise the overstatements and overused modifiers.

1. It was a fantastic book that I really liked a lot.
2. He's not real sure what to do with this perfectly terrible assignment.
3. Buffy was just devastated when she stepped on the ping pong ball and squashed it to bits; it was simply ghastly.

---

fig lang

42e Avoid unconscious echoes.

Sometimes, without realizing it, writers will produce rhymes and alliterations that become noticeable, and therefore distracting, to readers: *It made no sense; the album only cost ninety-nine cents; Sid's simple suggestion was certainly a sensible solution.* Read your paper aloud to find and revise unconscious echoes.

Paragraphs

¶/no ¶

43 EFFECTIVE PARAGRAPHS

A paragraph is a group of related sentences usually developing a single idea. Now and then paragraphs may consist of a single sentence; however, in formal writing, most contain several.

43a Recognize various paragraph structures.

A paragraph is a set of sentences related structurally; that is, the sentences fit together in a certain way: they have a relationship to one another.

Use topic + development structure. One common structure is "topic + development." The most general statement comes first, followed by specific detail and examples. (See "General to Specific" under Coherence.) For example:

TOPIC (GENERALIZATION)

Every detail of the cell interested me.

DEVELOPMENT (SPECIFIC INSTANCES)

Sleep fled, and when the peephole was not in use I studied it all furtively.

Up there at the top of one wall was a small indentation the length of three bricks, covered by a dark-blue paper blind.

They had already told me it was a window.

Yes there was a window in the cell.

And the blind served as an air-raid blackout.

Tomorrow there would be weak daylight, and in the middle of the day they would turn off the glaring light bulb.

How much that meant—to have daylight in daytime!

Aleksandr I. Solzhenitsyn,
The Gulag Archipelago, 1918–1956

Use development + topic structure. It is possible to turn the common structure around so that the developmental sentences come first and the topic sentence comes last. (See "Specific to General" under Coherence.) ¶/*no*

DEVELOPMENT (SPECIFIC INSTANCES)

The Chevy was wheezing and squealing and dipping alarmingly over its right front wheel on each revolution.

Every throaty roar from the muffler when Chingo pressed down on the pedal was followed by a sharp bang and a flash of blue fire out the tail pipe.

Raul's Firebird was hissing and spitting hot water and steam through the radiator and grinding and clanging with spine-jarring metal crunches through every gear.

TOPIC (GENERALIZATION)

Neither car was in any condition for a race.

Use coordinate structure. When the developmental sentences are merely added to the topic sentence (either before or after it), the paragraph has a coordinate structure; each of the developmental sentences is merely another illustration of the topic. To show that the developmental sentences are similar and have the same relationship to the topic, we have given each of them the same number in this example:

TOPIC (GENERALIZATION)

1 Dr. Howe devised a slate with type on which Laura could set up any word she wished to use, but shortly afterwards the manual alphabet was introduced.

DEVELOPMENT (SPECIFIC INSTANCES)

2 This alphabet consists of simple movements of the fingers of one person's hand upon the palm of another person's.

2 It was invented by a group of Spanish monks who had taken a vow of silence and used it to communicate without breaking the vow.

Joseph P. Lash, *Helen and Teacher: The Story of Helen Keller and Anne Sullivan Macy*

¶/no ¶ **Occasionally use an implied topic sentence.** When the developmental sentences clearly imply the idea, it is sometimes possible to leave the topic sentence unstated. The readers are permitted to make the generalization themselves (after the writer has made it fairly obvious). For example:

> 2 In San Francisco, the police department began issuing plastic resuscitation devices and rubber gloves in response to officers' fears that they might be infected during the course of first aid work.
>
> 2 In Los Angeles, some medical personnel refused to care for infected patients, and laboratory technicians worried that they could contract the disease by handling blood samples and transfusions.
>
> 2 And in New York, employees at a major national shipping company refused to handle a shipment of blood and biopsy specimens when they noticed the return address was marked "AIDS Foundation"—an independent research group that is delving into the Acquired Immune Deficiency Syndrome, a deadly disease that has already claimed 520 lives and shows every sign of claiming untold more.
>
> "The AIDS Hysteria," *Newsweek*, 30 May 1983, p. 42

We have labeled these sentences *2* because they are all second-level examples of an implied topic sentence ("There is a growing hysteria over AIDS"). Since the examples make the point almost too obvious, there is no need for a topic sentence here.

Use subordinate structure. In the subordinate pattern, each developmental sentence adds only to the sentence immediately above it. To show that each developmental sentence is of lower (or subordinate) level, we have given each one a different number:

TOPIC (GENERALIZATION)

1 In Mexico roadrunner meat is sometimes eaten.

DEVELOPMENT (SPECIFIC INSTANCES)

2 It is prescribed as a medicine by curanderos, or folk healers, in recognition of the bird's formidable ability to digest poisonous animals.

3 In the town of Ojinaga in Chihuahua, Crispina Gonzales de Martinez, a 92-year-old curandera, told me that tuberculosis could be cured by eating a stew of roadrunner meat, onions, tomatoes, and garlic. ¶/*no* ¶

4 This elixir is also good for backaches, itches, boils, lung problems, and leprosy, she claimed.

Martha A. Whitson, "The Roadrunner, Clown of the Desert," *National Geographic*, May 1983, p. 702.

Note that each sentence refers to something in the sentence above it. Sentence 2 (an instance of the bird being eaten) comments on sentence 1, the topic sentence. Sentence 3 adds to sentence 2, describing a medicinal stew to be made with roadrunner meat; and sentence 4 adds other diseases the stew will cure.

ACTIVITY 1

Explain the subordinate structure of the following paragraph. How should its sentences be numbered? Why?

From behind a tree a trumpeter stepped to the edge of the ring. Blowing on a make-believe bugle he sounded a call and the bull rushed in—a boy with a plain serape over his shoulders, holding with both hands in front of his chest the bleached skull of a steer complete with horns. Between the horns a large, thick cactus leaf from which the thorns had been removed, was tied. It was at the cactus pad that the matadors and picadores aimed their wooden swords and bamboo spears.

Ernesto Galarza, *Barrio Boy*

Use mixed coordinate-subordinate structure. The most common pattern is a mixture of coordinate and subordinate structures. In a mixed pattern, some of the sentences are similar and bear the same relationship to some sentence above them; other sentences are subordinate and add only to the sentence immediately above themselves. For example:

¶/no ¶

TOPIC (GENERALIZATION)

1 The tall grass of the Hill Country stretched as far as the eye could see, covering valleys and hillsides alike.

DEVELOPMENT (SPECIFIC INSTANCES)

2 It was so high that a man couldn't see the roots or the bottoms of the big oaks;

3 their dark trunks seemed to be rising out of a rippling, pale green sea.

1A There was almost no brush, and few small trees—only the big oaks and the grass, as if the Hill Country were a landscaped park.

2 But a park wasn't what these men thought of when they saw the grass of the Hill Country.

3 To these men the grass was proof that their dreams would come true.

4 In country where grass grew like that, cotton would surely grow tall, and cattle fat—and men rich.

4 In country where grass grew like that, they thought, *anything* would grow.

Robert A. Caro, *The Years of Lyndon Johnson; The Path to Power*

In this example by Caro, there are several levels of coordination and subordination. The third sentence ("their dark trunks seemed to be rising out of a rippling, pale green sea") was introduced with a semicolon. The fourth sentence we have labeled *1A* because it reintroduces the idea of the first sentence and includes the ideas in the second and third sentences. The whole paragraph has a subordinate structure, but the last two sentences, labeled *4*, are coordinate.

43b Make sure your paragraphs are coherent.

Make sure each sentence relates to the main idea in a paragraph and that the relationship between one sentence and another is clear. A paragraph is incoherent at any point where the reader is unable to follow the progression of ideas.

Coherent paragraphs have a unified idea. A paragraph is a unit; it develops a single idea. Without a unifying idea, your paragraph becomes a series of unrelated sentences. There should be nothing irrelevant in your paragraph, and the unifying idea should be obvious to your readers. ¶/*no* ¶

INCOHERENT PARAGRAPH

> The computer is a very useful device today. The future of technology is now upon us. Typical home computers have as much as 64K of memory. Even though you may not have much math aptitude, you will find that you can understand most computers today. Many companies are now offering machines at very low costs. One of the biggest and best known companies is IBM. The heart of the computer is the silicon chip, which makes it all possible.

The writer might claim that this paragraph is "about" computers, but it is really only a loose collection of sentences on the subject of computers; it has no *central* idea. Each of the sentences in this paragraph could start a separate paragraph. To revise a paragraph like this, you must reconsider the point you are trying to make; is the paragraph to be about uses of computers, about cost, about silicon chips? Revise your paragraphs until each one contains a single idea to which every sentence is related.

Use topic sentences to increase paragraph coherence. The topic sentence states what the paragraph is about. One of the simplest ways to show your readers that a paragraph is both unified and coherent is to write it with a topic sentence. Topic sentences can appear first, last, or in the middle of a paragraph. Not every paragraph needs a topic sentence, but obviously one way to help your readers follow the thread of your ideas is to use topic sentences.

In the following paragraph, we have italicized the topic sentence:

> *Animals that we do not use for food also act as carriers of radioactive particles.* A study at the Hanford Reservation showed, for example, that jackrabbits had spread radioactivity over a wide area. They picked up the material by burrowing near trenches where radioactive waste was buried. They obvi-

¶/no ¶

ously ate or ingested some of this material, since traces of radioactive isotopes were found in their feces. Such traces were also found in the feces of coyotes and the bones of dead hawks—animals which had apparently eaten the radioactive jackrabbits.

Dr. Helen Caldicott, *Nuclear Madness*

ACTIVITY 2

Outline the paragraph by Caldicott above to show the relationship of the ideas.

ACTIVITY 3

Analyze for topic sentence. Where is the topic sentence in the following paragraph? How can you tell? Explain the relationship of the sentences in this paragraph. What is its structure?

As a businessman, I was a bit surprised to learn that the handgun industry markets its products just like any other business, despite the fact that the product is potentially deadly. A typical handgun moves from the factory to the street almost as if it were toothpaste or chewing gum. By paying a modest license fee, a manufacturer buys the right to produce and sell handguns. There are no restrictions on quantity, quality, or size. Beyond minimal recording and reporting requirements, little else is required to keep the license. The manufacturers sell the handguns to dealers, who pay only a $10 annual licensing fee to sell to the public.

Pete Shields with John Greenya,
Guns Don't Die—People Do

Use transitional signals to help the reader follow your ideas. Not every sentence needs a transitional signal; the more closely related your ideas are, the less you will need other signals. But the transitional signal is a good device to use any time you want to revise for greater coherence and readability. Remember, though, that transitional signals cannot add coherence if the sentences themselves are not related. Note the use of time signals in the following paragraph:

Shortly after noon we arrived back at the smoking oven and dumped a truckload of corn into the hole. *Then* we covered it for the night. *Next day at dawn* Susanne and I met the three of them at the oven. ¶/no ¶

Jake Page and Susanne Page, "Inside the Sacred Hopi Homeland," *National Geographic*, November 1982, p. 613

STANDARD TRANSITIONAL SIGNALS

FOR ADDITION

again, also, and, and then, besides, finally, first, further, furthermore, in addition, lastly, moreover, next, second, secondly, too

FOR COMPARISON

also, as, by the same token, in comparison, likewise, similarly, then too

FOR CONCESSION

after all, although it is true, at the same time, granted, I admit, I concede, naturally, of course, while it is true

FOR CONTRAST

after all, although, and yet, but, by contrast, however, nevertheless, on the contrary, on the other hand, otherwise, still, yet

FOR EXAMPLES AND ILLUSTRATIONS

by way of illustration, for example, for instance, incidentally, indeed, in fact, in other words, in particular, specifically, that is

FOR RESULT

accordingly, as a result, consequently, hence, in short, then, thereafter, therefore, thus, truly

FOR SUMMARY

as I have said, in brief, in conclusion, in other words, in short, on the whole, to conclude, to summarize, to sum up

FOR TIME

afterwards, at last, at length, hence, immediately, in the meantime, lately, meanwhile, of late, presently, shortly, since, soon, temporarily, thereafter, thereupon, while

¶/no ¶ **Repeat key words and concepts to help the reader follow the development of your paragraphs.** You can gain coherence within (and between) paragraphs by repeating key words, ideas, synonyms, and pronouns. In the following paragraph, we have marked several different kinds of repetitions. The italicized words indicate the subject of the paragraph, *the box*. The parentheses indicate the specific transitional signals for sequential order. And the chain of pronouns referring to the box is marked in bold print:

> With his own hands he had made a *gift* for her at school, a small wooden *box*. At first glance **it** appeared somewhat crude. (First), **its** hand-sawn edges were not quite perfect, the bottom piece being the most uncertain. (Then too), one of the wire brads that held **it** together had gone in at an angle, leaving a sharp protrusion. (Secondly), the little brass hinges for the lid were slightly misaligned so that the lid didn't quite fit right. (And finally) the lacquer that covered **it** had gone on a little unevenly so that in spots **it** was still sticky. (But all things considered), she said, he had made a fine *box*.
>
> Elaine Meyers, "The Gift"

ACTIVITY 4

What coherence techniques are used in the following paragraph? Mark the paragraph to highlight the techniques.

> While it's true that a computer is a very complex piece of technology, it is a machine that really does only three very simple things; it adds, subtracts and moves numbers electronically from one place to another. Before it can do these things, though, it has to get the numbers from somewhere. It may also have to permanently store the numbers it will work on—or the results of its calculations—somewhere else. It must know what its user wants it to do, which means it must be able to understand instructions and sequences of instructions. Finally, it has to present its data to its user in a form the user can understand, which means the machine must have communications capability.
>
> "Now about That Computer," *Computer Buyer's Guide and Handbook*, Guide No. 11, p. 9

Use transitional sentences to increase coherence between paragraphs. One way to increase coherence between two paragraphs is to provide a transitional sentence, either at the end of one or the beginning of the next one. For example: ¶/*no* ¶

> Until recently, the two dominant forces in the home videogame world were Atari and Mattel. If a consumer was looking for something inexpensive or simply wanted the most variety of games published, the Atari Video Computer System was the choice. If, on the other hand, a higher level of graphics was important or the enthusiast simply craved the best sports simulations available, Intellivision was the intelligent choice. *But, with the introduction of ColecoVision all this has changed.*
>
> "The Game Machines Grow Up,"
> *Computer Buyer's Guide and Handbook*, p. 158

Although the paragraph is a comparison of Atari and Mattel's Intellivision, it ends with a reference to ColecoVision. The last sentence is a transition to the next paragraph (and the rest of the article), about ColecoVision.

43c Develop each paragraph logically and fully.

A plan of development helps the reader follow the sequence of ideas. You must develop your paragraphs based on the overall purpose of your composition. There can be many variations on developmental plans; nearly anything is possible as long as the reader can follow what you are doing. The following plans are standard:

TIME ORDER (CHRONOLOGICAL/NARRATIVE)

Begin at the beginning and proceed to the end, or begin at the end and " flash back" to the beginning. Many stories begin *in medias res*, "in the middle of things." As long as the reader can follow the order of events, many different time orders are possible. Use transitional devices and other techniques to help the reader follow.

¶/*no* ¶

POSITION ORDER (SPATIAL/DESCRIPTIVE)

Much depends on the effect you are trying to achieve. For dreamlike or surrealistic images, random details may work. But for informative writing you need a plan the reader can understand. Select a point of reference and then move in an orderly fashion away from or toward the observer. That is, describe the farthest objects first and then describe those closer to the observer, or start with those closest to the observer and then move in a clockwise fashion, and so on.

ORDER OF IMPORTANCE (CLIMACTIC)

Only one plan really works when presenting ideas, examples, illustrations, or arguments. Since they have no "natural" order; begin with the least important and end with the most important idea. It is possible to write a paper with some other plan (ending with the weakest point, perhaps), but experience tells us that it is best to end on a strong point.

GENERAL TO SPECIFIC (DEDUCTIVE)

In paragraphs with topic sentences, it is common to have the topic sentence first, followed by the specific examples or details that illustrate it.

SPECIFIC TO GENERAL (INDUCTIVE)

It is possible, though less common, to present the specific details first, leading up to the generalization at the end of the paragraph. Sentences about Agatha Christie, Helen MacInnes, and Marjorie Allingham, for example, might lead to a generalization about mystery writers.

Specific details help to develop each paragraph fully. A difficult problem for writers concerns the amount of information in each paragraph. A paragraph is "underdeveloped" when the reader feels there is not enough information. It is not enough to make general statements; you must supply specific details for the reader, usually the more the better. Most of us have seen rocket launches, and therefore only a detailed description is likely to interest most readers. For example:

> Far in the distance, almost out of sight, like an all-but-transparent fish suddenly breaking into head and tail, the first stage at the rear of the rocket fell off from the rest, fell off and was now like a man, like a sky diver suddenly small. A new burst of motors started up, some far-off glimpse of newborn fires which looked pale as streams of water, pale were the flames in the far distance. Then the abandoned empty stage of the booster began to fall away, a relay runner, baton just passed, who slips back, slips back. Then it began to tumble, but with the slow tender dignity of a thin slice of soap slicing and wavering, dipping and gliding on its way to the floor of the tub. Then mighty Saturn of the first stage, empty, fuel-voided, burned out, gave a puff, a whiff and was lost to sight behind a cloud. And the rocket with Apollo 11 and the last two stages of Saturn V was finally out of sight and on its way to an orbit about the earth. Like the others he stayed and listened to the voices of the astronauts and the Capcom through the P.A. system. ¶/*no* ¶
>
> Norman Mailer, *Of a Fire on the Moon*

How much detail is enough? How specific must the details be? Rough-draft paragraphs are more likely to be underdeveloped than overdeveloped. The amount of development depends on the impression you are trying to make. Mailer is trying to recreate his *impression* of the launch to help the reader experience the sensations of actually witnessing the launch. However, in a paper on the costs of the space program, a very different description might be written.

43d Start with an effective introduction.

An introduction should raise the reader's interest, it should introduce the thesis or topic of your paper, and it should form a transition to the rest of your composition. If you have trouble getting started, you may find it easier to skip over the introduction until later, after you have completed your rough draft. But when you come back to work on the introduction, be generous with the care and thought and work you put into it.

¶/*no* ¶

INTRODUCTORY STRATEGIES

CONTRAST OR REVERSAL

Explain what people should *not* do, for example, in a paper on buying a home computer.

DEFINITION

Explain the legal definition of *malpractice* in a paper on patients' rights.

DESCRIPTION

Describe the great damage of the mudslides of Utah in a paper on homeowners' insurance.

DRAMATIC INCIDENT

Describe the explosion of the *Challenger*, in a paper on space industries.

HISTORICAL BACKGROUND

Give the history of the various sightings of "Nessie," starting with AD 565, in a paper on the Loch Ness Monster.

QUESTION OR PROBLEM

Start immediately with the thesis question and expand on it, or ask some other relevant question. For example, ask whether arms reduction can be forced by arms increases in a paper on the arms race.

QUOTATION

Use a relevant quotation from your research or from a book of quotations or some well-known source like the Bible.

REFUTATION

Discuss the misconception that old age is a time of mental and physical decrepitude in a paper on age discrimination.

SETTING THE SCENE

Describe the effects of napalm attacks on the jungles of Vietnam in a paper on the ethics of warfare.

TELLING A STORY

Narrate a brief personal experience with a car wreck, for example, in a paper on highway safety.

UNUSUAL FACTS AND FIGURES

Give some figures on America's changing ethnic patterns in a paper on immigration policies.

FAULTY INTRODUCTORY STRATEGIES

Empty introductions. It is a mistake to write an introduction that seems to wander or only vaguely specifies the thesis. The finished introduction should not give the appearance of a writer thinking out loud. The introduction has serious work to accomplish, and you must revise until it is as interesting and informative as you can make it.

One-sentence introductions. Almost as bad as the empty introduction, the one-sentence introduction also gives the impression of an author unable to find a beginning. Such one-sentence introductions are almost never as effective as carefully thought-out, well-developed beginnings.

Lazy introductions. Some writers assume that the reader knows things, and therefore the writer can take short-cuts. Even though the subject may have been assigned by an instructor, your paper must stand on its own. There should be no references to "this assignment" or "an assignment like this." The introduction should not be written with the assumption that the reader has read the title of the paper. The title is not part of the introduction, and there should be no implied references to information in the title: "*This* is an interesting subject" or "*These people* have a fascinating history."

Self-conscious introductions. It is a mistake to call attention to yourself as the writer: "I don't know how to begin this, so I'll just start" or "I'm not really an expert on this subject, but I'll do my best." Such beginnings sound apologetic at best and start the paper on the wrong tone; at worst they sound immature.

Cute introductions. Most educated readers find the writer's efforts to be "cute" insulting. Serious papers that start

¶/no ¶ with inappropriately droll stories or highly imaginative beginnings ("Have you ever imagined what it might be like to have a long sticky tongue for catching flies?") usually produce a dour reaction.

43e End an essay with an effective conclusion.

The word *conclusion* has two meanings; one is simply "the end." And it is necessary to find an effective way to end your composition. But it also means "a deduction." Your paper must not only reach an end, it must come to some *conclusion*. The conclusion is never merely an ornament stuck on the end of a paper; it is the *point* of the paper. Save something for your conclusion. Conclusions that are too short or weak neither end nor deduce well enough.

CONCLUDING STRATEGIES

CALL FOR ACTION

End a paper on waste in government by urging readers to write to their representatives about it.

CONTRAST OR REVERSAL

End a paper on fad diets by contrasting medical advice on healthful dieting.

DRAW A DEDUCTION

After presenting data on the question of whether marijuana is harmful (for example), draw a deduction based on the facts. A deduction is not an opinion; it is a *necessary* conclusion, based on the data.

DISMISS OPPOSING IDEA

End a paper on rape by dismissing the myth that some victims enjoy it.

FINAL ILLUSTRATION

End with a good example, story, or argument. It is sound advice to save something for the conclusion; don't use up all your good material in the body of the paper.

PREDICTION

End a paper on the competition between American and Japanese automobile manufacturers by predicting what may happen in the future.

QUOTE RELEVANT AUTHORITY OR SOURCE

End your paper on modern warfare with a relevant quotation from the Bible, for example.

RELEVANT QUESTION

End by asking (and answering) the thesis question or some other related question. For example, in a paper on the MX missile, end with the question—If we do gain a temporary nuclear superiority over the Russians, how long will it last?

REVIEW OF MAIN POINTS

A brief review of main points makes a good beginning for a conclusion that will analyze and evaluate the evidence in a paper.

RETURN TO THE BEGINNING

If a paper on the whaling industry (for example) starts with a description of blue whales peacefully swimming, the ending can bring back this peaceful scene as a hope for the future.

FAULTY CONCLUDING STRATEGIES

One-sentence conclusions. Few one-sentence conclusions sound effective, especially in formal papers. In personal experiences, occasionally the one-sentence ending may work for humor, irony, or mystery. But for reports, research papers, and other impersonal kinds of writing, the fully developed ending is almost always preferred.

Summaries. The summary ending is a cliché—so overworked that it amounts to a fault in many cases. A brief review of main points is always permissible, especially in a long

¶/*no* ¶ or complex paper; but in shorter papers, the ending that does nothing more than restate what has already been said is likely to disappoint readers.

Tacked-on moral or lesson. Obviously, nothing should appear "tacked-on" in an effective composition. Avoid telling readers what they are supposed to "learn" from your composition. ("So you can see that it is very dangerous to go hunting with a borrowed gun.") Such endings give the appearance of forcing the obvious on the reader.

Contrived endings. "I woke suddenly; it had all been a dream!" Past a certain age, few readers care for sudden, implausible, "hokey" endings. Such endings suggest the writer has abandoned his or her commitment to the reader and instead of a forceful ending has settled for something "amusing" or "clever."

Self-conscious endings. "I guess I should end this. . . ." "Well, I can't think of anything else to say, so. . . ." Such references to yourself as writer can only produce an immature tone. Few readers will appreciate having their attention called away from the subject matter of your composition toward you as author.

Introduction of new subjects. The function of the conclusion is to bring the paper to an end; this is not the place to introduce a new subject. For example, a paper on the dangers of nuclear waste should not end with the sudden introduction of "other dangers" like possible meltdowns or nuclear terrorists.

Reasoning

44 EFFECTIVE EVIDENCE

To reason about anything, you must analyze and interpret information, weigh evidence, and reach conclusions. Conclusions should not be merely your personal opinions about the subject; if you use standard reasoning procedures, your readers should agree with your conclusions.

44a Use sound reasoning to evaluate evidence.

We reach conclusions and make judgments in one of two ways: inductively or deductively. Given a number of similar experiences, we make generalizations about those experiences. For example, if you begin to sneeze and itch every time you are near a cat, you may eventually conclude that you are allergic to cats. This is called *inductive reasoning*, the process of moving from specific instances to a general rule. However, once you have arrived at a general conclusion, that you are allergic to cats, you then apply it to new instances. You enter a room in which there is a cat, and you know that you must keep away from it if you are to avoid itching and sneezing. This is called *deductive reasoning*, the process of applying the general rule to particular instances.

These two processes represent the basic ways people reason. Notice that in the inductive method you can arrive only at various degrees of probability, not at absolute truth. You have, in the example, experienced only some, not all, cats. Inductive reasoning, then, is based on the reliability of the evidence and on the conclusions you draw from that evidence.

On the other hand, deductive reasoning relies on the truth of the generalization and on how that generalization is applied. This method is based on the *syllogism*. A syllogism contains a major and a minor premise, which when properly stated, lead to a conclusion. For example, "All dogs like bones. Rover is a dog. Therefore Rover will like bones." The syllogism is often stated in abbreviated form: "Rover will like this bone,

I am sure, because all dogs like bones." The syllogism is valid, even though one of the premises has been left unspoken (Rover is a dog). *Valid* means that the syllogism is properly constructed: the major premise makes a statement about all members of a group, and the minor premise identifies a member of the group. Therefore, whatever is true of the group must be true of its individual members. The syllogism can be *valid* even if we use fantastic premises. For example, "All dogs can fly. Rover is a dog. Therefore Rover can fly." The syllogism is valid because the premises are properly stated. If it were true that all dogs could fly, we would have to conclude that Rover too can fly. Thus *valid* only means *logical*, stated according to the rules of logic. *True*, on the other hand, means *real*, agreeing with reality.

ACTIVITY 1

Identify the following statements as *inductive* or *deductive*.

1. First Marjorie told me, then Larry told me, and now you are telling me: apparently everyone knows my secret!
2. American warships have the most sophisticated electronic equipment in the world; it should not be possible to hit one with a missile.
3. Athletes need a special diet, so you better not eat that donut if you want to play basketball.
4. Everyone I know likes Michael Jackson, so you probably will like him too.
5. Podiatrists, proctologists, ophthalmologists—there must be a medical specialist for every part of the human anatomy!

ACTIVITY 2

Identify the following statements as *valid* or *invalid*.

1. Our dog hates cats, so you better keep your Siamese inside.
2. I'm sure Benny's grandmother can bake a chocolate cake for us; all grandmothers can bake chocolate cakes.
3. All students are interested in education; you are interested in education; therefore you are a student.

4. Students enjoy time off from studies, and since you are a student, you will enjoy spring break.
5. All bankers worship money; Mr. Quimby is not a banker; therefore he does not worship money.

44b Follow standard procedures for evaluating primary and secondary evidence.

Primary evidence is first-hand data. If you conduct experiments, collect answers to a questionnaire, or do other "hands-on" research, you have primary evidence. If you read books and articles about other researchers' work, you have secondary evidence. Both kinds of evidence must be carefully evaluated.

Determine the distribution of evidence. In general, the more evidence there is, the more credible it becomes. In arguments for which there is good evidence on both sides, the weight of the evidence becomes the determining factor. If there is more evidence on one side than on the other, most people will conclude that the "heavier" side is correct.

Evaluate the sources of evidence. Reliable sources written by experts and aimed at educated readers have more credibility than popular sources aimed at general audiences. Professional journals like *College English*, authoritative works like the *Oxford English Dictionary* and the *Encyclopaedia Britannica*, highly respected newspapers such as the *New York Times*, and magazines like *Time* and *Harper's* are credible sources. Other publications, such as small local newspapers, movie magazines, and encyclopedias designed for children should generally be avoided in college work.

Some kinds of evidence are less reliable than others. Information gathered through questionnaires, for example, is often questionable. Respondents frequently are self-selected and may not be typical of the general population. Respondents sometimes say whatever they believe the researcher wants to hear. Many respondents fail to understand the questions. Frequently only a small percentage of those asked respond.

Use timely data. Research is cumulative; recent studies usually subsume older ones. In order to be sure your information is current, always use the most recent data possible. Your research must begin where you are; work backwards from today's date when collecting information.

Determine the relevance of data. Objective papers have no room for side issues. Use only material that is clearly relevant to your thesis.

Distinguish between "probable" and "certain" data. Most investigations today, especially in secondary research, use only probable data and reach probable (versus indisputable) conclusions. For most of the investigations undertaken in school, you can only hope for reasonable or probable results.

Use statistical data with care. Avoid statistical generalizations such as "most students prefer to wear blue jeans"; use the exact statistic instead (75 percent of students in our sample were wearing blue jeans). Follow standard procedures when collecting statistical data; make sure your sample population is representative of the entire population, and make sure the sample is large enough to support your conclusions. It is a good idea to present statistical data in charts.

Define the terms in your research. Research cannot reach valid conclusions unless the terms are clearly understood. When necessary, define key terms. When reading, make sure your sources all mean the same thing when they use similar terms.

Accept the simplest explanation. Researchers must remain skeptical of strange or bizarre assumptions. "Occam's Razor," the rule of simplicity, requires that researchers accept the simplest explanation, the explanation that requires the fewest assumptions. Thus you should resist assumptions about monsters, ghosts, or supernatural phenomena until you have very convincing proof.

Remain impartial. Objective investigations require impartial investigators. You should not undertake research for the purpose of "proving" you are correct; researchers must be prepared to accept whatever conclusion the data indicate.

Avoid research questions in which you have a personal interest, or any biased research question or procedure.

Evaluate "common knowledge" carefully. Common knowledge is information widely known among educated people. But students must not assume too much "common" knowledge. Any and all information you acquire from source material must be documented, whether it is common knowledge or not. Only information certain to be well known by most educated people should be treated as "common knowledge."

Do not mistake assumptions, inferences, or premises for facts. Assumptions are basic, fundamental beliefs. We assume that animals will die if they consume enough toxic materials. Inferences are deductions or conclusions based on data. We infer (conclude) that the animals did die because they ate the toxic substance. If the animals did not die, we would not change our assumption; we would suspect our inferences about the toxic material were inaccurate (i.e., it wasn't really as poisonous as we thought, or the animals didn't eat as much of it as we thought). It takes much more evidence to change an underlying assumption than to change an inference.

Premises are the ideas or questions being tested in research; a "premise" is a "hypothesis." In the rat experiment, the premise may be that given *n* quantities of toxic substance *x*, rats will die. None of these beliefs about toxic substances and animals is a "fact."

Facts are objective data; we test facts by referring to reality. What was in the food? How much was present? Did the rats actually eat it? How much did they eat? Factual data must be observable by the senses or testable by physical means—chemical analysis, observation of rat behavior, autopsies on dead rats.

ACTIVITY 3

Identify the possible error in each of the following statements as confusion between primary and secondary sources, faulty distribution of evidence, unreliable source, ambiguous terminology, outdated material, Occam's Razor, biased researcher, faulty assumption of common knowledge, irrelevant data, confusion of probability with certainty, improper use of statistical data, or mistaking assumptions, inferences, or premises for facts.

1. The candidate wanted to discuss issues like the economy, foreign policy, and national defense, but the reporters kept asking about his personal relationship with his beautiful young secretary.
2. Since the zoo's large python was found in the cage that had held two white rabbits, no one suspected that the rabbits had been stolen.
3. I have found some excellent articles written in 1980 about America's space shuttle, and since they are so good I shouldn't need any other information.
4. I plan to write a research paper proving that addictive drugs should be legalized for the good of society.
5. The basis of my research is the answers to a questionnaire sent to a thousand students.
6. Since you have had one car accident, you are not allowed to take the car, because you may have another.
7. It is not possible to discuss the morality of bombing "innocent civilians" until we can distinguish between "terrorists" and "freedom fighters."
8. Because the dead man had been found decapitated, a bloody ax in his right hand, in a room locked from the inside, the police listed his death as a suicide.
9. After reading an interview in *TV Guide*, we can conclude that the actor Tom Selleck is a heck of a guy.
10. Because I saw a bright light hovering above our house, heard a humming noise, and suddenly felt strange, I am convinced that what I saw was a UFO.

---

45 VALID ARGUMENTS

In dealing with everyday matters, most people generalize freely and draw conclusions based more on intuition and experience than on facts and logic. However, you must be on guard against them in the sources you read and in your own writing.

45a Avoid fallacies caused by insufficient evidence.

Avoid making large, unsupported generalizations. Many errors in reasoning arise from making generalizations based upon too little evidence. This problem, often called a *hasty generalization*, occurs when it is assumed that what is true of one person or in one situation is true of all people or all similar situations. Do not generalize from the few people you know to "people in general" or "most people" or "everyone." It is an overgeneralization to say that "most people prefer light entertainment to heavy drama." Even if you believe such a thing, there is no way to verify it. Limit your generalizations to what you actually know: "most of my friends prefer light entertainment to heavy drama"; "of ten students who were asked, nine said they preferred light entertainment."

Do not select only data that support your conclusion. Ignoring evidence that challenges or contradicts your opinion is "cardstacking." It means stacking the deck (stacking the evidence) so that only one conclusion is possible. If you are interested in whether cigarettes cause cancer, you must not disregard evidence about people who have smoked all their lives without getting cancer. You must account for *all* the evidence, not just that which supports your thesis.

Do not argue from negative premises. Avoid reasoning that something must be true if we cannot prove it false; nor should we reason that something must be false if we cannot prove it true. Reasoning on the basis of what we do not know is called *argumentum ad ignorantium*. The fact that we cannot prove whether extraterrestrials have or have not visited earth should not be the basis for any conclusion.

Avoid faulty cause-and-effect reasoning. Do not assume that one thing causes another just because one follows the other. Arguing that one event must have been caused by a preceding event solely on the basis that one happened after the other is called the *post hoc ergo propter hoc* fallacy (literally, "after this, therefore because of this"). One thing *may* cause another, but there is no *necessary* relation between events that follow each other in time.

45b Avoid fallacies caused by irrelevant information.

Avoid attacks on the source of an idea. Avoid suggesting that an idea is not good because the person who gave it is not good. It should be possible, for example, for criminals to have good ideas about law and crime prevention, despite their personal behavior. Attacks on the person instead of on his or her ideas is called *argumentum ad hominem* (literally, "appeal to the person").

A related fallacy is called the *genetic* fallacy; it suggests that ideas coming from places we dislike or think inferior must be bad ideas. A good idea can be valid no matter where it comes from. Ideas that come out of Russia, for example, should be judged on their merit and not their origins.

Another related error is called *guilt by association:* assuming that anyone who associates with those we dislike must be as bad as those we dislike. It should be possible for loyal, patriotic Americans to have friends who are Communists without being suspected of being Communists themselves.

Use emotional appeals with restraint in objective writing. Descriptions or pictures of starving people, wounded soldiers, sick children and so forth play on human emotions. Such appeals are called *argumentum ad misericordiam* (literally, "appeal to pity"). There is nothing wrong in arguing that we should help the unfortunate, but using pathetic material to persuade people is an error. Most people feel such appeals are manipulative; they make us feel guilty. Raising guilt in those you are trying to persuade often backfires; they become angry instead.

Avoid sloganeering and other appeals to popular senti-

ment. Using traditional or popular slogans such as "my country right or wrong" forces people to respond to group identity. Appealing to popular sentiments or prejudices is called *argumentum ad populum* (literally, "appeal to the people"). Politicians who campaign with slogans about the goodness and wisdom of the American people are using *ad populum* appeals.

A related fallacy is called *bandwagon*, arguing that an action or idea is good if many people approve of it (an appeal to group pressure). Some bandwagon appeals are described in *plain folks* language: plain, ordinary people eat hamburgers and pizza, not quiche. Other bandwagon appeals are described in *snob* language: if you want to be an important person, you must wear designer clothes.

Avoid citing inappropriate authorities. When experts are quoted, you must be sure they are really experts. Often celebrities who have no real expertise are quoted. Frequently experts in one field are quoted as if they were authorities in some other field. Using inappropriate authority is called *argumentum ad verecundiam* (literally, "appeal to authority").

Avoid arguing something other than the main point. A *straw man* argument is one in which you create some generalization to attack instead of the specific point of the argument. In an argument about the costs of education, for example, you may be tempted to create a "straw man" called "the modern student." Then you can attack this straw man, instead of the main question, the cost of education. ("The modern student is lazy and doesn't deserve education. The modern student doesn't use the education already available, so further costs are unnecessary.")

A related fallacy is the *red herring* argument. Instead of arguing the main point, writers may sometimes switch to a minor or secondary point. Then when the writer proves or disproves the minor point, it looks as if the argument has been won.

Avoid excuses based on what others do. The fact that others may cheat on their income tax is no justification for your doing it. This argument is called *tu quoque* (literally, "you also").

45c Avoid fallacies caused by ambiguity.

Avoid circular reasoning. In *circular* reasoning, the same idea appears in both subject and predicate: "The reason it is so hot today is that the temperature is so high." Circular reasoning is also called *begging the question*, meaning that instead of answering the question we have only restated it in different form. For example: "We know it is winter because it is no longer fall." Or, "Criminals should be punished because what they do is against the law."

Avoid misusing the definitions of words. Word meanings and connotations can be misused. The word *religious*, for example, can refer to piety, the study of the bible, or membership in a church. But it can also mean "dedicated," "persevering," "conscientious," as in the sentence "We study our computer manuals religiously." The sentence means only that these computer users are serious about their work, working hard to learn; it does not mean that they "worship" the computer. Arguing over the meanings of words or misusing their meanings is called *equivocation*.

Do not use false metaphors or false analogies. The two things being compared in a metaphor or analogy often are not very similar. For example, "War in Central America would be like the war in Vietnam, an endless struggle that we could not win." Only if Central America and Vietnam are very similar will this analogy be valid.

Avoid ambiguous language and data. You must avoid misusing implications. "Nine out of ten athletes prefer Gatorade" implies that 90 percent of all athletes have expressed an opinion, but that seems very unlikely. Using ambiguous terms or concepts is called *amphiboly*.

45d Avoid fallacies caused by faulty reasoning.

Avoid asking complex questions. Complex ("loaded") questions are worded so that they are not safe to answer. "Do you still take drugs?" Whether the answer is yes or no to this question, the speaker appears to be a drug-user. Often such questions are worded as "complex issues": "The President's inability to make decisions has pushed us to the brink of war with Russia." You must first determine whether the President is indecisive, then whether we are in fact on the brink of war, before you can attempt to connect the two ideas.

Avoid using either/or reasoning. A dilemma offers only two equally unattractive options. Arguing that we must *either* raise taxes *or* suffer an economic recession creates a *false dilemma.* The dilemma can sometimes be valid but only when there are truly only two possibilities.

Avoid conclusions that do not follow from your premises. Stating conclusions that do not necessarily follow from the premises is called *non sequitur* reasoning. The term is used any time the audience cannot "follow" or analyze how the speaker reached his or her conclusion. For example, "Since the window is open and letting in cold air, we may as well open the door too." Or, "Smith was seen going into the Courthouse: he must have committed some crime."

Avoid making excuses or giving self-serving explanations. Excusing yourself by blaming others is called *rationalizing.* For example, "I could have done better on the test, but it was too hot in the testing room." Or, "It isn't my fault that the cup fell and broke; someone left it where I was bound to hit it."

Avoid extending arguments to ridiculous conclusions. Do not attempt to defeat an idea by extrapolating or extending it until some absurd conclusion is reached. For example, "One vitamin pill is supposed to be good for you, so I will have even more good by taking two pills, and perhaps I shall gain even more by taking several; and no doubt I will gain the greatest good by taking the entire bottle." Extending an idea in this way is called *reductio ad absurdum:* the idea is reduced to an absurdity by extending it beyond reason.

ACTIVITY 4

Identify the fallacy in each of the following statements. In some cases there may be more than one possible answer.

1. First it was learned that the U.S. had sold missiles to Iran, Iraq's enemy; then an Iraqi plane fired two missiles at an American warship: it's obvious that the two events were connected.
2. Butter pecan is the most popular ice cream flavor; therefore, you will probably like it.
3. The President is the father-figure of our nation, and we must all be obedient children.
4. Seventy-five percent of the women in our survey said they would date older men.
5. The congressman was asked whether he would ever give up his foolish reliance on the President's shaky promises.
6. There is no more serious problem than feeding the hungry, but look at the quality of welfare food. We should not spend another dime on fatty beef, excess corn, and generally unappetizing meals.
7. The reason smuggling is called a crime is that it is illegal.
8. Lloyd has been hanging around the computer nerds lately; I think he may be turning into one himself.
9. If you love America, don't knock it.
10. Because the President was unavailable, the reporters interviewed his wife about the latest developments in our foreign policy.
11. There's no use asking Alicia where to party; she's a total drip.
12. The senator must be a poor speaker, because after he had spoken all across the country, he lost the election.
13. How can you accuse me of reckless spending when your own spending is as wild as anyone's?
14. Since we don't know who ate all the candy, we will punish everyone in the room.
15. All elephants are dangerous creatures.
16. Either you like modern art, or you hate it; there is no middle position.
17. Our young soldiers have come home without arms and legs, blinded, suffering mental disorders; we owe them our charity.
18. This must be an excellent book since it was written by a famous professor at one of our greatest universities.

19. I'm failing my Earth Science class, but it's only because the professor dislikes me personally.
20. Our cows kept injuring their tails on the rough boards in their stalls, until my father solved the problem by amputating their tails.

Writing Assignments

46 RESEARCH PAPERS

There are many different kinds of writing situations that call for research papers of one sort or another. In general, they all call for the use of evidence to substantiate a thesis and the use of documenation to show where you found the evidence. Research papers test your ability to analyze, evaluate, and draw conclusions from evidence. You will not be asked to come up with a startling new discovery; however, if you proceed systematically and carefully, much of the difficulty of research can be reduced, and you can teach yourself to become an independent researcher.

46a Begin your search for a specific, limited research question.

If your instructor has not given you a specific research question, you can use the assignment to study a field that interests you. Use the writing process to begin thinking about broad areas that are generally familiar to you. You should not select totally unfamiliar subjects, but neither should you select "old hat" subjects you already know thoroughly. Start your search by listing general areas that might yield workable topics: the President, the economy, nuclear weapons control, human rights, education, history, religion, business, or other broad fields. (See **1a-d.**)

Narrow a general topic to a specific research question. You cannot write a paper "about" Israel; you must narrow your focus to some question that not only interests you but that also may interest your readers. After you have decided on a general subject, begin to brainstorm. (See **1d.**) Ask yourself questions about the subject. You can ask the journalist's questions—*what, when, how, where, why?*—to get yourself started. If, for example, you are concerned about the environment and have in mind a general idea about pollution, the following are some preliminary questions you could ask yourself:

What is *pollution?*
What do my readers need to know about pollution?
What kind of pollution is most disturbing to me: air, water, chemical, nuclear, a combination?
What have I heard about pollution or read recently that made a particular impression on me? (Why pick this subject?)
What did it have to do with dioxin? acid rain? PBB?
What do I know about each one of these?
What are the observable effects of each?
What are the intangible—moral, ethical, psychological—effects?
Can I discuss or find out about a particular geographical area where one of these pollutants has appeared?
What causes pollution?
Who causes pollution?
Who is supposed to monitor pollution problems?
What's being done about it?
What should be done about it?
How can I find out more?

From a general concern about pollution, you must narrow your focus to a specific problem with dioxin in Midland, Michigan, or Times Beach, Missouri, for example. A good research paper must be thorough, a detailed analysis of a worthwhile question, and that is why you must find a very limited question—one you can investigate fully (See **1e-f.**)

Before deciding exactly what your research question should be, let the research itself help you. Go to the library; do some preliminary reading on the subject. Your preliminary reading will help you to see what other researchers have already done. You can determine from preliminary reading what is *worth* researching.

ACTIVITY 1
Select a general subject area you would like to research. Write out a list of every possible question you can think of related to your subject.

46b Use a search strategy to build a master bibliography.

The master bibliography is a researcher's tool; researchers attempt to discover all the evidence that has ever been published on their subject. A master bibliography can contain hundreds of items. For most school work you need not be so exhaustive, but you do need to find as many books and articles as you can for your master bibliography. From this material you will later produce a working bibliography, a much more concise list of materials actually used in your paper.

There are two kinds of research evidence: primary and secondary. *Primary evidence* is first-hand data, evidence collected in experiments, field work, "hands-on" data. *Secondary evidence* is published information about the research others have done. Most library material is secondary evidence, but the library does have some primary material. If you are writing about a novel, for example, the novel itself is the primary evidence; what critics have said about it is secondary evidence. If you are researching Louis, Mary, and Robert Leakey's anthropological work in Kenya's Olduvai Gorge, their writings are primary sources; anyone else's writings about them are secondary sources.

Start with general sources first. In order to build a working bibliography, plan a *search strategy.* The simplest search strategy usually starts with the most generalized sources and proceeds to more specialized ones. In general, this means (1) starting with the general encyclopedias, almanacs, and dictionaries for background material; (2) checking any specialized encyclopedias, bibliographies, or handbooks that may apply to your topic; (3) using first the general and then the specialized indexes for magazine, journal, and newspaper articles; (4) and finally, perhaps, using the card catalog to find books and other sources. It may be a good idea to leave books until later in your search, after you have built up some background familiarity with the subject. This advice, of course, depends on your subject and on your own level of expertise.

The point is to be systematic, plan your search strategy, and then stick with it.

46c Use reference materials: almanacs, dictionaries, encyclopedias, periodical indexes, computer data bases, card catalog.

In addition to general encyclopedias like the *Americana*, *Britannica*, and *Collier's*, there are many special encyclopedias, dictionaries, and almanacs you should investigate. For example:

ALMANACS, DICTIONARIES, ENCYCLOPEDIAS

Current Biography, 1940–
Dictionary of American Biography, 1928–37; supplements 1944–1980
Dictionary of American History, 1976–78
Encyclopedia of Philosophy, 1967
Encyclopedia of Religion and Ethics, 1908–27
Encyclopedia of World Art, 1959–1968
Facts on File; a Weekly World News Digest, 1940–
Information Please Almanac, 1947–
The Mythology of All Races, 1916–32
New Grove Dictionary of Music and Musicians, 1980
Oxford English Dictionary, 1888–33, and supplements
Statistical Abstract of the United States, 1878–
Webster's Third New International Dictionary, 1976
World Almanac and Book of Facts, 1868–

Use periodical indexes to find newspaper, magazine, and journal articles. Most journals, magazines, newspapers, and other periodicals are indexed and kept up to date with supplements. You can find recent magazine and newspaper articles by looking up subject headings in the index. Two helpful general indexes are the *Readers' Guide to Periodical Literature* and the *New York Times Index*. The *Readers' Guide* lists articles from over one hundred magazines; entries are by subject, author, title, and cross-references that suggest related information. For example:

READERS' GUIDE ENTRY

TELEVISION stations, Black
TV first at Howard [first television station owned and operated by a black university; WHMM] I. J. Poole. Black Enterprise. 11: 22+ D '80.

This entry shows that under the heading "Television stations, Black" there is an article, "TV First at Howard," described in brackets and written by I. J. Poole in volume 11 of the magazine *Black Enterprise;* the article starts on page 22 and has more than one page (+); it was published in December of 1980 (D '80).

The *New York Times Index* refers to articles that have appeared in that newspaper from 1913 to the present. For example, in the *New York Times Index* for June 16 through June 30, 1981, you will find the following:

NEW YORK TIMES INDEX ENTRY

CABLE Cars
Dean Havron article recounts ride in cable car up rocky summit of Pico Bolivar, Venezuela's highest peak; travel tips; illustrations; map (L), Je 28, X, p.1.

This entry shows that under the heading of "Cable Cars" there is a listing for an article by Dean Havron. The entry gives a brief description of the article, indicates other information in the article, tells you that it is a long (L) article (over two columns), and that it appeared on June 28, section 10 (X), page 1.

Check the front of each index for an explanation of its system of symbols and abbreviations. In addition to the general indexes, there are many others. For example:

SPECIAL INDEXES

Applied Science and Technology Index, 1958–
  Previously titled *Industrial Arts Index*, 1913–57
Art Index, 1929–
Biography Index, 1946–
Biological and Agricultural Index, 1964–
  Previously titled *Agricultural Index*, 1919–64

Book Review Digest, 1905–
Book Review Index, 1965–
Business Periodicals Index, 1958–
Current Index to Journals in Education, 1969–
Education Index, 1929–
Engineering Index, 1884–
Essay and General Literature Index, 1900–
General Science Index, 1978–
Humanities Index, 1974–
Previously titled *Social Sciences and Humanities Index*, 1965–73, and *International Index*, 1907–65
Index to Legal Periodicals, 1908–
Music Index, 1949–
Nineteenth Century Readers' Guide to Periodical Literature, 1890–99
Poole's Index to Periodical Literature, 1802–1906
Public Affairs Information Service Bulletin, 1915–
Social Sciences Index, 1974–
Previously titled *Social Sciences and Humanities Index*, 1965–73, and *International Index*, 1907–65
United States Government Publications: Monthly Catalog, 1895–

SOCIAL SCIENCES INDEX ENTRY

Television and children
See also
Television advertising and children
Television programs–Children's programs
Lessons from videogames and media: effects on the young [symposium] bibl *J Commun* 34:72–167, Spr '84
Sex-role differences in children's identification with counter-stereotypical televised portrayals. B. Eisenstock. bibl *Sex Roles* 10:417–30 Mr '84

This entry suggests under the heading "Television and children" that the researcher might also look under two other headings in the index, "Television advertising and children" and "Television programs" under the subheading "Children's programs." Two articles are listed: one is in the *Journal of Communication* and appeared in volume 34 on pages 72 through 167 in the spring of 1984. The article was of corporate authorship (symposium), and it contains a bibliography (bibl). Full names of journals to which abbreviations refer can be found in a list at the front of the index. The second article was written by B. Eisenstock and appeared in volume 10 on pages 417 through 430 of the March 1984 publication of the journal *Sex Roles*. It also contains a bibliography.

ELECTRONIC INDEXES AND COMPUTERIZED DATA STORAGE

Your library may have a *computerized card catalog*. Operating the terminal usually requires nothing more than typing in an access number and the title or author of a book.

ERIC (Educational Resources Information Center) is a computerized data bank for teachers and students studying to be teachers. Find ERIC documents in *Current Index to Journals in Education* and *Resources in Education*. ERIC documents can be ordered in hardcopy (print) or microfiche (explained below).

If you have ever spent time thumbing through the *Readers' Guide* or the *New York Times Index*, you will appreciate the great speed and ease with which you can use *microfilm indexes*. The *Magazine Index* covers many of the popular or general magazines; furthermore, many of the current issues covered in magazine articles have already been researched for you in "Hot Topics," a monthly bibliographical printout. The *National Newspaper Index* covers papers like the *Christian Science Monitor*, the *New York Times*, and the *Wall Street Journal*. The *Business Index* covers several hundred magazines, journals, and newspapers. The *Legal Resource Index* covers law journals, law newspapers, and other publications relevant to law. Some libraries now offer computer searches to students. For a small fee you can get a computer-generated bibliography on nearly any subject.

Learn to use *microform readers*. Most libraries already have material in microform (microfilm on reels or spools, and microfiche, microfilm in small sheets the size of an index card). Back issues of newspapers and magazines for example, are often kept in microform. If you discover, for example, in researching the problems of the American steel industry that an important article, "Big Steel's Winter of Woes" by Christopher Byron, which appeared in *Time* magazine on January

24, 1983, is in microfiche, it is an easy matter to go to the microfiche catalog, locate *Time* (the entries are arranged alphabetically and by date), and read the article.

MICROFICHE CATALOG ENTRY

Time		
New York, N.Y.	Vol. 121 Issue:4	Fiche: 1 of 2
January 24, 1983	Pages: 1–92	ISSN:0040-781X

The entry says that the microfiche contains pages 1 through 92 of the January 24, 1983, edition of *Time* magazine and that there is another "fiche" that contains the rest of that edition (one of two).

Use the card catalog to find books and other materials. The card catalog is the major guide to a library's books, classified three ways: by subject, title, and author. Before using the catalog, you will save yourself time and effort if you find out first how your subject is listed. Find the *Library of Congress: Subject Headings.* Go through the *Subject Guide,* looking under likely headings. For example:

Occultism in literature
sa Mysticism in literature
Supernatural in literature
x Occultism
xx Mysticism in literature
Occult sciences
Supernatural in literature

This entry shows that "Occultism in literature" is not found under "Occultism" (*x* in this case means error). The *Subject Guide* tells you to see also (*sa*) "Mysticism in literature" and "Supernatural in literature." It also shows you that there are other headings in the *Subject Guide* (marked *xx*) that are cross-referenced to this entry. Not only does the *Subject Guide* save you time and effort with the catalog, it can also give you many ideas for research by showing you how to analyze various subjects.

Figure 46-1 shows a subject card from the card catalog.

FIGURE 46-1 Card Catalog Subject Card

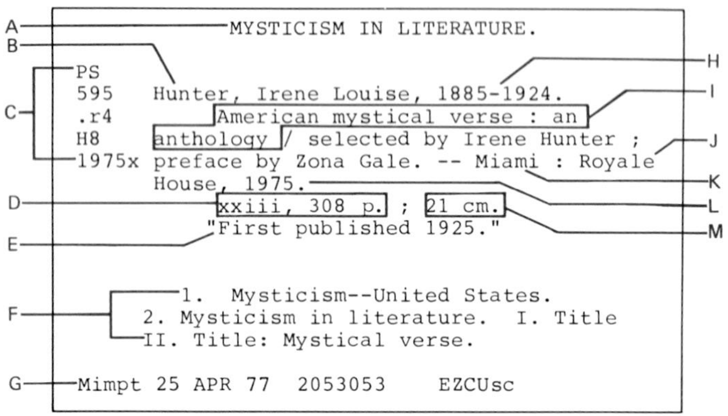

A. Subject heading
B. Author's name
C. Library of Congress call numbers
D. Number of preface pages and number of pages
E. Publishing history
F. Other cards for this book
G. Library information for ordering catalog cards
H. Author's birth and death dates
I. Title
J. Publisher
K. Place of publication
L. Date of publication
M. Height of book in centimeters (1 centimeter = .04 inch)

Cards in the "Author" and "Title" sections contain the same information except that the former is headed with the author's name and the latter with the title of the book.

As you examine the cards, be selective. Information on the card will often suggest whether the book may be useful. The title is not necessarily descriptive of the contents of the book. If chapter headings are listed, see how they relate to your topic. Look at the date of publication. The book may be too old for current information but may be useful as background or history. If the book looks promising, record its author and title, the place and date of publication, and the call numbers on an index card.

46d Begin preliminary reading and begin compiling a bibliography.

Make an index card for each source that looks useful. This is your working bibliography, to be revised as your research continues. The 3 × 5 index cards work best.

At the top of the card write full bibliographical information: author, title, place of publication, and publisher; if dealing with a magazine, date, and page numbers (figure 46-2). See also bibliography forms on pages 306–311.

FIGURE 46-2 Bibliography card, for a book (Heng and Shapiro) and a magazine (Farrell)

Heng, Liang and Judith Shapiro. Son of the Revolution. New York: Alfred A. Knopf, 1983.

Farrell, Robert E. "The Dark Side of Henry Kissenger." Business Week 25 July 1983: 9.

Follow the researchers' rule: find the most recently published material. Proceed from the most recent material backward. Avoid hopping around in the research; some material may be unavailable when you go to the library, but you must make sure that in the end your references cover the time period from the most recent backwards. Remember that books may be recalled or ordered from other university libraries.

ACTIVITY 2

Using the subject you chose for activity 1, or another if you prefer, go to the library and conduct a thorough search. Write bibliography cards for at least a dozen sources, preferably more. See pages 306–311 for model bibliography entries.

46e Take notes that summarize, paraphrase, or quote exactly.

Use a separate note card for each fact you find and write only on one side. (See figure 46-3.) Code your note cards to correspond with your bibliography cards: place the author's name in the upper-right-hand corner to refer to the card containing the bibliographical information. If you have more than one work by the same author, you can create a number code that refers to author and work. In figure 46-3, for example, the Farrell card is coded 5-1; the number 5 has been assigned to the author Farrell, and the number 1 indicates that the material comes from the first of two or more works by him. Sort and label your cards according to the divisions of your research.

Read source material critically. Be selective in reading your sources. Look at chapter headings and the index to find relevant material. The first time through, read quickly, *looking for* information, facts, opinions, examples that relate to your topic.

Record significant information on note cards. Limit your note-taking to material that is important in answering your research question. Use one card for each idea or fact, and give a page number for each idea, fact, or direct quote you put down. Use your time in the library to read and *assimilate* material. When you find useful material, write in your own words a shortened version of what it says. (See Paraphrases and Summaries below.) The less you copy, the more you will have to use your own words for your notes. The more you use your own words, the more you will have to think about what your sources are saying.

When you are taking notes, extract only the relevant data. Restate information and ideas as you understand them. Quote only when the information is important in its original form—for example, statistical data, the exact wording of a document, or an especially well-written statement of explanation. If you decide to quote from a source, copy the material *exactly* and make sure you indicate page numbers. Put the

FIGURE 46-3 Coding for note cards

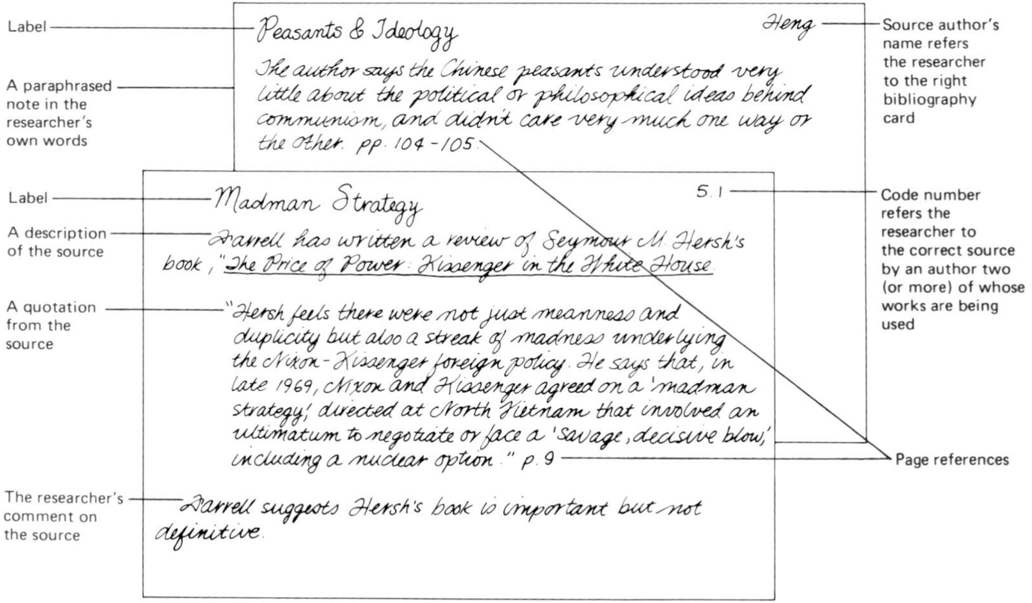

Label
Peasants & Ideology
Heng
Source author's name refers the researcher to the right bibliography card
A paraphrased note in the researcher's own words
The author says the Chinese peasants understood very little about the political or philosophical ideas behind communism, and didn't care very much one way or the other. pp. 104-105.
Label
Madman Strategy
5.1
Code number refers the researcher to the correct source by an author two (or more) of whose works are being used
A description of the source
Farrell has written a review of Seymour M. Hersh's book, "The Price of Power: Kissenger in the White House.
A quotation from the source
"Hersh feels there were not just meanness and duplicity but also a streak of madness underlying the Nixon-Kissenger foreign policy. He says that, in late 1969, Nixon and Kissenger agreed on a 'madman strategy,' directed at North Vietnam that involved an ultimatum to negotiate or face a 'savage, decisive blow,' including a nuclear option." p. 9
Page references
The researcher's comment on the source
Farrell suggests Hersh's book is important but not definitive.

material in quotation marks so that there will be no doubt that it is quoted. (See section **29** for guidelines on quoting.)

PARAPHRASES AND SUMMARIES

A *paraphrase* restates the material of the original in approximately the same number of words. All the information contained in the original is included but in different language. When writing a paraphrase, you may need to use some of the key terms from the original, but in general, make sure you use your own words and sentences. Remember, too, that you must give a reference note.

A *summary (or précis)* condenses the original. Generally only the most important points are recorded; examples, digressions, and so forth may be omitted. You must cite the source and use your own words.

ORIGINAL

A piece of liver is suspended from the top of a wire-cage so that the liver rests on the floor inside the cage, loosely held by a thread. A hungry cat in the room with the cage, but outside it, sees the liver and walks over to the cage. It hesitates for a time and its head moves up and down as though studying the string. Then it jumps on top of the cage, catches the string in its mouth, raises the liver by joint use of mouth and paw, and leaps down with the meat at the end of the string in its mouth.

Arthur Koestler, *The Act of Creation*, p. 570

NOTE-CARD SUMMARY

Koestler

A piece of liver hangs from a thread inside a wire cage. A cat outside the cage studies the string and then jumps on the cage and pulls up the liver with its mouth and paw. (570)

SUMMARIZED INFORMATION IN A PAPER

Koestler indicates with a story about a cat that animals possess problem-solving intelligence. In the experiment, a cat quickly solves the puzzle of how to retrieve a piece of liver attached to a string inside a cage. After studying the problem briefly, the cat hops up on the cage and draws the meat up using its mouth and paw (570).

The idea must be documented with Koestler's name and the page reference, so that readers will know where the information came from. It must have a bibliography reference.

NOTE-CARD PARAPHRASE

> Koestler
>
> Koestler uses a thread to suspend a bit of liver inside a cage. A cat entering the room sees the liver, approaches the cage and appears to think about the problem of how to get the meat. After a while, it jumps on the cage and pulls on the string with its mouth and paw, raising the liver. It retrieves the meat and jumps down with it in its mouth. (570)

The paraphrase may pick up some of the key terms, but essentially it must be in your own words.

PARAPHRASED INFORMATION IN A PAPER

Faced with a puzzle in which liver is tied to a string inside a cage, Koestler's cat seems to look the situation over briefly, and then solves the problem by jumping onto the cage and pulling the string up with its mouth and paws (570).

ACTIVITY 3

Using a long paragraph or two or three short ones from a magazine, write a highly condensed summary of it in two or three sentences. Then write a paraphrase of the same material.

46f Conduct research to develop, and then answer, a thesis question.

Having read a number of sources, it is time to decide exactly what your paper will accomplish, what question it will answer. If you have examined a narrow, two-sided issue and looked at the material on both sides, evaluate the evidence and determine which side, if either, is the stronger. The general rule is that when your thesis question can be discussed thoroughly and answered based on the data you have found, your central research has been completed.

46g After completing the central research, begin to put the paper together.

Since students are limited by time and resources, there must come a time to stop (or do less) researching and start putting the paper together. While writing the paper, you may need to research small, specific subpoints, but that does not mean you should delay beginning to put the paper together.

Organize your material: make a working outline. Gather together notes on the same topic or subtopic, grouping the cards into coherent sections. Organize your points in order of importance, from least to most important. Construct a preliminary outline based on the organization of your notes. List the major divisions along with their subdivisions to establish what ideas you will be dealing with and what supporting material you have. Incorporate any shifts or changes of focus into your outline.

If you are required to turn in an outline with your finished paper, you may place it ahead of the paper. However, especially if you do not have a title page, you may wish to place the outline last, after the bibliography (check with your instructor). The title of your paper should appear on your outline, regardless of where the outline itself appears. There are several kinds of outline styles, but the roman outline is standard. (See section **2d.**) Your outline will help you decide whether you have enough research to support your conclusion.

Evaluate the evidence. You must evaluate your sources, examine contradictions, examples, conflicting statements, and the logic in your data. (Review sections **44,** Effective Evidence; and **45,** Valid Arguments.) Be critical. Ask yourself, for example:

1. Is there enough material on each point? Will this amount of information seem convincing?
2. What are the assumptions and implications in the research?
3. How old is this information? Are these the most recent data?
4. Who are the authorities? Has the information come from recognized experts writing in respected publications?
5. Are the terms defined clearly; are all the sources using the terms the same way? (If not, you may have to clarify for the reader.)
6. Is all the information relevant?
7. If there are statistical data, do you understand what they mean? How they were gathered?

8. What are the relative merits of the arguments: which are stronger, which less significant?

Write a descriptive title. Most research papers do not require a title page (check with your instructor), but if you do use one, center the title, your name, and other identifying information in the middle of the page. Without a title page, place all identifying information and the title on the first page of your paper itself. Research titles should be descriptive and informative; often the research thesis or question is the title. Avoid vague, inaccurate, or amusing titles.

Write an effective introduction. The introduction should appeal to reader interest and make clear what the paper is about. (See section **43d** for introductory strategies.) In the introduction, state the thesis or ask the thesis question. The question can come first, thus informing the reader immediately of the purpose of your paper; or the question can come last, forming a transition to the body of your paper. The introduction sets the tone for the rest of the paper.

Present the evidence. Organize the information in order of importance—ending with the most important. Present concessions to the opposing view first. Making concessions establishes that you have researched the issue thoroughly, not just hunted for material that supports your thesis. Conceding worthwhile opposing positions also establishes your credibility: a researcher must be impartial, pointing out strengths and weaknesses on both sides of an issue.

You should not assume that the reader will follow you, inferring the relationships between ideas. As you move from one thing to another, give the reader a signal: *then too, however, on the other hand, nevertheless.* (See section **43b** for other transitions.)

The heart of any research paper is the evidence, facts, and details. A research paper is usually a compilation of material, and there is no need to hide that fact. You cannot have too much documentation (references). It is possible to have too many direct *quotations*, but you can reduce this number by using more summarizing, more paraphrasing, more extracting of data from sources—as long as you give references. But you cannot present the reader with unassimilated data. You must tell the reader what the data mean, show the reader how to weigh the evidence. You are not required to "prove" anything: your job is to discover information, analyze it, and evaluate it for the reader. Even though it may all seem perfectly obvious to you, you must not assume the reader can understand.

Write an effective conclusion. The conclusion of a research paper is the culmination of everything that precedes it. In the conclusion you must answer your thesis question, and you must help the reader understand *why* you reach your conclusion. It isn't enough, for example, to say, "This evidence shows that it was unwise to give the Panama Canal to Panama." You must help the reader understand why this is the correct conclusion. Review the main points for your readers. Save something for the conclusion—a final example, or quote, or something else that will give strength to the end of the paper. (See section **44e.**)

46h Use illustrations, drawings, tables.

Use drawings, charts, or tables, but keep them simple. (See figure 46-4.) If they are small, they can be inserted into the paper where you mention them. If they will not fit (you must not have part of an illustration on one page and part of it on the next) or if there are several of them, put them at the end of the paper, after the conclusion, in an appendix.

Draw figures in ink, using a ruler and compass for straight lines and curves. Type in any words. Tables of numbers should be done on the typewriter. All figures should be self-explanatory; but explain them anyway, and make sure to position them after, not before, the explanations. Figures need a descriptive label underneath: *Fig. 1 Diagram of Stress Patterns in Steel.* Tables of numbers should have a label (caption) above:

Table II

Numbers of Athletes Earning High Salaries

If the drawing or table is based on one in a source, or if it is one you create using figures from a source, you must identify the source directly below it.

FIGURE 46-4 Sample of a figure with a footnote

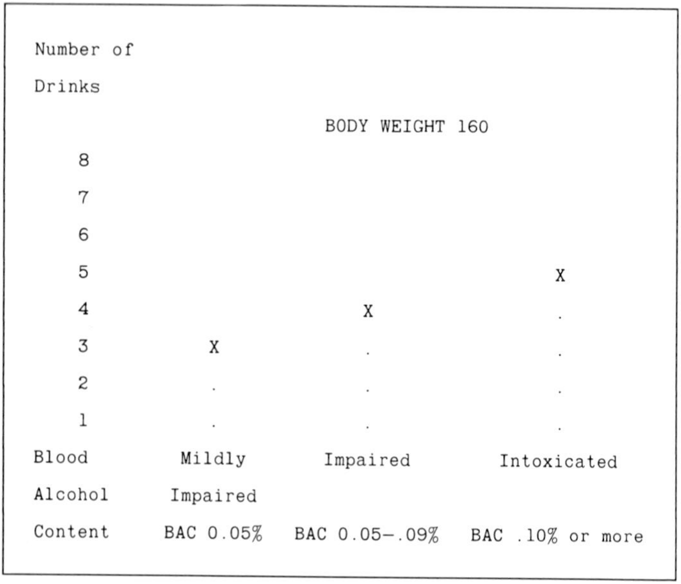
Number of
Drinks
BODY WEIGHT 160
8
7
6
5
4
3
2
1
X
X
X
Blood
Alcohol
Content
Mildly
Impaired
BAC 0.05%
Impaired
BAC 0.05–.09%
Intoxicated
BAC .10% or more

Fig. 1 Alcohol Impairs Driving, Figures from Consumer's Report, Aug. 1983: 353.

46i Avoid plagiarism: document all evidence.

Document everything. Paraphrases, borrowed words, even ideas need a reference. The only exception to this rule concerns so-called common knowledge, information most educated people should know or could easily verify with general reference materials. For example, if you wrote that Sally Ride was the first American woman in space, that might not require a note. If, however, you paraphrase her views on the evolution of the stars, you must show where you found the information. Experts talking to other experts may assume a great deal of "common knowledge," but students writing for a general audience must be careful. When in doubt, give a reference.

Do not document whole paragraphs of paraphrased material. It is better for every sentence to have a reference than to mislead the reader. If the last sentence of your paragraph requires a reference, write the sentence so that the reference falls inside the sentence. If you must use a whole paragraph or more of source material, do not paraphrase: *copy* the material in an indented quote. (See **29e.**)

Supply clarifying information in content notes. A content note contains explanatory information. Usually such notes are not essential but can be helpful if they clarify small points for your reader. Treat content notes as endnotes. Mark the information in your paper with a superscript (a raised note number) and put the note itself on a separate "Notes" page at the end of your paper. (See an example of a content note on p. 9 of the model research paper.)

Provide a bibliography. Two widely used documentation styles—those of the Modern Language Association (MLA) and the American Psychological Association (APA)—use the limited bibliography. That is, the bibliography contains only those sources actually cited in the paper. Anything not actually used in your paper must be excluded from the bibliography. The bibliography appears at the end of the paper and is called *Works Cited* in MLA style and *Reference List* in APA. (There are significant differences between the two styles, many of which are discussed in this section.)

Do not plagiarize. Plagiarism is the use of someone else's ideas or words without giving credit. You are free to copy, paraphrase, summarize, and use source material as long as you document it. There is no rule in research that says you should not quote much or you should not use source material much. The source material is the evidence, and you cannot have too much evidence, *as long as it is fully documented.* The following, however, are not acceptable:

1. Copied material *without quotation marks* is plagiarized. (See **29a, 29c-e** for quotation guidelines.)
2. Summarized or paraphrased material *without documentation* is plagiarized.
3. Borrowed ideas *without documentation* are plagiarized.
4. Paraphrased material that is *too close to the original* is plagiarized.

Plagiarism violates the operating principle of research: the only way researchers can use secondary materials is to keep clear at all times which are the words found in the source material and which are the words of the researcher who is writing the report.

ORIGINAL

> Writing a program amounts to making a listing of very exact instructions in a language "understood" by your computer. The fundamental language understood by any computer is called "machine language." This is not a good language for people, however, so higher level languages like BASIC have been invented.
>
> Thomas Dwyer and Margot Critchfield, *A Bit of Basic*, p. 14.

PARAPHRASE TOO CLOSE (PLAGIARISM)

```
To write a program you must make a list of very exact
instructions in a language your computer understands.
The fundamental language understood by your computer is
its machine language. But machine languages are not
good languages for people, and therefore higher level
languages like BASIC have been devised (Dwyer &
Critchfield, 14).
```

The more terms and concepts taken from the original, the more the paraphrase looks like copying. Here the "paraphrase" is very close to the original; without quotation marks it looks like the writer is claiming most of this for his or her own, even though a reference has been given. The writer should have quoted Dwyer and Critchfield directly here.

46j Understand how to use MLA in-text documentation.

TEXT REFERENCES

The documentation style introduced by the Modern Language Association in 1984 replaces footnotes or endnotes with in-text references. Enough information is given in the text (the research report itself) so that a reader can find the source in the Works Cited list. Thus, much documentation can be reduced to an author's name:

> In a recent study, Bellmont found no occurrences of anorexia.

Direct quotations can be identified with a parenthetic reference to name and page number:

> Certainly no one can favor "the imposition of a foreign policy backed with the threat of warfare" (Masters 97).

This in-text style does away with notes (except for content notes to the reader). Learn how to incorporate documenting information smoothly into your writing just as you learn to incorporate the words and ideas of your sources. Follow these guidelines:

Use author's name. Most of your references should give the author's name in your text instead of in a note.

According to Adolph Kline, the world's oil reserves cannot last another century. This assumption is sharply rejected by Richardson, who insists there is enough oil to last forever.

Give all authors' names unless there are more than three authors.

That we can never be too critical of public figures is the point made by Anderson and Boyd in Confessions of a Muckraker.

The idea of "resource wars" was first suggested in 1945 (Horton, Peters, and Rigby).

For more than three authors, give only the first name followed by *et al.*

A good source for the student is Literary History of the United States (Spiller et al.).

For authors with the same last name, give full names in your text, or give the authors' initials in a reference note.

According to Alan Withers, the new nonfiction amounts to a journalistic art.

In the opinion of at least one writer, the new nonfiction is a journalistic art (Withers, A.).

If you use authors with the same last name and the same initial, give full names.

But Adrian Withers asserts that the problem of art in journalism raises serious questions about objectivity and the nature of truth in reporting.

Use name and title. If there is more than one book by the same author in your bibliography, you must include the titles in your references.

In <u>World Resources</u>, Burford suggests that wars over the world's dwindling resources will begin early in the next century, an idea he repeats in <u>The Approaching Global Holocaust</u>.

Use page numbers. When making reference to a specific part of a source, you must give a page number in the reference. When the page number comes at the end of your sentence, the sentence period should be placed after the parenthesis. Note that page numbers are not identified with *p.* or other markers. If additional references are made to the same source, you need only the page number. Do not precede page numbers with a coma.

Mrs. Ellson's letter alleges that her husband was "a brute, a savage brute" (Horton 57). Later (78) she accuses him of having an affair with her sister. The sister, Elvira Clay, says of Mrs. Ellson, "Nell was so jealous of him, she imagined he had affairs all the time" (Denning 102).

Use shortened titles. To keep references as brief as possible, shorten titles, but make them unambiguous so that the reader can recognize them in the Works Cited. For example, additional references to Burford's work could use shortened forms:

We will run out of oil first, he says (<u>Resources</u> 81). And, since we view oil as a military resource, the United States may be first to resort to warfare (<u>Holocaust</u> 213).

For references to books of the Bible, use standard abbreviations.

"He that hath an ear, let him hear what the Spirit saith unto the churches. . ." (Rev. 3.11).

For references to plays, poetry, or other works with numbered sections or lines, give all the relevant numbers that would help a reader find the source: section, part, act, scene, line. Do not use *l.* or *ll.* for *line, lines.*

"O, what a rogue and peasant slave am I!" (Hamlet II.ii.534).

The line is from the play, *Hamlet*, act two, scene two, line 534. You may use arabic numerals if you prefer: 2.2.534.

"An aged man is but a paltry thing, / A tattered coat upon a stick. . . " ("Byzantium" 9–10).

The lines are from Yeats' "Sailing to Byzantium," lines 9 to 10.

Note: The sentence period follows the note in these short examples. Long (more than three lines) indented quotes are treated differently: the parenthetic note falls outside the last sentence, after the sentence period.

WORKS CITED LIST

The Works Cited lists entries alphabetically, the first line of each entry starting at the left margin, the second (and all subsequent) lines indented five spaces. Main elements of each entry are separated with periods.

For most works alphabetize authors' names last name first.

Tobias, Andrew. The Invisible Bankers. New York: Pocket, 1982.

For works whose author is a group or organization, give the name in normal order. Do not include the article with group names: *The Society of International Rogerians* should be listed as *Society of International Rogerians.*

For unsigned or anonymous works, begin with the title. Do not drop articles from titles, but disregard them in alphabetizing. An anonymous work called *The Earliest Indians* should be alphabetized as if it started with *Earliest.* Do not label such works as Anonymous or Anon.

BOOKS

BOOK, ONE AUTHOR

Adolph, Robert. The Rise of Modern Prose Style. Cambridge, Mass.: MIT UP, 1968.

University Press is abbreviated UP.

BOOK, MORE THAN ONE BY SAME AUTHOR

Booth, Wayne C. Modern Dogma and the Rhetoric of Assent. Notre Dame: U of Notre Dame P, 1974.

---. The Rhetoric of Fiction. Chicago: U of Chicago P, 1961.

Subsequent books by the same author use three hyphens in place of author's name.

BOOK, MORE THAN ONE AUTHOR

Anderson, Jack, and James Boyd. Confessions of a Muckraker: The Inside Story of Life in Washington During the Truman, Eisenhower, Kennedy and Johnson Years. New York: Random, 1979.

Only the first author's name is presented in reverse order. The name of the publisher (Random House) may be shortened.

BOOK, MORE THAN THREE AUTHORS

Spiller, Robert E., et al. <u>Literary History of the United States: History</u>. 3rd ed. New York: Macmillan, 1963.

Note the edition number.

BOOK, PART OF SERIES

Hatfield, Henry, ed. <u>Thomas Mann: A Collection of Critical Essays</u>. Twentieth Century Views Critical Series. Englewood Cliffs: Prentice, 1964.

BOOK WITH EDITOR

Adams, Hazard, ed. <u>Critical Theory Since Plato</u>. New York: Harcourt, 1971.

BOOK WITH TRANSLATOR

Perelman, Chaim, and L. Olbrechts-Tyteca. <u>The New Rhetoric: A Treatise on Argumentation</u>. Trans. John Wilkinson and Purcell Weaver. Notre Dame: U of Notre Dame P, 1969.

BOOK IN MULTIVOLUME WORK

Wiener, Philip P., ed. <u>Psychological Ideas in Antiquity to Zeitgeist</u>. Vol. 4 of <u>Dictionary of the History of Ideas: Studies of Pivotal Ideas</u> 4 vols. New York: Scribner, 1973.

BOOK, REPRINT

Clarke, Arthur C. <u>The Challenge of the Sea</u>. 1960. New York: Dell, 1966.

ESSAY IN BOOK

Young, Richard. "Invention: A Topographical Survey."
In Teaching Composition: 10 Bibliographic Essays,
Ed. Gary Tate. Fort Worth: Texas Christian,
1976. 1–43.

BOOK, INTRODUCTION

Grommon, Alfred H. Foreword. A Long Way Together:
A Personal View of NCTE's First Sixty-Seven Years.
By J. N. Hook. Urbana: NCTE, 1979.

ARTICLES AND OTHER SOURCES

POPULAR MAGAZINE, WEEKLY

Quinn, Jane Bryant. "The Real-Estate Exchange."
Newsweek 11 July 1983: 12–13.

Page numbers always follow the colon. For inclusive pages, give full numbers from 1 to 99: 9–12; 27–35; 91–99. For numbers larger than 99, shorten the second number: 105–07; 325–37 (but 195–203; 398–401). The same principle applies to inclusive dates: 1986–87; 1899–1901.

MAGAZINE, MONTHLY

Schiller, Andrew. "The Coming Revolution in Teaching
English." Harper's Oct. 1964: 82–84.

Abbreviate months except May, June, July.

MAGAZINE, NO AUTHOR GIVEN

"The Upheaval in Health Care." BusinessWeek 25 July
1983: 44–48+.

The plus sign indicates additional, nonconsecutive pages.

JOURNAL, TECHNICAL, OR SPECIALTY MAGAZINE PAGED BY VOLUME

Putman, John J. "China's Opening Door." National
Geographic 164 (1983): 64–83.

Collier, Richard M. "The Word Processor and Revision
Strategies."
College Composition and

Some periodicals begin each issue where the last one ended. If the first issue ends with page 175, the next issue will begin with page 176. Because a bound volume of such periodicals may contain several issues, and because there may be more than one volume for a given year, it is necessary to provide the reader with the volume number, *34*, the year (*1983*), and the page numbers, *149–55*.

JOURNAL, TECHNICAL OR SPECIALTY MAGAZINE PAGED BY ISSUE

Howitt, Doran. "Whither Electronic Mail?" InfoWorld
6.27 (1984): 28–29.

When each issue of a periodical begins with page 1, it is necessary to know both the volume, *6*, and the issue number, *27*, since every issue is likely to have pages 28–29.

ENCYCLOPEDIA ARTICLE

Fraser, Francis Charles. "Whale." Encyclopaedia
Britannica. 1974 ed.

"Chickamauga Dam." Encyclopedia Americana. 1976 ed.

Because encyclopedias (and many other general references) arrange entries alphabetically, no page numbers are necessary.

NEWSPAPER ARTICLE

Granat, Diane. "Parent-Power Groups Demand Bigger
Voice in School Policies." New York Times 11
Nov. 1979, sec. 12: 4.

 Do not use *The* in newspaper titles in the Works Cited list.

DISSERTATION

Hazan, C. L. "The Relative Effectiveness of Two Methodologies in the Development of Composition Skills in College Freshman English." Diss. North Texas State, 1972.

DISSERTATION ABSTRACTS INTERNATIONAL

Moore, M. L. E. "A Descriptive Survey of Secondary English Teachers' Attitudes Toward Language Norms & Variations." DAI, 39 (1979): 6052–53A.

BIBLE VERSES

The New English Bible with Apocrypha. Oxford UP: Cambridge UP, 1970.

Only editions other than the King James edition of the Bible require a bibliographic entry.

BULLETIN OR PAMPHLET

Thorp, Margaret Farrand. Sarah Orne Jewett. University of Minnesota Pamphlets on American Writers, No. 61. Minneapolis: U of Minnesota P, 1966.

GOVERNMENT PUBLICATIONS

U.S. Central Intelligence Agency. National Basic Intelligence Factbook. Washington: GPO, 1980.

GPO stands for Government Printing Office.

U.S. Cong. House. Committee on House Administration. National Publication Act of 1980. 96th Cong., 2nd sess. H. Rept. 836. Washington: GPO, 1980.

LEGAL REFERENCES

United States v. Whitmire, 595 F. 2d 1303 (5th Cir. 1979).

Use the following research paper as a format model. Note that title pages are optional (ask your instructor). Instead of a title page, you can give your name, the instructor's name, the course number or other information, and the date on the first page of your paper. This information should begin one inch from the top of the page, at the *left* margin, and be double spaced, according to MLA guidelines.

Optional title page

Are Humpback Whale Sounds a Form

of Meaningful Communication?

by

Holly Adrian

Research Paper

Professor Walsh

English 201B

November 24, 1988

Are Humpback Whale Sounds a Form
of Meaningful Communication?

I. The background to the question "are humpback sounds a form of meaningful communication?"
   A. The history of whale communication studies
   B. A definition of meaningful communication
   C. The types of sounds whales produce
      1. The description of the song
      2. The description of social sounds
II. Rejecting the thesis
   A. Rejection of song as a form of meaningful communication, not following rules of verbal communication of other species
      1. The song produced only during one season
      2. The song produced only by males, an instinctive reaction so that sexes can differentiate each other
      3. The song always produced in the same situations
   B. Rejection of social sounds as a form of meaningful communication
      1. Social sounds used for catching food
         (a) Formation of bubble net
         (b) Confusion of prey with sounds
      2. Sounds used for echolocation
   C. Unintentional cues guiding the results of research
      1. Bias from feelings on the subject

2. Clever Hans effect: experiments ruined by unintentional cues and rewards

III. Accepting the thesis

A. The song as a form of meaningful communication

1. Monotony, repetition as a criterion

(a) Message relayed, understood by all

(b) Message not forgotten

2. Song as a form of music, music as a form of meaningful communication

B. Social sounds as a form of meaningful communication

1. Proof from listening to social sounds

2. Increase in vocalization rate in social situations

(a) Increase of vocalization rate with addition of new whales to group

(b) Increase of vocalization rate when whales become trapped

(c) Correct response to replayed social sounds

IV. Thesis question reviewed

A. Summary of main points

B. Possible meanings of the question

C. Closing statement

Heading for paper without title page

Holly Adrian

Professor Walsh

English 201B

November 24, 1988

Are Humpback Whale Sounds a Form of Meaningful Communication?

Introductory strategy

Humpback whale (Megaptera novaeangliae) sounds were first heard by eighteenth-century whalers, who believed the moans were the restless souls of drowned sailors. Throughout the years, many myths and legends grew up about these mysterious sounds which penetrate the wooden hulls of ships. Humpback sounds were not correctly identified until World War II when they were recorded by a United States navy enemy submarine detection device (Schreiber 32). These newly classified sounds sparked an interest in whale research, consequently causing new sounds to be discovered throughout the 1960s and '70s. With an increase in research, a controversy developed over the question, Are humpback whale sounds a form of meaningful communication? Researchers are split over the answer to this question: some believe that the whales can communicate, yet others believe the sounds are nothing more than an instinctive reaction.

Thesis question

Definition of terms

In order to analyze this question, a definition for meaningful communication must be formulated. For this paper's purpose, meaningful communication is a technique for intentionally and effectively expressing ideas to others. All whale researchers seem to have their own ideas on what meaningful communication is, so the definition above is a composite of these ideas. By use of this definition, in order for whale sounds to be considered communication, the humpback must intentionally produce a sound in an attempt to convey a message or feeling to others.

Humpback whales produce basically two types of sounds which may be involved in this meaningful communication--"songs" and "social sounds." The song consists of repetitive patterned moans, whooshes, and isolated clicks arranged in various phrases and themes (Payne and McVay 590); consequently the phrases and themes are stereotypically repeated for a whole year without any variation (Payne 10). Social sounds, in contrast with songs, are various clicks, moans, and other such noises which are not repeated in a series (Silber 1986).

Negative view of hypothesis

Some researchers disqualify the humpback songs as a possible form of communication because they are only produced during one season; therefore, they are considered to be nothing more than an instinctive reaction. "The regular repetition of humpback song only during calving and mating season certainly suggests that the song merely facilitates mating" (Whitehead and Moore 2203). Besides being sung only during one season, the sound is produced by only one sex. "Only single, unmated, young, sexually mature males produce song" (Winn and Winn 112). Researchers such as Whitehead, Moore, Winn, and Winn believe that meaningful communication would be produced by both sexes and for the whole year; therefore, the song is considered to be an instinctive reaction.

At the Fifth Biannual Conference on the Biology of Marine Mammals of 1985, James Darling also hypothesized that the humpback song is merely an instinctive reaction. "The song is a product of sexual selection: the male whales 'sing' during mating season, by instinct, so that a differentiation between sexes can be distinguished" (74).

Author's name in text

Some researchers even go as far as saying that the humpback songs lack communication traits because the same sounds are always produced in identical situations. Winn and Winn (89) discovered that "whales always make the same sound in their song before surfacing." Also, the song is very monotonous: the themes and vocalizations do not change for a whole year (110). All known vocal languages seem to exhibit a variety which these whale songs lack.

Researchers who reject the communication abilities of animals hypothesize that social sounds are tools used for catching food, not a form of communication. "Humpback whales often catch prey by 'bubble feeding.' A series of sounds and bubbles are released, forming a pattern; the whale then comes up, open-mouthed, through

Adrian 4

the pattern and catches the concentrated fish or zooplankton in the area" (Johnson and Wolman 35). In other words, the humpback whale uses social sounds to confuse prey and keep them in a concentrated area; therefore, the social sounds are being used as a tool for catching food, not as a form of communication.

Direct quote requires reference

James Prince, in his 1985 book Languages of the Animal World, hypothesized that social sounds are nothing more than an echolocation device. "The humpback whale uses pulsed sounds for echolocation. Low-frequency sounds are used to detect prey and other obstacles because they travel through the water many miles away. High-frequency sounds appear to be used as echolocation in the dark because they stay in the immediate vicinity of the humpback" (63). Donald Griffen, 1974, also explored the echolocation possibilities of humpbacks and discovered similar results. "Baleen whales emit low pitched sound that suggests orientation by echolocation. The frequencies which make up the pitches seem to contain ultrasonic as well as audible components" (274). Therefore, both of these researchers believe that social sounds are created as a biological location device, not as meaningful communication.

A major problem of whale research, particularly when studying social sounds, is that some researchers unknowingly let their feelings guide the outcome of the experiment, the so-called clever Hans effect.[1] There is

Superscript for content note

a possibility that researchers may give unintentional cues or read more into the results of an experiment than really exists. When studying social sound, the researcher usually has to come into fairly close contact with the whales in order to examine the behavior exhibited when making such sounds. This close contact may unintentionally bias the results of the experiment; the whale may act differently if it realizes that it is under observation. "Unintentional, minimal movements affect the research greatly. Cues and rewards both destroy many well-intended experiments" (Pfungst 23). Therefore, if research is not conducted in an objective manner, the experiment's results may mirror the researcher's feeling on the subject.

Transition to favorable view

Researchers supporting communication abilities of whales refute these arguments (about the redundancy of sounds in whale song) by stating that a humpback's vocalization is monotonous in order that the message in the song can be relayed and understood by all. "Song redundancy suggests the need for specific information; also, constantly repeating the message ensures that specific themes [are] remembered" (Guinee and Payne 69).

Roger Payne, one of the leading whale researchers, believes that humpbacks use their song as a form of communication. To a group at the University of Iowa, Roger Payne said:

Indented quote

> The question of why whales sing may, in fact, have no answer. It is possible that the

> whales don't know themselves. After all, why do people sing? Could you answer someone who demanded to know why you sing? Speech is just one way to communicate. Another way is through music. . . . Whether or not we subscribe to a whale's song as music, it was created by a form of life that composes and does so within a set of laws of form as complex and strict as our laws for composing sonnets--a form of life that has filled the vaults of the oceans with music for millions of years--filled them with untold arias, cantatas, and recitatives that echoed and faded away, never to be heard again.
>
> Indirect reference
>
> (qtd. in Crail 222-23).

Payne believes that humans cannot dismiss the whale song as a meaningless biological process, unless they do the same with their own songs.

A few researchers believe that just listening to social sounds is proof enough to justify the fact that the sounds are a form of meaningful communication. "How can we explain those alternating voices and such diversity of modulation except by concluding that it is actually conversation?" (qtd. in Crail 213), Jacques Cousteau once asked.

Not only are the sounds very diversified, they also seem to influence others to answer back. "Vocalization in a group increases with the addition of new whales to

Ellipsis for omission

the group . . ." (Silber 2079), suggesting that whales

Adrian 7

do vocally interact with each other. Vocalization rates also increase in situations in which humpbacks become trapped (Winn, Beamish, and Perkins 154). Other whales are usually observed near the trapped whale after it emits a series of social sounds. This suggests that the entrapped whale cries for help, therefore lending strength to the argument that communication does exist (155).

Peter Tyack's experiments also appear to confirm the communication abilities of whales. "Recordings of humpback social sounds, including those of battling males, got an unexpected response when played in Hawaiian [mating grounds]: time after time, whales charged the boat when the various sounds were played" (Tyack 69). The whales must have understood the sounds of challenge and responded to them. Tyack believes that this is clearly a case of communication abilities.

Evaluation of arguments

Overall, the amount of evidence is fairly even supporting each side of the argument, although there is slightly more information in favor of whale communication abilities. The two types of sounds analyzed in communication studies are songs and social sounds. There are four basic reasons why songs are not possible forms of meaningful communication: songs are not produced during more than one season, songs are only produced by males, the songs' sounds are produced in identical situations, the songs are very monotonous. In short, the songs appear to be instinctive behavior.

On the other hand, songs may be considered a form of communication if we believe that monotonous repetition is a way to make the message understood and remembered. Then too, "song" is a form of music--music according to Payne is a form of communication. In addition to songs, whales emit social sounds. Social sounds are not considered communication because they are used as a tool to catch food, they are used for echolocation, and experiments on them may be unintentionally biased. However, there are four reasons supporting social sounds as a form of meaningful communication: just listening to the sounds is proof enough; the vocalization rate of a group increases with the addition of new whales; vocalization rates of individuals increase when they become trapped; and whales correctly respond to social sounds.

Concluding strategy

The answer to the question, Are whale sounds a form of meaningful communication? may never be found; however, the existing experiments are creating a good groundwork for future animal communication studies. The answer to the question is important because someday, there may be a possibility of interspecies communication. Some researchers believe whales may already be attempting to communicate with humans, as well as members of their own species. David Starr, in 1986, stated that "the creatures of Earth may already be trying to converse with us." If Starr is correct, the future may bring interspecies communication with our neighbors of the sea.

Notes

[1] Named after a famous nineteenth-century horse who appeared to be able to spell, do mathematical problems, and many other marvels, until it was discovered his trainer was unconsciously cuing him with minimal movements.

Works Cited

Crail, J. Apetalk and Whalespeak. Los Angeles: Tarcher, 1981.

Darling, James. "Fifth Biannual Conference on the Biology of Marine Mammals." Bioscience, 34.2 (1981), 74.

Griffin, Donald R. Listening in the Dark. New York: Dover, 1974.

Guinee, L., and K. Payne. "Rhyming to Remember." Science Digest, 93.4 (1985), 69.

Johnson, J. H., and Wolman, A. A. "The Humpback Whale," Megaptera novaeangliae. Marine Fisheries Review, 46.4 (1984), 30–37.

Payne, Roger. Communication and Behavior of Whales. Denver: Westview, 1980.

Payne, Roger S., and S. McVay. "Songs of Humpback Whales." Science, 173 (1971), 587–97.

Pfungst, Otto. Clever Hans (the Horse of Mr. Von Osten). New York: Holt, 1965.

Prince, James H. Language of the Animal World. Nashville: Thomas Nelson, 1985.

Schreiber, O. W. "Whale Sounds." Journal of the Acoustical Society of America, 21.1 (1952), 32.

Silber, G. K. "The Relationship between Social Vocalization to Surface Behavior and Aggression in the Hawaiian Humpback Whale (Megaptera novaeangliae)." Canadian Journal of Zoology, 64 (1986), 2075–80.

Adrian 11

Starr, David. "Calls of the Wild: Forget Aliens. The Creatures of Earth May Be Trying to Converse with Us." Omni (1986), pp. 52–55, 102–08.

Tyack, Peter. "More News from the Sea." Science Digest, 91 (1985), 24.

Whitehead, H., and M. Moore. "Distribution and Movement of West Indian Humpback Whales in Winter." Canadian Journal of Zoology, 60.9 (1982), 2203–11.

Winn, H. E., P. Beamish, and P. J. Perkins. "Sounds of Two Entrapped Humpback Whales (Megaptera novaeangliae) in Newfoundland." Marine Biology, 65 (1979), 151–55.

Winn, L. K., and H. E. Winn. Wings in the Sea: The Humpback Whale. UP of New England, 1985.

Note that this is a "limited" bibliography, not Holly's master bibliography. These are the sources actually used in the paper. Other sources that Holly may have read but did not cite in her paper have been omitted from the Works Cited list. Make sure that every Works Cited entry has a matching reference in your paper.

46k Understand how to use other documentation styles.

APA STYLE

Another method of documentation, adapted from the *Publication Manual of the American Psychological Association* (1983), is sometimes used in business, education, and various sciences.

Follow APA guidelines for text references. This style uses in-text (parenthetical) citations of author and date of publication. If the author's name has been mentioned, only the date appears in parentheses.

```
Howard Hughes' giant wooden troop-carrying seaplane,
sarcastically nicknamed the "Spruce Goose," also had an
estimated cost, $9.8 million for the first plane
(Barlett, 1979, p. 118).
```

or

```
Barlett (1979, p. 118) states that Howard Hughes' giant
wooden troop-carrying seaplane, sarcastically nicknamed
the "Spruce Goose," also had an estimated cost of $9.8
million for the first plane.
```

These text citations guide the reader to full publication information in a References list at the end of the paper.

For parenthetical references, supply the author's last name followed by a comma, the date of publication followed by a comma, and the page number or numbers if necessary. Quoted material, paraphrases, and references to specific pages all require page numbers. In parenthetic notes, page numbers are identified with *p.* (page) or *pp.* (pages), but see below for a different treatment of page numbers in the reference list. If the source has two authors, give both last names

(Jones and Eckdahl, 1985, p. 317). If there are more than two, supply all authors' names in the first reference, but only the first author's name and *et al.* in subsequent references (Thrall, et al., 1960, p. 12). If no author is given, use a recognizable abbreviation, usually the first word or two of the title, and its date of publication ("Implications," 1981). If there is more than one source in a reference, list the authors in alphabetical order (Hanauer, 1982; Kolcum, 1982).

Follow APA guidelines for the reference list. The sources cited in your text are listed in the References. The list itself is arranged in alphabetical order by authors' last names or by the first word of the title if no author is given.

Here are typical entries, the first for a book, the second for an article in a journal. Notice the order of information, punctuation, and capitalization:

BOOK

Roth, P. (1983). The anatomy lesson. New York:
Fawcett.

Use only the initial, even if the author's full name is given on the title page. For titles of books, essays, articles in magazines and newspapers, capitalize only the first word, the first word of a subtitle, and any proper names.

JOURNAL ARTICLE

Bell, A. H. (1982). The trouble with software: An
English teacher's lament. Curriculum Review, 21,
497–499.

Capitalize all significant words in the title of a journal or magazine. Do not put quotation marks around the title of an article. Underline the volume number. Do not add *p.* or *pp.* or other labels to page numbers of journals. (See below for use of *p.* and *pp.* with magazines and newspapers.)

Underline the titles of books, magazines, journals, newspapers, and journal volume numbers. Articles, essays, and chapter titles *are not* put into quotation marks:

Bean, J. C. (1983). Computerized word-processing as an aid to revision. College Composition and Communication, 34, 146–48.

Roman numerals that appear as volume numbers of books and journals should be changed to arabic numerals (volume 7, not VII). But do not change roman numerals that are part of a title:

Auten, A. (1982). Computer literacy, part III: CRT graphics. The Reading Teacher, 35, 966–969.

Do not shorten inclusive page numbers.

Here are sample References entries in APA style. Compare them to the entries for the MLA Works Cited.

BOOKS

BOOK, ONE AUTHOR

Adolph, R. (1968). Rise of modern prose style. Cambridge, MA: Massachusetts Institute of Technology Press.

Give state names only when cities may not be well known or may be mistaken for other cities with similar names. Use official two-letter postal abbreviations for state names. Spell out names of university presses and associations.

BOOK, MORE THAN ONE BY SAME AUTHOR

Booth, W. C. Modern Dogma and the Rhetoric of Assent. Notre Dame: University of Notre Dame Press, 1974.

Booth, W. C. The Rhetoric of Fiction. Chicago: University of Chicago Press, 1961.

Repeat author's name for subsequent books. Disregard articles *A*, *An*, and *The* when alphabetizing.

BOOK, MORE THAN ONE AUTHOR

Anderson, J., & Boyd, J. (1979). Confessions of a muckraker: The inside story of life in Washington during the Truman, Eisenhower, Kennedy and Johnson years. New York: Random House.

Use the ampersand (&) in the References list, but not in your paper. Note the inverted order of both authors' names. Note the capitalization in the title (first letter of title, first letter of subtitle, and proper nouns). Remember to supply the names of all authors of a work in the References list.

BOOK, PART OF SERIES

Hatfield, H. (Ed.). (1964). Thomas Mann: A collection of critical essays. (Twentieth Century Views Critical Series). Englewood Cliffs, NJ: Prentice-Hall.

Note the designation of editor.

BOOK, LATER EDITION

Leggett, G., Mead, C. D., & Kramer, M. (1988). Prentice Hall handbook for writers (10th ed). Englewood Cliffs, NJ: Prentice Hall.

Shortened forms for publishers are preferred except for university presses.

BOOK WITH TRANSLATOR

Perelman, C., & Olbrechts-Tyteca, L. (1969). The new rhetoric: A treatise on argumentation (J. Wilkinson & P. Weaver, Trans.). Notre Dame: University of Notre Dame Press.

This reference assumes you used the English translation. If you used the non-English (original) source, give the original title, followed by the English title in brackets. Note the translators' names in normal order.

BOOK IN MULTIVOLUME WORK

Wiener, P. P. (Ed.). (1973). Psychological ideas in antiquity to Zeitgeist (Vol. 4 of Dictionary of the history of ideas: Studies of pivotal ideas). New York: Charles Scribner's.

BOOK, REPRINT

Clarke, A. C. (1966). The challenge of the sea. New York: Dell. (Originally published 1960).

In-text references to a reprinted work should give the dates for each printing: (Clarke, 1960/1966).

BOOK, INTRODUCTION

Grommon, A. H. (1979). Foreword. In J. N. Hook, A long way together: A personal view of NCTE's first sixty-seven years. Urbana, IL: National Council of Teachers of English.

ARTICLES AND OTHER SOURCES

POPULAR MAGAZINE, WEEKLY

Quinn, J. B. (1983, July 11). The real-estate exchange. Newsweek, pp. 12–13.

For popular (nontechnical) sources, use *p.* and *pp.* for *page* and *pages*.

POPULAR MAGAZINE, MONTHLY

Schiller, A. (1964, October). The coming revolution in teaching English. Harper's, pp. 82–84.

 Do not abbreviate months.

POPULAR MAGAZINE, NO AUTHOR

The upheaval in health care. (1983, July 25). BusinessWeek, pp. 44–48, 56.

Discontinuous pages are set off with commas.

JOURNAL, TECHNICAL OR SPECIALTY MAGAZINE PAGED BY VOLUME

Putman, J. J. (1983). China's opening door. National Geographic, 164, 64–83.

The page numbers run continuously through such periodicals, each new issue beginning where the previous one ended.

JOURNAL, TECHNICAL OR SPECIALTY MAGAZINE PAGED BY ISSUE

Howitt, D. (1984). Whither electronic mail? InfoWorld, 6(27), 28–29.

It is necessary to know the issue number (27), since every issue is likely to have pages 28–29.

ESSAY IN BOOK

Young, R. (1976). Invention: A topographical survey. In G. Tate (Ed.), Teaching Composition: 10 Bibliographic Essays (pp. 1–43). Fort Worth: Texas Christian University.

ENCYCLOPEDIA ARTICLES

Fraser, F. C. (1974). Whale. Encyclopaedia Britannica.

Chickamauga Dam. (1976). Encyclopedia Americana.

NEWSPAPER ARTICLE

Granat, D. (1979, November 11). Parent-power groups demand bigger voice in school policies. New York Times, sec. 12, p. 4.

DISSERTATION

Hazen, C. L. (1973). The relative effectiveness of two methodologies in the development of composition skills in college freshman English. Unpublished doctoral dissertation. North Texas State University.

DISSERTATION ABSTRACTS, INTERNATIONAL

Moore, M. L. E. (1979). A descriptive survey of secondary English teachers' attitudes toward language norms & variations. Dissertations Abstracts International, 39, 6052A-6053A.

BULLETIN OR PAMPHLET

Thorpe, M. F. (1966). Sarah Orne Jewett (University of Minnesota Pamphlets on American Writers, No. 61). Minneapolis: University of Minnesota Press.

GOVERNMENT PUBLICATIONS

U.S. Central Intelligence Agency. (1980). National basic intelligence factbook. Washington, DC: U.S. Government Printing Office.

Committee on House Administration. (1980). National publication act of 1980 (96th Cong., 2nd sess. House Report 836. Washington, DC: U.S. Government Printing Office.

LEGAL REFERENCES

U.S. v. Whitmire, 595 F. 2d 1303 (5th Cir. 1979).

The excerpts on the next page show the APA style of documentation.

APA DOCUMENTATION STYLE

Space Shuttle: Worth the Cost?

The new space age began, by coincidence, exactly twenty years after they first got under way with the one-orbit trip of Soviet cosmonaut Uri Gagarin on April 12, 1961.

> A little chipped on the outside but dead on course, the space shuttle Columbia hurled itself into orbit early Sunday morning atop the most powerful rocket engines ever fired. . . . It was the first manned American spaceflight since 1975, and the first flight ever of a space vehicle designed to be flown again after it returns to earth. ("Shuttle Blasts Off," 1981, p. 44)

The space shuttle Columbia looks like a short, fat, commercial jet with small wings. Its appearance is

References

Banks, H. (1982, July 19). Overloaded shuttle. Forbes, p. 33.

Barlett, D. L. (1979). Empire. New York: W. W. Norton.

Dooling, D. (1981, June/July). Estimates vary on cost of space shuttle. Space World, p. 19.

Dooling, D. (1981, June/July). Space shuttle opens new range of missions. Space World, pp. 15-19.

Dooling, D., & David, L. (1982, April) The 1983 space budget. Space World, pp. 4-7.

Golden, F. Touch down Columbia. (1981, April 27). Time, pp. 16-23.

47 WRITING ABOUT LITERATURE

Writing about literature is one way to understand and appreciate creative works. Ideas, patterns, images, and the emotional power of a work of literature may not be clear until you try to express your thoughts about it in writing.

47a Begin by reading closely and analyzing the assignment.

The first step in writing about literature is to read the work closely. Make sure you understand the plain sense of each sentence before you begin to search for deeper meanings. You must be sure you know who the characters are and what each is doing, what the relationships among characters are. In the end you must be able to say in detail what is going on in the work of literature and why.

Next consider the nature of the assignment. Are you free to select your own topic, to develop your own focus? If the assignment has been left open, look for something that particularly impresses you: a character, a scene, the setting, the use of language, a particular pattern of images, or a symbol. Think of a question that seems especially relevant to the work you are reading. For example, "What is the significance of the image patterns of light and darkness in the play *Macbeth*?" or "What is the structure in John Irving's *Hotel New Hampshire*?" Your paper will be more effective if you write about something to which you have a strong reaction.

47b Analyze characters in a work of literature.

You gain information about characters in literature from what they say, what they do, what others say about them, what they think, and what the narrator says about them. The characters set the story in motion; they cause the action to happen.

In many literary works, someone tells the reader what is going on. Such works are said to have a **narrator.** The narrator is sometimes actually one of the characters, like Huckleberry Finn, who tells the story; in other cases, the narrator is simply an unidentified voice that comments on the characters and action. Do not assume that the narrator is simply the author; the narrator is as much a part of the story as the other characters, and many interesting insights can be reached by analyzing the narrator's function. Some narrators seem to be omniscient, knowing everything, even what is going on inside the other characters' heads or what has happened in the past before the action of the story or what will happen in the future. Other narrators are much more objective, telling the reader only what a real observer could actually know.

If you decide to write about a character, ask yourself the following questions:

1. What does the character look like? Is the character's appearance significant?
2. What kind of language does the character use? What does he or she sound like?
3. Does the character fit into a category? Is it a type or a stereotype?
4. Is there anything about the character that makes it unique?
5. How does the character relate to other characters in the work?
6. Does the character compare or contrast with other characters?
7. What does the character think about him- or herself?
8. What do others think about the character? Do these two views conflict in any way? How?
9. Is the character you are analyzing a major one?
10. Does the character change during the course of the work? How? If so, what causes the change?
11. What is the character's motivation?

12. How do you relate to the character? Is the character appealing, memorable? Do you care about the character?
13. How does the author reveal the character to you?
14. How does the character fit into the plot? The meaning?
15. Is the character a minor one? If so, what is the character's function in the work? Would the work be the same if this minor character were omitted?
16. What is the personality of the character? What values does he or she hold?
17. Does the character have any flaws, any poor personality traits, habits, or behaviors?

47c Analyze setting in a work of literature.

Setting refers to the time and place in which an action occurs and also to the prevailing political, moral, and social attitudes of the society in which the characters live. Setting can be a major element in a piece of literature; for example, it is crucial to the story that the children in William Golding's *Lord of the Flies* are on an island, cut off from civilization. Setting is important in drama and fiction and long narrative poems such as Homer's *Iliad* and also in shorter works such as Sandburg's "Fog" or Sylvia Plath's "The Colossus." Following are some questions you might ask about setting:

1. What is the setting—time, place, atmosphere?
2. Does the setting change? Why?
3. What effect does the setting have on the characters, on the plot, and on the mood or tone?
4. Is the setting realistic? If not, why not? What effect does a nonrealistic setting have?
5. How do you get your sense of the setting? From the author? From the characters?
6. How does the setting reinforce the meaning?
7. How do the characters react to the setting?
8. Does it control them, or vice versa?
9. Does the setting conflict with the motives of the characters? How?

10. If not located in the present or in a world with which you are familiar, what comparisons and contrasts can you make with your own world?
11. What atmosphere is created by the setting?

47d Analyze actions and structure in a work of literature.

Action can be defined as the events that occur in literature and **structure** as the order of events, how they are organized. To illustrate, in Shakespeare's *Henry IV, Part 1,* there are serious scenes about the king and his son in conflict, both verbal and physical, with a group of rebels who are trying to take over the throne. Within this same play, there are a number of comic scenes, laid in a tavern or in the countryside, that deal with Falstaff and his criminal cronies. Particularly in the first half of the play, Shakespeare alternated between the serious and the comic. The individual scenes make up the play's action; the alternation of comic and serious scenes has to do with structure. A legitimate question is Why? What effect is achieved? How does that kind of structure add to the meaning of the play? The same kinds of questions can be asked about action and structure in fiction or poetry. Why, for example, does an author of a piece of fiction choose a particular sequence of actions? Does he or she depart from chronological development—go back in time or jump forward? Why does a poet select a particular sequence of images or ideas? How do they relate? What is the progression?

In some works of literature, one thing happens after another, and the reader is drawn along wondering what will happen next. Such works are called **episodic**; episode follows episode with no particular reason or with only the thinnest excuse as in some adventure stories or comedies. This kind of structure of actions can be very entertaining, although only loosely controlled by any overriding purpose.

More tightly structured stories are said to have a **plot.** The plot is a sequence of cause-and-effect events, the overriding purpose of the actions. In many stories, the characters face some kind of problem or complication they must deal with. In a mystery tale, for example, the plot is usually to solve the mystery. Plots can be very simple or they can be quite complex, with many twists and turns and unexpected developments. The traditional structure of a plot has three stages of development: the *exposition*, which tells the reader essential information for understanding the story, setting forth the situation as the story begins; the *conflict* or climax, which introduces some problem or complication the characters must deal with; and the *dénouement* or resolution, in which the plot conflict is resolved. The *climax* is the high point of the story, the point of greatest intensity; action leading up to this point is called rising action, and action leading away from this point toward the resolution is called falling action. Not all plots are this neat, but in a well-written story, you should be able to say not only what happens but why it happens and how the actions of the characters lead to the ending.

Don't rely solely on summarizing the actions or the plot. Instead, focus on the elements and the order of the action and the way they contribute to understanding the work. Here are questions on structure:

1. What is the structure? What are the main parts and how are they arranged?
2. Are there separate series of actions?
3. How do the actions relate? How do they come together?
4. Is the work episodic? That is, is it simply a series of incidents with no strong connection among them?
5. Does the author stick to a chronological development? Does the author go back or ahead in time? Why? What effect does this have?
6. Does the story have a plot? Is the plot plausible; do the actions arise naturally from the motives of the characters? Is it believable, given the premises of the story?
7. What is the structure of the plot? Is the plot simple or complex? Does it have a traditional exposition, conflict, and dénouement?
8. If a poem, what form has the author chosen?

9. How does this form fit the content?
10. Are there particular patterns of images, meter, rhyme scheme, and grammar? What effect is made by these patterns?
11. What are the divisions of the poem? What effect is achieved by dividing the work this way?

47e Analyze the use of language in a work of literature.

Writers select words and arrange them to convey precise meanings and elicit specific kinds of responses. We learn about characters through their use of language. We learn about action, setting, atmosphere, and meaning through the words and word patterns writers have chosen. Sometimes an author's intentions are clear and easy to grasp; other times you must work hard to decipher a consistent meaning.

The language of literature is both denotative and connotative. (See section **40b.**) A writer might describe a graveyard at midnight, using literal language about the darkness, the stillness, the sound of a dog howling, the open grave. If you read actively, participating in the literature, your own mind will add fearful emotions, thoughts of the undead, loneliness, and isolation.

In a similar way authors use words as *symbols*. Roughly defined, a symbol is that which stands for itself and also suggests or means something else, as the flag is a symbol of a country, which in turn might suggest patriotism or hate, the stars and stripes or a swastika. The writer's use of *metaphoric language* is similar: the metaphor identifies one thing with another and transfers qualities of the second to the first. For example, Macbeth says, "I have fallen into the sere, the yellow leaf." He identifies himself with the leaf, and one of the qualities of a yellow leaf is old age.

Here are questions on language:

1. Is there anything remarkable about the language, anything that catches your attention?

2. What tone is achieved by word choice? Personal, distant, angry, sympathetic, bitter, and so forth?
3. Does the tone change?
4. Are characters differentiated by their use of language?
5. Are there specific images that are particularly effective?
6. Is there a discernible pattern of images?
7. How do the images add to the meaning?
8. Is there a controlling symbol in the work? How does the author use it?
9. What is the author trying to accomplish with its use?
10. Are there specific metaphors that are especially effective?
11. Do any seem contrived, forced, artificial?
12. Is the language clear and simple? Difficult? Complex?

47f Interpret the meanings in a work of literature.

Meaning cannot be isolated from character, structure, language, and the other elements that comprise a work of literature: all must be taken into account when you attempt to discuss an overall meaning. The work itself is its own meaning, and your interpretations are influenced by your own experience, knowledge, and biases. But you can analyze what you think the author is trying to accomplish, and you can try to assess what a work means to you.

The more complex the literature, the deeper its meaning is likely to be. At the simplest level, meaning is related to plot. If we ask what *Hamlet* is about, we may get an answer such as "*Hamlet* is about a prince who must deal with the murder of his father." But at a deeper level we can discuss the play's **theme,** which has to do with power and fate, the degree to which we are in control of our lives versus the control exerted over us by events and external forces.

Most works of literature have a point beyond simply the resolution of the plot. The theme is an overriding meaning the reader deduces from the story: that war is brutal, perhaps, or that love makes life endurable, or some other meaning. The theme is not simply the lesson to be learned from the story, like the moral at the end of a fable. Different readers will find different themes in the same story. The theme is the controlling idea that lets the author select and exclude characters, actions, and details. It is the set of values, the ideas about life and human affairs that the author brings to the story. Sometimes the theme can seem to arise despite the plot, almost in contradiction to it, as when a powerfully moving tragedy leaves the reader with a sense of hope and the possibility of a better world.

Here are questions that help in discussing meaning:

1. What basic issues are dealt with?
2. What are the conflicts, either within a character, among characters, or between characters and outside forces?
3. Are there resolutions to these issues or conflicts? What are they?
4. Does the author offer no resolution but simply observe?
5. Is a consistent philosophy presented? What is it?
6. Are there dominating ideas or concerns? What?
7. Does the work have broad-reaching implications, or is it limited in time or situation?
8. What is the theme of the story? How are the characters and the plot related to the theme?
9. What is the historical background of the work?
10. Is there biographical information about the author that would influence the meaning of the work?
11. Is the work self-contained, or are outside sources needed to understand it?
12. What is your personal overall response? Why do you react as you do?

47g Decide what approach to take in an essay about a work of literature.

Once you have discovered an element to write about, you need an approach, a way to organize your thinking, and ultimately your writing.

THE ANALYTICAL PAPER

Analysis means dividing a whole into its parts. Analysis can be narrow or broad. For example, in a drama you could analyze an individual scene to discuss its movement, its actions, its language, its characters, its function, and how it relates to the rest of the play. On the other hand, you could analyze the structure of the whole play, demonstrating how each act or scene contributes to the overall impression. Similarly, you could analyze an individual character's personality, motivation, conflict, actions, or relationship with other characters. Or all the characters of a work could be classified into different categories and then analyzed as to their functions in the work as a whole. Poetry often lends itself to different kinds of analysis: structural, linguistic, imagistic, metrical, and others.

THE INTERPRETIVE PAPER

In an interpretive paper, you must decide on the meaning not only of the whole work but also of the individual elements in the work. You might focus on the meaning of a certain image or series of images, you might discuss various ambiguities of language, or you might concern yourself with how a poem's form serves the poet's purpose. In drama and fiction, character, action, setting, structure, and language all lend themselves to interpretation; you can write about what they mean in themselves and how they contribute to the sense of the whole work. Critical interpretation, then, asks you to discover meaning within the text and to demonstrate how the author accomplishes that meaning.

THE PAPER OF PERSONAL REACTION

If your instructor asks you what the work meant to you, or if, in an open assignment, you wish to respond personally to the literature, the emphasis shifts from the objective to the subjective. That is, the focus is on your personal relationship to the text. For example, you might write on how the work relates to your experience, your value system, your views of life. You might compare similar emotional experiences in your life to those expressed in a poem. Perhaps you know characters like those developed in a book or play. The text does not disappear in a personal reaction paper, but the focus is on how the text relates to you.

THE EVALUATION PAPER

Evaluation requires judgment: something is good, mediocre, or bad; it works or it does not work. The first question to ask is what are the criteria for judging the literature? To answer this question, think about the author's purpose and your reaction to what was written. There is a difference between a personal opinion and a judgment based on criteria and evidence others can verify. The important things to take into account when making critical judgments are the context of the work, when and where it was written, and its purpose. When these have been established, you can apply specific criteria in making an evaluation. Remember that any judgment must be well supported by quotes and paraphrases from the text.

THE COMPARISON PAPER

Comparisons within a given work or of one work to another can be worthwhile. The key here is to find a controlling reason for making the comparison, a point you want to make. For example, the point of comparing a character's behavior in a crisis at the beginning of a novel and in another crisis later might be to show growth or change in that character. The possibilities with this approach are numerous, from comparing one book with another to comparing syntax in two lines of poetry. Another possibility is to compare your interpretation of a literary work to that of a critic or to that of your instructor.

The following paper should be read as a model of how to use and document material from a work of literature to substantiate a thesis. The paper is essentially a study of character, particularly the relationship between two characters. This relationship is compared to a similar relationship between other characters. Read the paper to see how the character study develops a theme in the play.

Mary Lou DiBaldi

English Literature

May 1, 1988

The Servant/Master Bond

The evil, suffering, and injustice shown throughout _King Lear_ made the play very depressing to read. However, there were some positive elements. One of these was the bond that existed between servant and master as demonstrated by Kent, the Fool, and several other servants.

Kent offers not only the service required of a servant but also love and commitment:

> Royal Lear,
> Whom I have ever honored as my King,
> Loved as my father, as my master followed,
> As my great patron thought on in my prayers--
> (1.1.139-42)

At first I thought Kent was laying it on rather thick (like Goneril and Regan), but soon I realized that he spoke with truthful devotion. Kent was willing to risk his life to offer his king sound advice.

> Answer my life my judgment,
> Thy youngest daughter does not love thee
> least,
> Nor are those empty-hearted whose low sound
> Reverb no hollowness. (1.1.151-53)

And a line later,

DiBaldi 2

> My life I never held but as a pawn
> To wage against thy enemies, nor fear to
> lose it,
> Thy safety being the motive. (1.1.155-157)

Of all the people present, Kent was the only one to speak out against Lear's rash judgments. He was more concerned with Lear's future than the consequences to himself.

Even after Kent is banished, he returns under disguise to serve his master.

> Now, banished Kent.
> If thou can serve where thou dost stand
> condemned,
> So it may come, thy master whom thou lovest
> Shall find thee full of labor. (1.1.4-7)

When the disguised Kent comes upon Lear, he offers service to Lear's authority, "to serve him truly that will put me in trust" (1.4.14-15). Kent stays in Lear's service, first as a messenger and later as a companion during Lear's madness and the storm. Kent finally reveals his identity to his king and explains how he has been with him from the first (5.3.289-90).

The Fool offers similar service to his master by acting as Lear's counsel and conscience; his images and riddles are an attempt to get Lear to face up to responsibility and to look beyond himself.

> Why, after I have cut the egg i' the middle
> and eat up the meat, the two crowns of the

DiBaldi 3

> egg. When thou clovest thy crown i' the
> middle and gav'st away both parts, thou
> bor'st thine ass on thy back o'er the dirt.
> (1.4.160-3)

The Fool describes the faithfulness of a true servant as he contrasts his service with that of a knave.

> That sir which serves and seeks for gain,
> And follows but for form,
> Will pack, when it begins to rain,
> And leave thee in the storm.
> But I will tarry; the Fool will stay,
> And let the wise man fly,
> The knave turns Fool that runs away,
> The Fool no knave, perdy. (2.4.76-83)

The Fool stays with Lear during the outside storm, and the inside storm of Lear's oncoming madness. The Fool only leaves when his job is done, when he has gotten Lear to look beyond self-pity.

Finally, the servants in Gloucester's castle speak out against the injustice to Gloucester. Cornwall's own servant rebukes his master when Cornwall is blinding Gloucester.

> Hold your hand, my lord!
> I have served you ever since I was a child;
> But better service have I never done you
> Than now to bid you hold. (3.7.74-7)

Cornwall responds with his sword, and both the servant and Cornwall eventually die. It may seem contradictory

DiBaldi 4

that I have added this example when stressing the bond between master and servant. However, Cornwall's servant did risk his life by giving Cornwall good advice, just as Kent had earlier. The servant's sense of morality and justice prompts him to try to prevent his master from committing a terrible crime. But the bond between him and Cornwall is shattered by the latter's evil.

The second and third servants show true service as they follow Gloucester, at some risk to themselves, to offer him some help. "Go thou. I'll fetch some flax and whites of eggs / To apply to his bleeding face" (3.7.108-9).

Service, truth, duty, and honor are displayed in the bond between master and servant. In the midst of the turmoil and the overwhelming demonstration of man's wickedness, these positive elements offer some hope.

48 ESSAY EXAMS

The essay exam gives you an opportunity to show that you are an educated person, able to discuss an academic question. Unfortunately, essay exams do not allow much prewriting or rewriting. Such exams are, after all, tests; you are expected to produce a finished essay in a limited time. The exam tests two things: (1) your knowledge of the subject being tested and (2) your ability to write educated English. If you really do not know the subject or cannot write under pressure, there is little you can do about it except discuss these problems with your instructor.

Prepare yourself for the exam. Last-minute cramming is the least productive method of preparing for an exam. When the test is announced, review your notes and reread any sections of the text in which you need additional study. Be sure you understand all major concepts and technical terms, and learn to spell significant terms and the names of significant people. When you feel you know the material, try to put yourself in the instructor's place: What would you ask if you were giving the exam? Look at the text and your class notes for clues. Recall what the instructor stressed in the lectures, the important ideas in the reading. Practice writing answers about these ideas.

48a Read the test questions carefully.

Scan the test. Allot yourself time to answer questions depending on difficulty, relative value, and so on. Decide the order in which you will answer questions.

Make sure you understand the questions. Ask for clarification; never try to answer a question you don't completely understand. It's possible you don't understand because you haven't studied thoroughly, but it's also possible that the instructor can clarify the wording of the question for you.

No matter what question is asked, all essay answers require information, facts, details, examples. Imagine how the essay question might be worded on a multiple-choice or fill-in-the-blank test: the same information is required in the essay exam, except that you must express it in full sentences. For example, imagine an exam question that asks you to describe the origins of OPEC:

A RAMBLING, GENERAL ANSWER

OPEC means Organization of Petroleum Exporting Countries, and is a cartel of Middle Eastern nations that produce oil. Some of these nations are Saudi Arabia, Iran, and Kuwait. Together they form a cartel, a monopoly, by which they can control the price of oil. When OPEC says a barrel of oil will cost $40, then that's the price of oil because they control all the oil production and can just cut back production until they get what they want. The Western nations need oil and must pay whatever the cartel says. During the 1950's oil was so cheap because there was an oil glut, but then the OPEC countries got together and formed a cartel in 1960.

A BETTER ANSWER

OPEC was created in 1960 at a meeting between Saudi Arabia, Iran, Iraq, Kuwait, and Venezuela. Up to then, oil prices were set by the <u>buyers</u> of oil at less than $2 a barrel. The world had an oil glut, and the "seven sisters"--a cartel of big oil companies--kept prices low by refusing to buy from any country that tried to raise them.

Venezuela had only 7 percent of the world market, but oil minister Juan Perez Alfonso had studied the policy of the Texas Railroad (and Oil) Commission, from which he learned the principle--cut back on production to keep prices up. This idea was the heart of Alfonso's plan to unite the oil producers. The plan was well received by Saudi Arabia, but getting some other Middle Eastern States to cooperate was difficult. The world oil glut made any price increases seem impossible. But then, in 1960, without conferring with anyone, Exxon announced a cut in the price of crude, and the other companies quickly followed. This action outraged the oil countries, who overcame their long standing difficulties and sent ministers to the meeting in September of 1960 and announced the birth of OPEC.

The better answer has more specific (and accurate) information in it; and it does what the exam question asks: it tells how OPEC originated. The first answer has the key date correct, 1960, but it misses the important role of Venezuela in the formation of OPEC.

48b Understand what kind of response the exam question requires.

Think about what the question requires. We cannot guarantee what all exam questions mean, but in general the following questions are possible:

When the exam says *analyze* or *explain*, the answer requires an analysis of actions, events, or elements. "Explain why" calls for an analysis of both causes and effects; "explain how" calls for an analysis of process. "Explain the difference between a word processor and a computer" requires you to discuss the components and processes of each and the difference between data processing and information processing.

When the exam says *compare*, the answer requires a description of similarities and differences. A comparison requires you to give contrasts, whether the question uses that term or not. "Compare the 1985 Corvette with the 1965 Corvette" requires you to show how they are similar and how they are different. It is not enough to use vague general terms like "faster," "bigger," "more stylish," and so on; give specific details.

When the exam says *describe*, the answer requires details that support a general idea. "Describe Ronald Reagan's Presidential style" requires that you formulate a thesis and then give specific examples of what the President did and said that illustrate your thesis.

When the exam says *discuss*, the answer requires a controlling idea and a wealth of detail. Often the instructor has in mind a discussion similar to one in the text or one given in class. "Discuss Hamlet's character" requires you to state a thesis about Hamlet's character. You must refer to what Hamlet says or does that supports your thesis. Almost never does a "discussion" question invite you simply to give your own opinion without substantiation.

When the exam says *evaluate*, the answer requires you to express (and support) a value judgment. "Evaluate Joyce Kilmer's poem 'Trees'" requires you to judge whether the poem is good or bad. You must state what criteria you are using—structural or technical criteria, philosophical or moral criteria, and so on—and you must support what you say by quoting from the poem. You must either have memorized it or have a copy of it in front of you.

When the exam says *illustrate*, the answer requires detailed examples. "Illustrate Faulkner's theme of Southern decadence" requires you to describe the plots, themes, or scenes from several of Faulkner's novels as examples of "Southern decadence."

When the exam says *review*, the answer usually calls for a detailed chronology. "Review the events leading up to the Declaration of Independence" requires you to select and describe in as much detail as there is time for, in chronological order, things like the Stamp Act and the Boston Tea Party.

When the exam says *show that*, the answer requires substantiation of a particular point of view. "Show that the government's decision to go ahead with the MX missile is or is not correct" requires you to describe the details of the MX missile and give reasons why it should be called a mistake or a success. The more specific details you give, the better your answer.

48c Follow a strategy for writing an essay-exam answer.

1. Plan your answer. Spend a few minutes planning your answer. Reread the question carefully and jot down any ideas that come to mind. Arrange your ideas into a rough outline to provide a structure for your essay. Chronological and descriptive questions imply the order you should use. For anything else, use order of importance: save the most important reasons and examples for last.

2. Create a controlling idea. An essay is not a loose collection of ideas; there must be a controlling idea. If you have been asked to explain the cause of the Great Depression, you are not free to describe instead its effects. The answer requires a thesis statement: "The cause of the Great Depression was manipulation of the stock market by large banks," for example. (See section **1e–f.**)

3. Provide details, quotes, examples, specific information to support general ideas.

4. Do not write summaries unless asked to do so. A question asking you to evaluate the plot of a film requires you to say whether the plot is good or bad; if you merely summarize what happens in the film, your answer will be unresponsive.

5. Don't pad your answer. The instructore knows the answer to the question and is looking for specific information. If you don't know the answer, there is no way to fake it.

6. Don't try to switch the question or modify the wording. Don't create a "red herring," an answer that leads away from the exam question. If the question asks you to describe the level of readiness of the American armed forces, it is a bad idea to say that American readiness is not so good as Russian and then spend the rest of your time describing Russian readiness. Even if what you say is true, it does not answer the question.

7. Think of your reader; put variety, emphasis, and well-chosen language into your sentences. Remember that the writing too is part of the test—information alone will not bring a good grade if it is not well expressed.

8. Allow enough time to get to every question and to proofread your responses. Neat (readable) corrections are permitted on exams.

9. When you reach the end of your answer, stop. Exam answers do not need formal conclusions.

49 BUSINESS WRITING

49a Write effective business letters.

Cover letters for job applications, letters of request or refusal, of complaint, of gratitude, and of inquiry and follow-up letters are all business letters you may have to write at any time. The person to whom you are writing will form an image of you based on the letter you write, and this impression often affects that person's response to your letter.

Consider your audience. Most recipients of business correspondence are, like you, busy. Get to the point as quickly as possible. (The one-page letter is standard.) Usually short sentences and short paragraphs are most effective. Select language that is appropriate to your purpose and audience. Be courteous, even in a letter of complaint.

The sample letter on p. 355 shows a useful format for business letters.

49b Write an effective resumé.

A resumé is a list of information about a job applicant: academic credentials, work experience, and so on. There are no standard requirements for resumés, except that they ought to be accurate and provide information relevant to the application. Like the business letter, the resumé should be kept concise, two pages at most. The resumé by itself will not win a job for you, so there is no point in trying to make it seem long and impressive. It is meant instead to get you to an interview. Keep it neat and businesslike and make it show that your qualifications fit the job requirements. The resumé on p. 356 shows a useful format.

MODEL BUSINESS LETTER

Lawrence Masterson
907 High Road, Apt. 12
Emmy, Michigan 48902

January 9, 1989

Mr. Clay Torrence
Emtor Sports, Inc.
134 159th Avenue
New York, New York 10112

Dear Mr. Torrence:

For Christmas I received from a distant relative a "Home Tension-Stress Meter," model number 18956, made by Emtor Sports, Inc.

The meter worked only once, when I first tried it. Since then, it has become erratic: the needle spins around, reverses itself, pauses, and spins again, measuring 10, 80, 50, 100, or 20 pounds of tension on one pull. It continues to spin as long as I hold the pull, so that it never gives a final reading.

The box says the meter is guaranteed, but since I don't have a sales receipt, and we don't have an Emtor distributor here, I am writing to you for assistance. Should the meter be sent to you, or is there a customer service center where I could send it for repair or replacement?

Yours,

Lawrence Masterson

Lawrence Masterson

MODEL RESUMÉ

ANNE MARIE CUNNINGHAM
10 Chauncey Street
Boston, MA 59380
617-555-0218

EDUCATION: St. Christopher's High School, class salutatorian, graduated 1979
Lawter's Business School, 1979-1980
Massachusetts Institute of Technology, B.S.; major in petro-engineering; minor in chemistry, graduated 1984

EXTRACURRICULAR ACTIVITIES: High School Orchestra, violin; College Chemistry Club; Foreign Language Club; vice-president Young Engineer's Club; annual participant Boston Marathon

WORK HISTORY: Paper route 1973-1975
Office work, Cunningham Tool Co., 1975-1979
File clerk, computer terminal, Levitt Industries, 1979-1980.
Library assistant, Student Work Program, MIT, 1980-1982
Lab assistant, running chemical analyses, computer logs, Phillips International, Boston, 1982--present

SKILLS: Speak and write fluent Spanish and French; speak and read passable German and Arabic
Data processing, some programming, advanced chem lab skills, can do geologic surveys, field work

CAREER GOALS: Petro-engineer with large oil company or geologic survey company, possibly government work in energy, conservation, or environmental protection.

PLACEMENT FILE: Grade transcripts, recommendations, and other information will be forwarded from Placement Office, MIT on request.

REFERENCES:

Professor Lars Johannesen
Department of Geology
Massachusetts Institute of Technology
Cambridge, MA 02139

Ms. Adel Halstein
Director of Field Evaluation
Phillips International
Boston, MA 02116

Glossary of Formal Usage

Formal writing requires conventional language, and therefore, language choices that might be acceptable elsewhere are discouraged in this glossary. For example, some of the expressions discouraged here may be used in writing at the level of formality of some newspapers, magazines, and books aimed at popular audiences. Such expressions are not "bad" or "incorrect"; they are simply not found very often in formal writing. The same is true of many expressions here marked *nonstandard*, meaning only that they are acceptable in oral English in some situations but are not generally used in formal written English.

a, an Use *a* before words beginning with a consonant sound: ***a** man, **a** unit, **a** history of China.* Use *an* before words beginning with a vowel sound or silent *h*: ***an** elephant, **an** ox, **an** hour.*

accept, except *Accept*, a verb, means "to receive, or to take": *I **accept** your apology. Except*, a preposition, means "but": *Everything worked **except** the altimeter.*

ad Informal for *advertisement*. Avoid clipped forms in formal writing (*auto, exam, photo, plane*).

AD *Anno Domini*, "in the year of the Lord." It is redundant to write "in the year AD 1985." Note that *AD* precedes the number, and should be written in capital letters with no space between them and without underlining: AD. See *BC*.

adapt, adopt *Adapt* means to "change; alter to fit." *Adopt* means to "take, acquire." *They have **adapted** the old terminals to the new circuitry. We have **adopted** a uniform system of documentation.*

advice, advise *Advice* is a noun and means "a recommendation, or suggestion": *Our **advice** is to buy the cheaper model. Advise* is a verb and means "to give a recommendation or suggestion." *They **advise** us to buy the cheaper model.*

affect, effect *Affect* means "to influence." *The temperature **affects** the chemicals. Affect* also means "to pretend or take on airs." *She **affects** a wealthy lifestyle.* As a noun, *an affect* (*af' fect*) is an emotional response. *Effect* means "to bring about directly, make happen." *We will* ***effect*** *the repairs on your motorcycle immediately.* To *put into effect* is to make happen: *Your orders will be* **put into effect** *without delay.* As a noun, *an effect* is a result or outcome: *The* ***effect*** *of nitrous oxide on the metal was corrosive.*

aggravate Informal for *tease* or *annoy*. In its formal sense *aggravate* means "to make worse, to intensify negative conditions."

agree to, agree with *Agree to* means "to consent," and *agree with* means "to concur." *They* ***agree to*** *the test, and we* ***agree with*** *the need for the test.*

all of The *of* is usually unnecessary and is considered informal when applied to things measured by volume, degree, or time (i.e., noncount items). *She worked* ***all*** [not *all of the*] *day. We have bought* ***all*** [not *all of*] *the sulphur we need.*

all of a sudden *Suddenly* is more concise. *All of* **the** *sudden* is nonstandard.

all that Informal for *very*. *Their results weren't* ***very*** [not *all that*] *good.*

allude, refer *Refer* means "to mention or point out specifically"; *allude* means "to make indirect reference." *The report* ***alluded*** *to Iran as "a disruptive influence in the Middle East" but did not* ***refer*** *to Iran by name.*

allusion, illusion An *allusion* is an indirect reference (see *allude*): *Reagan's* ***allusion*** *to Carter was sarcastic. Illusion* means "ghost, imaginary vision, false appearance." *The magician created the* ***illusion*** *of a woman floating in air.*

alot Misspelling of *a lot*. Compare with *a little*.

already, all ready *Already* means "before, previously." *We had* ***already*** *mailed the check when their bill arrived. All ready* means "everything is ready": *The police are* ***all ready*** *for riots this summer.*

alright Misspelling of *all right*. Compare with *all wrong*.

altogether, all together *Altogether* means "completely, entirely." *All together* means "everyone is here, everything is assembled." *The scientists worked* ***all together*** *on the project until the work was* ***altogether*** *finished.*

alumna, alumnus Latin terms for female (*alumna*) and male graduates. Their plurals are *alumnae* (female) and *alumni* (male). Use the word *graduates* to avoid the Latin entirely.

among, between *Between* suggests two, *among* suggests more than two: *The argument was* ***between*** *the dean and the provost. The money was divided* ***among*** *the members of the team.* Formal writing requires, *The choice was between England* ***and*** [not *or*] *Germany.*

amoral, immoral *Amoral* means "neither good nor bad, without moral judgment or values." *Arithmetic is an* ***amoral*** *means of determining facts.* To say that someone is *amoral* means he or she is innocent, without moral values; animals are *amoral. Immoral* means "bad, that which is prohibited by moral law."

amount, number Use *amount* for measurement by volume: *amount* of wheat, *amount* of snow. *Number* is used for things that can be counted: *number* of people, *number* of tires. In general, use *amount* of money and *number* of dollars.

and etc. Redundant.

and which, and who Requires a preceding *who* or *which* clause. *He has written a book* ***which*** *explains the causes of revolutions* ***and which*** *I would like to read* [not *He has written a book explaining the causes of revolution,* ***and which*** *I would like to read*].

ante-, anti- *Ante-* means "before," as in *antedate. Anti-* means "against" as in *anti-Semitic. Anti-* requires a hyphen when the next letter is either a capital or the letter *i*: *anti-intellectual.*

 anymore In the sense of "today" or "now," *anymore* is nonstandard. ***Today*** [not *Anymore*] *students don't learn penmanship.*

anyplace *Anyplace* is an adverb: *Put the books* ***anyplace***. After a preposition, *place* is a noun: *You can live* ***in any place*** *you like.*

anyway Informal for *despite*, or *nevertheless*. Avoid using it as an all-purpose transition [not ***Anyway***, *I can't think of anything else to say*].

anyways, anywheres Nonstandard.

around Informal for *about* or *approximately*: *There are* ***approximately*** [not *around*] *one thousand affected cells nearby.*

as Nonstandard for *as though*, *that*, *whether*, or *who*: *It didn't seem* ***that*** [not *as*] *the number could be so low. The ones* ***that*** [not *as*] *were on top looked densely packed. I don't know* ***whether*** [not *as*] *I like it.*

as, for, since None of these is a good substitute when your meaning is "because." *We ordered new rheostats* ***because*** [not *as, for, since*] *the old ones burned out.*

as far as Not a substitute for *concerning*: ***Concerning*** [not *As far as*] *new work, we seem to have enough.* But note: ***As far as*** *new work* ***is concerned***, *we seem to have enough.*

as good as, as much as Informal for *almost*, *nearly*: *We were* ***nearly*** [not *as good as*] *caught when the door first opened.*

as if, as though Formal writing requires *were* as the verb with either of these, but *was* is accepted in less formal writing: *The substance behaved as if it* ***were*** [not *was*] *alive.*

assure, ensure, insure All three of these words share the same root, *-sure*, "to give guarantees." But traditionally, *assure* is limited to *oral promises*: *We* ***assure*** *you that the material will be ready. You have our* ***assurance***. Some writers use *insure* only when talking about insurance and reserve *ensure* for all other instances of making certain. *We will*

insure *our equipment for $50,000. We are making further tests to* ***ensure*** *that our conclusions are valid.*

at, to Avoid adding a redundant *at* or *to* to questions and statements about place. *Where is my pencil* [not *at*]? *I don't know where my pencil* ***is*** [not *is at*]. *Where are you* ***going*** [not *going to*]?

at this point in time Either *now* or *at this time* is less wordy and less pretentious.

awful Avoid using as an adverb (*awful* hard, *awful* expensive, *awful* bad).

a while, awhile Following a preposition, *while* is a noun. *We let the hot dogs cook for* ***a while*** *so that we could have time to talk. Awhile* is an adverb. *We talked* ***awhile*** *and then ate the hotdogs.*

bad, badly Use *bad* to describe emotions, state of health, or negative or unpleasant conditions, actions, and so on: *He felt* ***bad*** *all day. The beach looked* ***bad*** *after the storm.* Use *badly* as an adverb to describe actions. *They spoke English* ***badly***.

BC *Before Christ.* Avoid adding redundant *in the year* or *in the year of* with BC dates. *Confucius died in 479* ***BC.*** Note that ***BC*** (unlike *AD*) follows the date. It is typed without space between the letters and without underlining: BC.

being, being as, being that Nonstandard substitutes for *since* or *because.* ***Because*** [not *Being that*] *we lived in New Jersey, we visited New York often.*

beside, besides *Beside* means "next to"; *besides* means "in addition to." *The tanks were lined up* ***beside*** *the trucks. Many laboratories can do this kind of work* ***besides*** *ours.*

better, best Use the comparative (*better*) to express comparison between only two items. *He is the* ***better*** [not *best*] *of the two players.* Avoid oral constructions like the double comparative *more better, more slowlier*) and the faulty comparative (*more good, more soft*).

between you and I Unacceptable, pretentious for *between you and me*. See **10b.**

blame for, blame on Both are used in formal writing. *Don't be too quick to* ***blame*** *an employee* ***for*** *this; it's too easy to* ***blame*** *mistakes* ***on*** *workers.*

bias Nonstandard for *biased. They were* ***biased*** [not *bias*] *against anyone different from themselves.*

bored of Nonstandard for *bored by, bored with, tired of.*

bring, take It is nonstandard to use *bring* when you mean to "carry from a near place to a far one": ***Take*** [not *bring*] *these reports to Jackson when you go to see her.*

bursted Not accepted in formal writing as the past or past perfect form of *burst. By the time we got there, all the pipes had* ***burst*** [not *bursted*].

bust, busted Slang for *arrest* or *burst.*

but, hardly, scarcely Avoid constructions with other negatives (*didn't* have *no* tools *but* wrenches; *couldn't hardly* see the work; *hadn't scarcely* begun).

but what Informal. ***I don't doubt that*** [not *I don't know but what*] *we'll stay for another week.*

can, may Distinctions between *can* and *may* based on politeness are now ignored by many writers; both are acceptable.

cause is due to Redundant. *The* ***cause*** *of the revolution* ***was*** [not *was due to*] *poverty.*

censor, censure To *censor* is to deny permission to publish broadcast, write, or say something, usually because the censored material is offensive in some way. To *censure* is to express disapproval of an action.

cite, site *Cite* means "to refer to": *The footnote* ***cited*** *Shakespeare. Site* means "place": *The hill overlooking the town will become the* ***site*** *of a new factory.*

climactic, climatic *Climatic* means "of the climate"; *climactic* means "of the climax": *Our instruments measure any* ***climatic*** *changes. We waited for the* ***climactic*** *moment in the play.*

colloquial Spoken language. The word is often used to mean language acceptable in conversation but not in formal writing. Colloquial writing is informal. Note the word does not mean local or regional, though it has that connotation since oral language tends to be regional.

compare, contrast *Compare* means "to show similarities and differences." It is not necessary to say "compare *and* contrast," since *contrast* is already implied in *compare. Contrast* means "to show differences only." *After we had* ***compared*** *the two models, their advantages and disadvantages were clear to us. The* ***comparison*** *revealed that their* ***contrasts*** *were only minor.*

complected Nonstandard for *complexioned. The light-****complexioned*** [not *complected*] *soldiers were not suited for desert warfare.*

compliment, complement To *compliment* is to comment favorably upon: ***Compliment*** *them on their new schnauzer.* To *complement* is to balance or complete: *They played soothing music to* ***complement*** *the muted colors of the walls.*

consensus of opinion Redundant. *The* ***consensus*** *is that smoking is bad for you.*

contemptible, contemptuous *Contemptible* means "that which deserves contempt"; *contemptuous* means "feeling contempt for": *They were* ***contemptuous*** *of his* ***contemptible*** *maneuvers.*

continuous, continual *Continuous* means "without interruption": *The earth's rotation is* ***continuous****. Continual* means "happening frequently, but not without interruption": *No one can work with these* ***continual*** *annoyances.*

contrast from, contrast to Informal for *contrast with*: *The male cardinal has brilliant red feathers, in* ***contrast with*** [not *to*] *the female's gray-brown with a reddish cast.*

could of Nonstandard for *could have.*

credible, credulous *Credible* means "believable," such as a witness or testimony. *His manner was so sincere that the jury found him a highly* ***credible*** *witness. Credulous* means "believing too easily, gullible": *The child was* ***credulous*** *enough to believe that Santa would come down the chimney.*

data, media, criteria These plural words are sometimes used as singular words. In formal writing they are treated as plurals: ***These data are*** [not *this data is*] *insufficient. The* ***media have*** *been notified. The* ***criteria were*** *selected.* The singular form of *media* is *medium* (television, a communication medium . . .), and the singular of *criteria* is *criterion* (one *criterion* of success . . .).

dialect A language variation: language differences from group to group and from individual to individual; variations within a language are called dialects (Southern and Northern varieties of English, for example). See *Standard English.*

different than Formal writing requires *differ from* and *different from*: *The Eastern dialect* ***differs from*** *the Western. Southern speech is* ***different from*** *Northern.* But *than* is widely used in less formal writing.

disasterous Misspelling of *disastrous.*

disinterested, uninterested *Disinterested* means "impartial, unbiased": *The duty of the judge is to serve as a* ***disinterested*** *observer. Uninterested* means "having no interest": *They were* ***uninterested*** *in old horror films.*

due to the fact that Wordy for *since* or *because.*

egoist, egotist An *egotist* is a conceited person. An *egoist* is someone who believes in the theory of *egoism*—that human behavior is governed by self-interest.

emigrate, immigrate To *emigrate* is to leave one's country. To *immigrate* is to enter a foreign country.

eminent, imminent *Eminent* means "well-known, outstanding"; ***eminent*** physician. *Imminent* means "approaching": ***imminent*** danger.

enthuse, enthused, enthusing Informal derivatives from *enthusiasm*, these words are not recognized in formal writing but may appear in popular media.

equally as Nonstandard for *as: We were* ***as*** [not *equally as*] *surprised as they were.*

everyday, every day When context requires an adjective, *everyday* is correct: *Don't wear your* ***everyday*** *clothes to church.*

expect Informal for *suppose* or *believe: I* ***suppose*** [not *expect*] *you will need new filters for that pump.*

farther, further In formal writing, *farther* suggests physical distance: *We had walked* ***farther*** *than anyone else. Further* suggests degree or progress in time: *The* ***further*** *I read, the angrier I got.* Less formally, the words are interchangeable, except when you mean "additional": *It was clear that* ***further*** *surprises were in store.*

few, less *Few* suggests countable items: *few* trees. *Less* suggests items measured by volume or degree: *less* water, *less* heat.

flunk Slang for *fail.*

former, latter When there are only two items, formal writing prefers *former* and *latter* instead of *first* and *last: We elected Benson and Cheney, the* ***former*** *a biologist and the* ***latter*** *a chemist.*

frightened of, scared of Informal for *frightened by, afraid of.*

fun Nonstandard adjective for *enjoyable, pleasant.*

go and, take and, try and Informal. ***Go*** [not *go and*] *see what is in the box.* ***Try to*** [not *try and*] *lift the crates.*

good, well Use *good* to mean "attractive, promising": *This looks* ***good*** *to me.* Use *well* to describe actions: *The motor* *runs* ***well.*** *She writes* ***well.*** To describe state of health or general condition, use ***well:*** *You seem to feel* ***well.***

had ought, hadn't ought Nonstandard for *ought, should not. You* ***ought*** [not *had ought*] *to have that lanced. They* ***should not*** [not *hadn't ought to*] *light matches near the oil vats.*

hanged, hung *Hanged* means "executed by hanging": *The stranger was* ***hanged*** *for horse stealing. Hung* means "suspended": *She* ***hung*** *the crossbow in her locker.*

hang-up, hassle Slang for *problem, trouble, annoyance.*

he or she Write *he or she* when referring to a generic or hypothetical individual who could be either male or female. *The researcher should work until* ***he or she*** *begins to see a pattern in the data.* A better alternative is to write in the plural. ***Researchers*** *should work until they begin to see a pattern in the data.*

himself, herself, myself Not acceptable as substitutes for *him, her, me: The class couldn't decide between Alice and* ***me*** [not *myself*]. However, *-self* words are correct when used to refer to a preceding pronoun or to add emphasis: *She gave* ***herself*** *a shock. Alice* ***herself*** *did the work.*

how Nonstandard for *that: We were annoyed* ***that*** [not *by how*] *the computer kept saying "error."*

if, whether Use *whether* to express doubt: *They asked* ***whether*** [not *if*] *the prices were higher in the country.*

ignorant, stupid *Ignorant* means "uneducated, untaught"; *stupid* means "unintelligent, unable to learn": *Some very intelligent people are* ***ignorant*** *about matters they have not studied; this does not mean that they are* ***stupid.***

incidence, incidents An *incident* is an event: *There was an unfortunate* ***incident*** *when the two gangs collided. Incidence* means "rate of occurrence": *They have reported a high* ***incidence*** *of cancer of the lungs in cigarette smokers.*

infer, imply *Imply* means "to suggest": *He claims to be innocent, but the facts* ***imply*** *otherwise. Infer* means "to deduce": *From this evidence we* ***infer*** *that someone else was in the room.*

ingenious, ingenuous *Ingenious* means "clever"; *ingenuous* means "naive, innocent": *You are an* ***ingenuous*** *child. You will never be able to resist their* ***ingenious*** *maneuvers.*

in, into *Into* suggests from one place to another: *He walked* ***into*** *the room [from outside it] as if he owned it. In* suggests action at one place only: *He walked* ***in*** *the room [once he got inside it] as if he owned it.*

in the affirmative, in the negative Pretentious for *yes* and *no.*

in the area of Wordy and imprecise. *The experimental work was* ***in*** [not *in the area of*] *chemical properties of inorganic substances.*

in the neighborhood of Informal for *approximately. There were* ***approximately*** [not *in the neighborhood of*] *10,000 subjects with the symptom.*

in this day and age Wordy for *now* or *today.*

in regards to Not a substitute for *in regard to* or *as regards.*

inside of Redundant; *inside* is less wordy. *She is* ***inside*** [not *inside of*] *the house.*

in view of the fact that Wordy for *considering that, since,* or *because.*

irregardless Nonstandard. *They continued to work on the bomb* ***regardless*** [not *irregardless*] *of the danger to themselves.*

its, it's *It's* means "it is" or "it has": ***It's*** *now twelve o'clock. Its* is the possessive form of *it: The surface of the table has lost* ***its*** *shine.*

-ize Many *-ize* words are rejected by serious writers as pretentious invented terms (neologisms): *prioritize* (to set priorities), *finalize* (to make final). However, the linguistic principle is well established: *alphabetize, authorize, systematize, theorize.* Avoid inventing words in formal writing.

kind of, sort of In formal writing, *kind* and *sort* are singular and are followed by singular phrases: *kind of book, sort of plant.* The plurals for the examples are *kinds of books* and *sorts of plants.*

leave Nonstandard for *permit* or *let: Will you* ***let*** [not *leave*] *me do it?*

lie, lay The past tense of *lie* is *lay: Today I* ***lie*** *in bed; yesterday I* ***lay*** [not *laid*] *in bed all day.* See **11c.**

like, as Formal usage avoids using *like* in place of *as. Like* is a preposition or verb: *Your son looks* ***like*** *you. They* ***like*** *ice cream. As* is a conjunction: *They persuaded her to sing again* ***as*** [not *like*] *she had in the old days.*

loose, lose *Loose* means "free, unrestrained"; *lose* means "misplace" (an object) or "have taken from you" (property, rights, life): *Our ship broke* ***loose*** *in the storm; we can't afford to* ***lose*** *it.*

-ly Use *-ly* modifiers to describe actions: *work* ***carefully,*** *speak* ***slowly.***

might of Nonstandard for *might have.*

mighty Informal for *very. It soon became* ***very*** [not *mighty*] *hot.*

monsterous Misspelling of *monstrous.*

most Nonstandard for *almost* or *nearly:* ***Nearly*** *everyone* [not *most everyone*] *approves of charity. He hits the ball* ***almost*** [not *most*] *every time.*

must of Nonstandard for *must have.*

nice Avoid using *nice* as a vague word of approval. *Nice and* is informal: *The engine started* ***easily*** [not *nice and easy*].

not too distant future Wordy for *soon.*

no way Slang for *under no condition:* ***Under no condition*** [not *No way*] *would I do it.*

nowheres Nonstandard for *nowhere.*

off of, off from Redundant: *Take everything* ***off*** [not *off of*] *the floor before you leave.*

OK, O.K., okay Informal for *acceptable* or *yes.* All three spellings are used.

ourself Nonstandard: *She said we had to do the work* ***ourselves*** [not *ourself*].

outside of Informal for *except: There was nothing to do* ***except*** [not *outside of*] *clean up the place and leave.* Informal for *outside: We went* ***outside*** [not *outside of*] *the house.*

past history Redundant.

plan on Informal for *plan to: We* ***plan to*** *open* [not *plan on opening*] *a new branch office soon.*

predominate, predominant *Predominant,* an adjective, means "superior, dominant"; *predominate,* a verb, means "to control, to dominate, to prevail": *The* ***predominant*** *consideration was the cost of materials; this factor* ***predominated*** *in the discussion.*

prejudice Nonstandard for *prejudiced: He soon discovered that they were* ***prejudiced*** [not *prejudice*] *against his ideas.*

pretty Informal for *very, somewhat, rather: We thought the work was* ***very*** [not *pretty*] *hard.*

principal, principle *Principal* means "the chief or main thing," as the *principal* of a school, the *principal* battle in a war, the *principal* sum of money (on which interest is earned). *Principle* refers to "ethics, theories, guidelines, or moral qualities": *The* ***principle*** *of nonviolence is alien to most Americans.*

prophecy, prophesy *Prophecy,* a noun, means "a prediction"; to *prophesy,* a verb, means "to make a prediction."

rarely ever Redundant: *They* ***rarely*** [not *rarely ever*] *give surprise quizzes in math.*

real Nonstandard for *very: Their data looked* ***very*** [not *real*] *interesting.*

reason is because Redundant: *Later it was determined that the* ***reason*** *the bridge collapsed* ***was that*** [not *was because*] *unreinforced concrete had been used.*

reason why Redundant: *The report said the* ***reason*** [not *reason why*] *the engines stalled was worn oil seals.*

refer back Redundant.

repeat again Redundant.

right Informal for *very: They do a* ***very*** [not *right*] *good analysis of materials sent to them.*

said In phrases like *the* ***said*** *property, the* ***said*** *individual,* a legalism to be avoided in all but legal documents.

should of Nonstandard for *should have.*

sit, set *Sit* means "to take a seat"; it is usually followed by a place expression and does not take an object: ***Sit*** *down;* ***sit*** *in the chair. Set* means "to put or place" and always takes an object: ***Set*** *the books on the table.* See **11c.**

so Overused conjunction between sentences. Formal writing requires precise connectives: *We were tired from long hours of observation;* ***therefore*** [not *so*] *we postponed any additional sessions for one week. So* is informal in the sense of "very": *She thinks she is* ***very*** [not *so*] *smart.* But note that *so* can be used in the formula *so . . . that: He is* ***so*** *strong* ***that*** *he can do the work of two men.*

somewheres Nonstandard for *somewhere.*

slang Words or expressions not accepted by educated readers as part of the general language.

standard English Language that conforms to the conventions and traditions of formal written English; the English of most serious writers.

such a Informal for *very: We had a* ***very*** *good* [not *such a good*] *time at the party. He is a* ***very*** *poor* [not *such a poor*] *sport.* But not *such . . . that: He is* ***such*** *a poor sport* ***that*** *we don't want him on our team.*

suppose Nonstandard for *supposed: We were* ***supposed*** [not *suppose*] *to receive new supplies in a week.*

sure Informal for *very* or *certainly: It was* ***very*** [not *sure*] *hot.*

teached Nonstandard for *taught.*

that Informal for *very, so,* or *too: I never liked algebra* ***very*** [not *that*] *much.*

theirself, theirselves, themself Nonstandard for *themselves.*

this here, that there Nonstandard for *this, that.*

today's modern world, today's modern society, the modern world of today Wordy and redundant for *now* or *today.*

try and Informal for *try to: You must* ***try to*** [not *try and*] *brush your teeth regularly.*

type Informal for *type of: This* ***type of*** [not *type*] *word processor is very sophisticated.* Reword to avoid informal compounds with *-type* [not an academic-*type* job, a strange-*type* machine].

usage The traditions (conventions) of appropriate and effective language. Usage conventions tell writers what readers expect in different situations.

use to Nonstandard for *used to: We* ***used to*** [not *use to*] *live on Maple Street.*

was, were Formal writing requires *were* to express wishes, doubts, probability, conditions contrary to fact: ***Were*** *it not for her intervention, her employees would have lost their jobs. We wish it* ***were*** [not *was*] *true.*

ways Informal for *way: They drove a long* ***way*** [not *ways*] *into the country looking for strawberries.*

when Informal for *in which: An assault is any attack* ***in which*** [not *when*] *the threat of violence exists.* But note: *An assault* ***occurs when*** *violence is merely threatened.*

where Informal for *in which: They were revolted by the scene* ***in which*** [not *where*] *the snake ate the rabbit.* Also informal for *whereas: Today calculators are relatively cheap,* ***whereas*** [not *where*] *before they were very expensive.*

who, whom *Who* is used as a subject; *whom* is used as an object. See **10e.**

who, which, that See **10m.**

-wise Avoid using *-wise* as an all-purpose suffix meaning *concerned with* or *pertaining to* (transportation-*wise*, usage-*wise*).

would of Nonstandard for *would have.*

would . . . would Avoid redundant conditionals: *We knew that* ***if*** *we* ***did*** [not *would do*] *it, they* ***would*** *be surprised.*

Appendix

WORD PROCESSING: WRITING WITH A COMPUTER

WORD PROCESSING: WRITING WITH A COMPUTER

The computer revolution has been so fast and so radical that the general public is not as yet aware of the astonishing change it has brought about. Professional writers, journalists, academics, and students everywhere have come to rely on computers to a degree no one would have imagined ten years ago. The triumph of computers over typewriters is nearly complete. There are still those, of course, who stubbornly resist, but it is not much of an exaggeration to say that writing today means word processing on a computer. Then too, employers today expect new employees to be "computer literate"; certainly students who have computer experience have an advantage over those who haven't. The benefits are so enormous that within a generation we can expect the use of computers for writing to be nearly universal.

Why? Most of the psychological "pain" of writing evaporates with computers. Students need never fear "mistakes" in writing again. Revising, editing, rewriting a paper is now so simple it is nearly a pleasure. Freed from the anxieties and time-consuming drudgery of writing with a typewriter, students can focus on the artistry of trying different approaches, rearranging components, adding to and deleting from their drafts. The computer has made the writing process a creative activity of drafting and redrafting. And no matter how weak any student's typing or spelling skills, the computer can make finished papers look so professionally polished that teachers are not inclined to reach for the red pencil in order to fuss with insignificant matters of format and mechanics.

Much of this change is attributable to the word processing programs available on computers today. These programs assist writers by allowing them to retype, change, modify, move, delete, and in many other ways function like skillful secretaries who can alter a manuscript in seconds. It is not at all unreasonable today to expect students' writing to look like the work of skilled adults. The computer's ability to FIND, MOVE, DELETE, REPLACE anything can help students look for troublesome usage items like "its" and "it's" (though usually the operator still needs to know the difference). These programs take over most of the work of formatting the printed page, and they offer many other kinds of assistance to writers. Word processing programs put students in charge of their writing in a way that typewriters never did.

One other significant element in this change has been the computer printer. Early predictions that paper might cease to be necessary in the computer age have proved false. On most computer screens (monitors), lighted letters are harder to read than on the printed page. Even very expensive monitors with crystal clear letters do not make reading the screen much more desirable: the simple truth is that people do not like to read from video screens. It can be done, and certainly we all look at the screen from time to time; for very limited kinds of editing, using the screen is one option. But almost all writers report that editing, revising, proofreading—even just looking over the manuscript—is best done on paper. Thus the computer printer becomes the key component for most writers. The computer printer obediently types out copy after copy—as many as we like—of exactly what we typed, but much faster than most of us could ever type. Inexpensive "dot matrix" printers produce acceptable images for reading, as long as we remember to change the ribbon now and then. The very best printers can produce printed pages that far surpass typewritten pages; laser printers can produce work that looks typeset. Increasingly even the most humble kind of written task can be made to look like expensive printing. Students are discovering that beautifully prepared printed pages can bias their readers in favor of their writing—the better the paper looks, the better it is received by readers.

All writers work out their own habits and techniques for working with their computers; it is a highly individual and, some say, emotional relationship between writer and machine. However, for inexperienced writers the following suggestions may prove useful.

1. Don't be afraid to "waste" time or paper. The computer is excellent for freewriting, brainstorming, "thinking

out loud." You can use it like a journal, like a notepad, like scraps of paper to "scribble" ideas. The computer's ability to store infinite amounts of data makes it an excellent device for prewriting. (If you are one of those who *must* first write on paper and then type, go ahead. Sooner or later you will find yourself able to work directly on the computer, at a great savings in time.)

2. Save everything. There is no need to "throw away" (delete) anything on the computer. False starts, ideas that you abandon—save it all. You can never tell when an old "dead" idea may come alive again. Then too, if you don't deliberately "save" your document, your computer may not do it for you. It is wise to develop the habit of saving everything (this includes copying your entire disk now and then, as insurance against loss or damage).

3. Print out everything. Paper is the least expensive component of a computer system. Use your printouts exactly like notes—scribble on them, add new ideas, delete others; let your printouts help you find what you are trying to say.

4. If your word processing program permits "split screens" or "windows," you will find this a tremendous help in looking at two documents at once. You can have the document you are working on—your research paper, for example—in one "window" and your notes in another. And you can move material from your notes into your main document (it's called "cut and paste") with just a few keystrokes. This is one way to cull from your random notes; it is the bridge between brainstorming and outlining. The computer helps you organize your ideas.

5. If your word processing program has an automatic outline feature, by all means use it to help yourself think about your subject. These outliners act like a coach, automatically supplying the correct outline level and

number, and thereby suggesting to you what data you need and where it belongs in the outline. Furthermore, if you do use one of these outliners, you will appreciate the computer's ability to *revise* them; if you add to or delete from the outline, the computer will automatically adjust all the levels and numbers to account for your changes. This fact can be useful in allowing you to experiment with the organization of your paper, allowing you to see different relationships among major and minor points.

6. If you are collecting books and articles for your research paper, the computer is the natural place to store them. Placing items in alphabetical order—and *revising* that order—is a moment's work on the computer. Some sophisticated programs today will even do the alphabetizing for you, automatically. The computer printout can take the place of those little 3 × 5 notecards students used to make. Because the computer list can be revised as many times as necessary, it is the preferred method for building a bibliography. And once you have your list stored on the computer, it can be attached to your paper with a few keystrokes.

7. Unless you have a portable computer (in a generation, students everywhere will bring portable computers the size of notebooks to school), taking notes directly on the computer may not be possible. But even if you write them out longhand first, it is an excellent idea to copy them into your computer. Once stored in the computer (on disk), your notes can be manipulated, edited, incorporated into a draft of your paper. Since most writers become experts on the subjects they write about, meaning they continue to write about the same subjects, stored notes become a writer's data bank of research. Your notes can be used not only for your present paper but for future papers as well.

8. Learn to use all the features of your word processing program. You may not have a need for "line drawing" at the moment, but the day may come when you will appreciate the computer's ability to draw boxes, make charts, and so on. For example, some sophisticated programs today will automatically create footnotes and endnotes wherever you require them and, if you edit the pages, automatically renumber and move them to wherever they belong. Most word processors today include a spelling checker: you need never turn in a paper with a misspelled word on it again. Even if you are a very good speller, the computer will find errors you may miss. Many programs include a thesaurus. You can find more accurate, more effective words for the common, lackluster words in your rough draft. All word processors today have an automatic page numbering feature; not only will the numbers appear automatically, but if you revise the pages, the computer will *renumber* all the pages correctly.

9. Save your rough drafts. Instead of writing over your rough draft—so that it disappears under the new draft—save each draft under a different name (*Draft 1*, *Draft 2*, for example). Now and again writers discover they wish they had kept something deleted from an early draft. Occasionally writers decide that their first draft was the better one. In any case, since computer disks can store so much information, you can save any number of drafts very inexpensively. And unlike paper drafts, computer-stored drafts are highly accessible. Some programs, for example, have a "search" feature that will find for you the draft in which you mentioned "Tecumseh."

Computers have changed greatly since 1980; they are much more sophisticated and user friendly. Students need not fear that computers require specialized knowledge from their users. The truth is that word processing on a computer is no more difficult than typing on today's sophisticated electronic "typewriters" (which are themselves becoming more and more like computers). Even if are not a trained typist, you will find you quickly become familiar with the keyboard. And today's word processing programs were designed with the unskilled typist in mind: errors can be deleted with a single keystroke the moment you see them or later, after your paper is finished. No matter how awkwardly you type, you will find you can produce letter-perfect papers with a computer. Then too, *Brief Handbook for Writers* is based on a multiple-draft theory of composition. Students with computers will have a significant advantage over students who must struggle with typewriters or paid typists. The multiple-draft theory does not treat revision as a penalty for error; it is an inherent part of the writing process, and you should anticipate revising even if you are capable of "good enough" work in a single draft. The idea is to find ways to improve your drafts after feedback from classmates, friends, instructors—and the computer makes this idea work better than anything else.

Index

A

B

D

E

F

G

H

I

J

K

L

M

N

O

P

Q

R

S

T

Notes

Notes

Correction Symbols

ab	abbreviation problem	38
adj	adjective problem	4d, 15
adv	adverb problem	4e, 15
agr	agreement problem	9
awk	awkward	
cap	use capital letter	37
case	case problem	10
coord	coordination problem	16a–b, 20b
cs	comma splice	8
dm	dangling modifier	18
doc	documentation problem	46j–k
frag	unintentional sentence fragment	7a
fs	fused sentence	8
gloss	see usage glossary	
gr	grammar	5–6
hyph	hyphen problem	35
ital	italics (underlining) problem	36
lang	language-usage problem	41, 42
lc	use lowercase letter	37
log	faulty logic, invalid argument	45
mm	misplaced modifier	18b–d
ms	manuscript-format problem	3e
nos	number/numeral problem	38
pn ref	pronoun-reference problem	10
punct	punctuation problem	21–33
ro	run-on sentence	8
sp	spelling problem	39
shift	sentence-consistency problem	19
sub	subordination problem	16c–d
t	tense problem	12
vb form	verb-form problem	11
wordy	make more concise	20a
ww	wrong word	40, 41

Correction Symbols

¶/no ¶	use new paragraph/no new paragraph	43a–c
¶ coh	paragraph-coherence problem	43b
¶ devel	paragraph-development problem	43c
/ /	use parallel construction	20d
[ ]/no [ ]	use brackets/delete brackets	32
:/no :	use colon/delete colon	24
,̂/no ,̂	use comma/delete comma	21, 22
( )/no ( )	use parentheses/delete parentheses	33
./no .	use period/delete period	26
?/no ?	use question mark/delete question mark	28
“ ”/no “ ”	use quotation marks/delete quotation marks	29
;/no ;	use semicolon/delete semicolon	23
	delete	
^	insert	
?⃝	unclear	
#/no #	space/no space	

A Revision Checksheet

Use this checksheet to guide your revisions. Evaluate your paper. Revise, edit, and proofread to make sure your writing represents your best work. Be sure you let your draft **"cool off"** before starting to revise. **(3a)**

☐ **Assignment:** Does your composition fulfill the assignment? **(1a)** Is your writing **purpose** clear; will your readers understand your point of view? **(1b)** Mark your draft anywhere your **aim** can be made clearer for your readers. **(2a, 3a)** Have you followed the special requirements of assignments that call for **research (46)** or writing about **literature (47)**?

☐ **Title:** Does your composition have an effective title, **descriptive** and **informative**? Does the **tone** of your title suit the rest of your composition? **(2f)**

☐ **Introduction:** Do you have an effective **introductory strategy**? Have you avoided the problems of weak introductions? **(43d)**

☐ **Thesis:** Do you have a clear **thesis statement**? Is it specific, limited, worthwhile? Have you avoided problems of overly general, broad, intangible, trivial or overworked subjects? **(1e)** Mark your draft anywhere you can make it more accurately reflect your thesis statement. Consider whether you need to change your thesis to make it match your draft. **(2b, 3a)**

☐ **Ideas and Reasoning:** Have you thoroughly explored your **sources** of subject matter? **(1c)** Have you found a new and worthwhile idea to write about? **(1d)** Check your use of evidence. **(44)** Evaluate your data: do you have good data? Do you have enough? **(44a)** Have you followed the guidelines for primary and secondary evidence? **(44b)** Are your arguments valid? Have you avoided fallacies of reasoning? **(45a–d)**

☐ **Organization:** Mark your draft anywhere your **developmental strategy** can be made clearer to your readers. Check your outline; does it match your draft? Could a reader outline your draft? **(2c, 3a)** Does your outline reveal the logic of your organization, any weak spots? **(2e, 43)**

☐ **Point of View:** Revise your draft to make your language better reveal your **point of view**. Where is the evidence that you are concerned about your **voice, tone,** and **attitude**? **(2d, 3a)**